HITLER'S GIFT

HITLER'S GIFT

The True Story of the Scientists
Expelled by the Nazi Regime

JEAN MEDAWAR
and DAVID PYKE

Foreword by Dr. Max Perutz

ARCADE PUBLISHING • NEW YORK

FIRST U.S. EDITION 2001

Library of Congress Cataloging-in-Publication Data

Medawar, J. S.
    Hitler's gift : the true story of the scientists expelled by the Nazi regime / Jean Medawar and David Pyke. —1st North American ed.
        p. cm.
    Includes bibliographical references and index.
    ISBN 1-55970-564-7
        1. Jewish scientists—Germany. 2. Jewish scientists—Great Britain. 3. Jewish scientists—United States. 4. Science and state—Germany—History—20th century. 5. National socialism and science—Germany. 6. Science—Great Britain—History—20th century. 7. Science—United States—History—20th century. I. Pyke, David. II. Title.

Q141 .M385 2001
943.086'088'5—dc21   2001022143

Published in the United States by Arcade Publishing, Inc., New York
Distributed by Time Warner Trade Publishing

Visit our Web site at www.arcadepub.com

10 9 8 7 6 5 4 3 2 1

EB

PRINTED IN THE UNITED STATES OF AMERICA

Contents

Acknowledgements

In preparing this book we have been helped by many people and institutions, especially:

The Royal College of Physicians, Wellcome Trust, Wolfson College, Oxford, Bodleian Library, Oxford, Wiener Library, the Royal Society, Rockefeller Archive Center, Miss Tess Simpson, the Society for the Protection of Science and Learning, Professor Peter Lachmann FRS, Mrs Mary Blaschko, Professor Gus Born FRS, Sir Rudolf Peierls FRS, Professor Albert Neuberger FRS, Dr Cornelius Medvei, Mr Charles Perrin, Lady Simon, Mrs Frank Loeffler, Mr Ralph Blumenau, Sir Hans Kornberg FRS, Sir Bernard Katz FRS, Dr Nicholas Kurti FRS, Dr Werner Jacobson, Sir Joseph Rotblat FRS, Dr Marthe Vogt FRS, Dr Heinz Fuld, Dr Erwin Chargaff, Sir Hermann Bondi FRS, Sir Ernst Gombrich OM, Sir Karl Popper FRS, Mrs H. G. Kuhn, Herman Wouk, Sir Isaiah Berlin OM, Mrs Ilse Wolff, Dr C. F. von Weizsäcker, Mrs Jean Havill.

We would also like to thank our agent, Christopher Sinclair-Stevenson, for his support and help in finding a publisher; our editor, Anne Boston; and Peter Day, whose skill and enthusiasm were a major encouragement. We must also thank Richard Cohen for taking on *Hitler's Gift* and for his support throughout its writing. Finally, we are particularly grateful to Dr Max Perutz OM FRS for writing the Foreword. He and Mr Barry Davis read the manuscript for scientific and historical errors. Any that remain are the fault of the authors.

List of Illustrations

15. Rudolf Peierls and Francis Simon, c.1951 (Michael Nicholson Collection).
16. Erwin Schrödinger and Frederick Lindemann, 1933 (from *Refugee Scholars*, private publication).
17. Jews forced to scrub the streets (Imperial War Museum).
18. Max Perutz, 1990 (Dr Pyke's private collection).
19. Professor Chadwick and General Groves at Los Alamos, c.1944 (Michael Nicholson Collection).
20. Internees, Isle of Man, 1940 (from *'Collar the Lot'* by P. and L. Gillman).
21. Model of atomic pile built by Fermi and Szilard, Chicago, 1940 (American Institute of Physics).
22. Edward Teller, 1983 (Emilio Segrè Visual Archives).
23. Joseph Rotblat, 1995 (Dr Pyke's private collection).
24. Einstein and Szilard write to President Roosevelt, August 1939 (Time/Warner/HBO).

Foreword

By Dr Max Perutz

Some years ago I ran into one of my Viennese friends of the 1930s. He asked me:

'What do you think of Fifi?'

'Who's Fifi?'

'Don't you remember, the girl with the dachshund?'

'What about her?'

'Haven't you seen *Born Free*?'

'I've read it.'

'She emigrated to Kenya, abbreviated Josephine to Joy and married that game warden Adamson.' Had Fifi remained in Vienna, she would have continued to keep dachshunds: it was her emigration that enabled her to keep a lioness instead. That story is symbolic of the greater opportunities many of us found in our new homes.

Jean Medawar and David Pyke tell the stories of the selected group of Jewish scientists and physicians from Germany and Austria whom the Nazis dismissed from their academic posts and who settled in Britain and the United States. They describe some of the contributions to science and medicine which these men made both before and after their emigration. According to the authors, their emigration was Hitler's loss and Britain's and America's gain.

As one of the scientists included in the book, I must protest. Like

Fifi's, the gain was mine. Had I stayed in my native Austria, even if there had been no Hitler, I could never have solved the problem of protein structure, or founded the Laboratory of Molecular Biology which became the envy of the scientific world. I would have lacked the means, I would not have found the outstanding teachers and colleagues, or learned scientific rigour; I would have lacked the stimulus, the role models, the tradition of attacking important problems, however difficult, that Cambridge provided. It was Cambridge that made me, and for that I am forever grateful. The art historian Ernst Gombrich feels the same way. We all owe a tremendous debt to Britain.

It began with a remarkable act of selfless generosity on the part of British academics. Shortly after Hitler came to power, in March 1933, Sir William Beveridge, then director of the London School of Economics, and Lionel Robbins, one of its professors, were enjoying themselves in Vienna when they read the first news of Hitler's wholesale dismissal of Jewish teachers from German universities. Possession of even a single Jewish grandparent disqualified academics from teaching the German Master Race. Refusal to swear allegiance to Adolf Hitler was another ground for dismissal. Outraged, Beveridge and Robbins returned to London and convened the professorial council which decided to invite all teachers and administrators to contribute to an academic assistance fund for helping displaced scholars in economic and political science. Beveridge recalled: 'The answer to Hitler of British Universities generally was as immediate and emphatic as the answer of the London School of Economics.' On 22 May 1933, 41 prominent academics, including Maynard Keynes, Gilbert Murray, George Trevelyan and seven Nobel laureates in science and medicine wrote to *The Times* announcing the foundation of the Academic Assistance Council 'to raise a fund, to be used primarily, though not exclusively, in providing maintenance for displaced teachers and investigators, and finding them work in universities and scientific institutions.' Accommodated in two small offices in the Royal Society's rooms in Burlington House, it became as much a specialized labour exchange as an income provider. In 1936 the council's name was changed to the Society for the Protection of Science and Learning.

At the end of the Second World War, 2,541 refugee scholars were registered with the society, most of them Germans and Austrians. Other refugees came from Czechoslovakia, Italy and Spain. The society's income from its formation to the outbreak of war was nearly £100,000, equivalent to about £8 million today, most of it from private individuals. The City of London kept its coffers closed.

Hitler's Gift includes only refugee scholars who achieved academic distinction; there were others now forgotten, who created wealth. For example, one of my Viennese acquaintances who settled here was the young entomologist Walter Ripper. He and his wife moved into a house in a village just outside Cambridge. To earn some money, Ripper began to synthesize agrochemicals, mainly pesticides, in his garage. His business soon expanded into a small factory. After the war, its growing profits allowed Ripper to fly his own aeroplane to the Sudan to help cotton growers control their insect pests. Ripper met his death when he crashed his plane into a Greek mountain, but his firm continued to flourish. Its successors expanded until they employed as many as 250 people, and the firm is now part of a global conglomerate.

Scientists were not the only ones to whom Britain offered new scope and opportunities. In 1992 Sir Claus Moser, also German-born and an authority in social statistics and a prominent supporter of music, delivered a lecture on Britain's 'Life in the Arts and the Influence of Jewish Immigration'. His lecture is a tribute to the refugees' part in making London a world centre of music. According to him, they raised standards, heightened disciplined professionalism, discouraged dilettantism, widened artistic interest and increased support and participation. Moser found that the Amadeus Quartet, three of whose members were refugees, achieved a major musical transformation in England. He writes that the Glyndebourne Opera, though founded by John Christie, owes its high quality to Fritz Busch from Dresden and Carl Ebert from Berlin. The Edinburgh Festival was Rudolf Bing's brainchild in 1947 and was run from 1965 to 1978 by Peter Diamond, another ex-refugee. George Solti, an ex-refugee from Hungary has also exercised tremendous influence on London's music. Moser credits the Jewish immigrant musicians too with increasing the public's enthusiasm for music, so that about three million people now attend opera in Britain every year, and for raising the quality of British artists to a level that brings them engagements in opera houses around the world. The art historian Nicholas Pevsner was another German refugee who found an immensely fruitful field of activity here, an untapped treasure in the form of Britain's buildings whose architecture he recorded in a monumental series of volumes. Like scientists, musicians, artists and academics of all kinds found Britain a good country to live and work in.

MRC Laboratory of Molecular Biology
Cambridge
June 2000

Introduction

D. A. Pyke

This is a note to explain my life-long interest in the subject of this book.

I was born in 1921 so was aged nearly twelve when Hitler came to power. The event was probably not of interest to most children of my age but I had a father who was highly politically aware and so I was very interested in public affairs. Although the political atmosphere in England was calm and detached it was not difficult to see that what was happening in Germany was – or could be – enormously important to everybody. Although there had not yet been any rearmament Hitler's threats against political opponents, especially the Communists, and his actions against Jews was clearly serious and dangerous. Indeed his actions against Jews in academic life were obvious at once. A law of 7 April 1933 (only ten weeks after Hitler coming to power) dismissed most Jews in State institutions, and as all universities in Germany were run by the State that meant nearly all Jews in academic life. Most started to look for jobs abroad, many came to Britain where an organization to help them – the Academic Assistance Council – was very quickly created.

My father was Jewish. He was never in any sense a practising Jew, having no religion at all, but perhaps he was sensitized to the horror in Germany by that fact. I have never felt Jewish and think that my feelings about anti-Semitism, starting in 1933, are such as any decent person who had any idea of what was happening in Germany felt.

Enough information came out of Nazi Germany to make quite clear to anyone with eyes and ears something of the horror of con- centration-camp tortures – and this was long before the death camps and the policy of murdering all Jews.

On 30 June 1934 there was a flare-up in the Nazi leadership which gave some people the hope that it might be disintegrating. Ernst Röhm, the head of the SA and an old friend of Hitler's, together with other SA leaders was murdered, an action which Hitler supervised personally. I was so intrigued by this that three weeks later at a speech competition at my preparatory school I spoke on 'The rise and possible fall of Adolf Hitler'. I don't remember what I said – and I regret to say that the school magazine did not report the speech. At least I seem to have been thinking along the right lines, if a little optimistically.

The next time I can remember doing anything of relevance to the story of this book was in 1940. I was a medical student at Cambridge and was editor of the University Medical Society magazine. It was the time of internment when refugee Germans (and Italians) who had not been naturalized (naturalization took five years so many of the refugees had not had time) were interned in a panic action soon after the German attack in the West. Refugees at Cambridge were parti- cularly badly hit because, in the fear that some refugees might actually be Nazi spies, the east and south-east of Britain were thought to be specially vulnerable if there were an invasion. We did not quite know what was going on: no announcements were made, friends and teachers simply disappeared. It gradually emerged that they had been sent to internment in Liverpool and the Isle of Man. Without knowing if there had been any real danger of treachery (there hadn't) it still seemed harsh to intern all the refugees, including those previously graded by government committees as friendly, so abruptly and without telling their families what was happening to them. Everyone could see, especially after the fall of Norway in April when a traitor – Quisling – emerged to take over the government, and when alarmist stories of parachutists and spies spread, that it was reasonable for the British government to act. It was the severity and the manner of the action that aroused some criticism in the press and Parliament, especially after a few weeks when none of the internees had been released.

At that time some universities had their own Members of Parliament. The MP for Cambridge was A. V. Hill, a Nobel Prize winner and physiologist who was one of the founders of the Academic Assistance Council set up to help the refugee scholars and scientists. He started asking questions in Parliament from June onwards and offering, on behalf of the Royal Society, to help the government to screen refugee scientists so that known anti-Nazis could be released. It was, incidentally, a tremendous boost to the morale of the internees when they heard that at a time of extreme crisis for the country Parliament was occupying itself with their plight. Having no source of news they concluded from this that the situation couldn't be so bad. They were wrong, the situation was desperate, but even in such a situation the British Parliament was mindful of its duty.

I knew about A. V. Hill's actions and thought it would be nice to commission an article for my magazine, not stopping to think that he might have other and more important things on his mind. Here is the letter he sent to me:

29 October 1940

Dear Mr Pyke

Thank you for your letter of 26 October. I certainly do with you deplore the policy of indiscriminate internment of scientific and medical people (among many others) who could so well help us in our national effort. The 'distressing apathy' which you note among medical students in Cambridge about the internment of foreign doctors is shared by a large proportion of qualified medical people and the Home Office is not to be blamed so much as the medical organizations and the strict trades union attitude of the BMA for the attitude towards foreigners. Some of the medical people are much better and there is a committee of the Royal Society of Medicine which is taking an interest in getting medical people out of internment. The Royal Colleges, which might have taken, relative to their brethren, the same action that the Royal Society has taken for scientific people, have done nothing at all. The Home Office, I know, lives in terror of the medical profession or rather of their organizations because of the rigidity of their trades union attitude and the powerful influence they are able to exert. The Home Office indeed is far more liberal minded than the doctors.

There are now several hundred Polish doctors and an almost equal number of Czech doctors, both supposed to be our allies, as well as the hundreds of medically qualified refugees from Nazi oppression who have not got British medical qualifications. These are now kicking their heels and not allowed to follow their professions at all. If one says this one arouses the comment that there are plenty of British doctors out of a job or with practices greatly limited. That is perhaps true, but during this winter we are likely to have very extensive epidemics and every medical man may be needed, and anyhow we throw away annually some six thousand children's lives to diphtheria, who could be saved if we would put medical people on to preventive immunization. The situation is a sorry one. I am afraid, however, that I have far too much to do to be able to find time to write the article you want. Good luck to you, however, in your efforts to make your fellow medical students more liberal minded.

Yours sincerely
Professor A. V. Hill
MP for Cambridge University
Secretary R S

I was – and still am – overwhelmed that he spread himself so generously (he might have written an article in fewer lines!) in writing a private letter to someone of no importance. The letter was of a piece with the man and with the attitude of the British public at the time.

As this book shows, the British people's welcome to the anti-Nazi refugees came from a generous spirit. It also produced enormous benefits for the country. Twenty of the scientific refugees later won Nobel prizes and more than 50 became Fellows of the Royal Society. Nearly all the early workers on atomic energy were British or European Jewish refugees. In the arts, including especially music, the German contribution was enormous. Consequently Britain's gain was great. Sir Peter Medawar used to say that the three greatest Englishmen he knew were Ernst Gombrich, Max Perutz and Karl Popper – art historian, biologist and philosopher – all from Vienna.

So what started as an altruistic gesture, the rescue of German academic refugees, turned out to be a highly profitable venture. Germany lost and we gained a greater intellectual and artistic treasure than has ever moved from one country to another. Germany, which had been incomparably the top nation scientifically, damaged itself irretrievably, almost mortally in the sense that its scientific losses in U-boat and atomic warfare might have been crucial to the result of the war. The West was infused with a deep draught of academic strength which enormously strengthened Britain and set American science on the steep rise to its present world supremacy.

The trigger to write this book came from knowing Wilhelm Feldberg. He was a physiologist who had been thrown out of Germany immediately Hitler came to power and came to England.

He had worked on chemical neurotransmission (the chemical method by which nerve impulses pass from one nerve to the next, not via an electric current). When I went up to Cambridge he was one of several refugee scientists who taught us. Many years later my medical research interests took me in his direction. I saw him at the National Institute for Medical Research, Mill Hill, and got to know him well again. He was an overwhelmingly attractive personality. He had lost two wives, one son, his country and job and yet said: 'I have been so lucky.' He meant it – he had pursued his career of choice with great success and was surrounded and supported by the love of his family and friends and the admiration of his colleagues.

Another sweet and engaging one of our teachers was Hermann (later Hugh) Blaschko. He seemed to be part of the physiology department but we discovered later that he had no proper appointment and was surviving on tutoring fees. He did vital work studying the metabolism of substances in the brain.

Both these lovely men lived to be FRS, famous pharmacologists and died in their nineties, universally beloved.

Jean Medawar

I joined the project of writing this book for two reasons – one political one personal, as the widow of Peter Medawar OM, Nobel laureate.

In 1932, before the Nazis came to power I spent a holiday in the Black Forest. Already there were swastika flags flying although they were legally forbidden. That gave a feeling of menace and of danger which I never lost. I was thoroughly alerted when I was an undergraduate at Oxford and joined the Labour party in its opposition to appeasement, together with Peter, who although entirely committed to a scientific career, was far from immune to political issues. By virtue of his eminence then, and especially later, he encountered many of the refugee scientists, particularly those who came to Oxford like E. B. Chain, who worked in Howard Florey's department of pathology, where Peter also worked. Despite their junior status they did what they could to soften the lot of those who had been expelled or squeezed out from careers in Germany. My knowledge of German was an advantage.

That is the background of my interest in our subject. The foreground is the personal, working relationship with David Pyke. This came about through the initiative of his mother, Margaret Pyke, who as chairman of the Family Planning Association was always on the lookout for sympathetic talent and quickly spotted me. Soon afterwards, in 1959, she asked me to help David in the job of editing the journal *Family Planning*. This enterprise, generally regarded as a success, led to many other efforts, so it was natural that when the idea of writing this book developed it should become a joint enterprise between two people working together who had the same ideas and ideals concerning science, scientists and humane behaviour.

The more our work has gone on, the more we have come to admire the scientists who came to Britain and the West, and – quite as much – the academics of Britain who in 1933 were so quick to see the danger and so quick to act. They behaved with an intelligence, courage and decisiveness that should guide us all.

Their actions were an inspiration to the world then, have been ever since and should always be. We hope that by writing this book we may help to honour their names.

This, therefore, is the story of some of the scientists, almost all Jewish, who were driven out of Germany in the years before the Second World War. It is an account of their escapes, rescues and later careers rather than of their work. It is not a scholarly study. Of the hundreds of refugees, we have written about only 40. They include most of the outstanding figures and those we have known and interviewed.

I

German Science Before Hitler

In the first 32 years of the Nobel Prizes (1901–32)
Germany won one third of all the prizes in science,
33 out of 100, Britain 18 and the USA 6.

From the nineteenth century German science led the world; its reputation in chemistry, physics, biology and medicine was rivalled, if at all, only by Britain. If scientific success can be measured by the award of Nobel Prizes, Germany's record far outshone that of any other country. Of all 100 Nobel Prizes in science awarded between 1901, when the awards were founded, and 1932, the year before Hitler came to power, no less than 33 were awarded to Germans or scientists working in Germany. Britain had 18 laureates; the USA produced six. German and British scientists together won more than half of all Nobel Prizes. Of the German laureates, about a quarter of the scientists were of Jewish descent, although the Jewish population made up no more than 1 per cent of the German people at the time.

There were special circumstances that fostered this pitch of achievement in German science, linked to German society and the development of the nation as a whole. The German empire came into being in 1871 with formidable military power inherited from Prussia, the founder state. It was Prussia, led by Otto von Bismarck, after three lightning wars in the 1860s and early 1870s against Denmark, Austria and France, who established its king as German Emperor and stamped its authoritarian, militarist character on the new German nation.

A surge of confidence and national pride accompanied the creation of the German Reich, based on the Prussian army's power and the combined potential of Germany's unified people and resources. With a population bigger than that of France or Britain, and territories expanded by its war gains, Germany was in the ascendant – the most powerful nation in Europe.

Bismarck's recognition that military strength must be matched by industrial and economic efficiency set the scene for the founder years and the decades before the Great War, which saw a tremendous growth. The government encouraged research-driven industrial development, and German businesses led the world in running research departments alongside their manufacturing plants – a pattern which American industry later adopted with spectacular success. Industry courted the best academics for research and its practical application, and technical skill was supplied by *Technische Hochschulen* (technical universities). Conversely, the state-run universities favoured scientists who had worked in industry – a cross-fertilization which had enormous benefits for Germany's industrial growth. Chemistry led the way, and became a byword for progress and wealth.

Soon after his accession in 1888, Wilhelm II dismissed Bismarck, the architect of Germany's greatness. The Kaiser, who regarded himself as leader of the nation's civil as well as its military life, was vain and unstable – perhaps hardly surprising in a man who gloried in the title of 'All Highest'. What he did have, however, was a respect for science and learning, whose achievements had done so much to advance Germany's industrial strength and enhance its prestige and military power.

This interest increased with Wilhelm's acquaintance with Walther Nernst,[1] one of the founders of physical chemistry and director of experimental physics at Berlin University. Confident and decisive, Nernst was always open to new ideas, which he discussed with the Kaiser over meals and meetings at the Palace – a relationship which symbolized science's high standing in Germany. The Kaiser expanded on Nernst's proposals to set up a national science establishment, and the result was the creation of the Kaiser Wilhelm Society, whose Founding Convention in January 1911 described chemistry and natural science, not colonial expansion, as 'the true land of boundless opportunities'. By the 1920s a network of Kaiser Wilhelm Institutes (KWI) for chemistry, physical chemistry, physics and medical research, first in Berlin and then elsewhere in Germany, had become world leaders and are still, under the name of Max Planck Institutes.

Science entered a great age, with scientists as the new heroes in an environment uniquely shaped to draw out greatness. Public respect for science was close to reverence, hard to conceive from today's perspective of popular scepticism about the benefits of modern technology. Some described their work as if it was akin to a religious calling, and their faith seemed justified. In medicine and biochemistry they were defeating the scourges of disease and infant mortality. In applied chemistry they were revolutionizing industry. And in physics they were on the verge of discoveries which would open the way to a new universe.

The research that led to Germany's pioneering industrial production of synthetic dyes, reaping enormous commercial returns, also brought biological and medical breakthroughs. In medical science the great figures were Robert Koch, Rudolf Virchow and Paul Ehrlich – respectively the discoverer of the bacterium causing tuberculosis in 1876, the founding father of pathology and the originator of the chemical treatment of disease. It was the beginning of what Otto Warburg called 'that great age in which medicine and chemistry forged their alliance for the benefit of all mankind'. He and another outstanding biochemist, Otto Meyerhof, were awarded Nobel Prizes for work on the chemistry of muscle and on respiratory enzymes respectively. Their learning was passed on to others, such as Hans Krebs, who went on to become Nobel laureates.

Berlin, centre of imperial power and scholarship, dominated the scientific scene, with its world-famous university and the new Kaiser Wilhelm Institutes; it was also the seat of the Prussian Academy and the National Physical Laboratory. In the capital city brash new wealth jostled with imperial pomp and the old governing class of the Prussian military and landowning aristocracy. It was also the artistic and cultural capital, with a flourishing salon society which cultivated creativity and honoured the great scientific intellects along with philosophers, writers and musicians.

At the new Kaiser Wilhelm Institute for Physical Chemistry and Electrochemistry in Berlin, Fritz Haber, its director, showed how original research applied to technology could transform the nation's fortunes. But for him, Germany would almost certainly have lost the First World War within a year. His discovery of how to make ammonia, a crucial step in the manufacture of nitrates, which are a vital component of explosives, saved Germany, starved of the nitrates it had previously imported from Chile. A further consequence of Haber's work was the manufacture of artificial nitrate fertilizers, which are used today by farmers all over the world. Finally, Haber's research on the gases released from the industrial process produced poison gas in the form of chlorine, an unprecedented example of what science mobilized for war could do. Haber became a national hero for his war work, and he was awarded the 1918 Nobel Prize for his work on nitrates.

In theoretical physics, Germany shone brightest of all, contributing more revolutionary discoveries than any other country in any science, at least until the United States took over as science's world leader half a century later. The 'golden age' of physics began at the turn of the century; Berlin was central to its development, as Max Planck was to its success. Universally respected for his absolute integrity and devotion to German science, Planck was famous for his formulation of the quantum theory, recognizing that energy exists in quanta or finite amounts and was not, as had been thought, a continuum. This theory, published in 1900, was a foundation stone of atomic physics, leading Niels Bohr to postulate that quantal changes of energy were involved when electrons were lost or moved from one orbit round the atomic nucleus to another. Personally and scientifically Planck was thoroughly conservative and recoiled from his own findings, which clashed with the tenets of classical physics, and he preferred to look for ways to reconcile them.

The young Albert Einstein, working alone in Zurich, was inspired by the revolutionary implications of Planck's discovery; his famous paper on the photoelectric effect, published in 1905, confirmed Planck's quantum theory. His special theory of relativity challenged Newton's laws of physics, which had been unquestioned for two centuries. The theory of relativity seemed so outlandish that at first hardly anyone understood its importance; Planck was among the few who did, and in 1913 he and Walther Nernst, Berlin's two senior scientists, persuaded Einstein to join them in Berlin as head of the KWI for Physics. Original in every utterance and totally unconventional, Einstein added the shock of genius to Berlin's scientific establishment.

Another champion of Einstein's new theories was Max von Laue, a former student of Planck's, who won the Nobel Prize in 1914 for his discovery that crystals diffract X-rays, which proved that X-rays are electromagnetic waves. Von Laue was from an old landowning family of East Prussian nobility, the traditional backbone of the Prussian army, and not at all the sort of person to go in for science. He always had the bearing and bark of a Prussian officer, though he tried to soften this impression by taking elocution lessons.

Walther Nernst was awarded the Nobel Prize in 1920 for discovering the third law of thermodynamics: the merging of total and free energy which occurs as absolute zero temperature is approached. The realization of this principle came while he was lecturing to his students during his first term in Berlin in 1905, and he was never slow to proclaim 'his' law. He also enjoyed being an entrepreneur, and a patent he took out on an improvement to a type of electric lamp made him a wealthy man.

Women who worked in science at the time were exceptional. Despite his conservatism, Planck appointed Lise Meitner, from Austria, as his assistant in 1912, and she enjoyed a long and fruitful working relationship with Otto Hahn. She was a physicist and Hahn was a chemist, but they are generally known as the discoverers of nuclear fission, the basis for the atomic bomb, in 1938 – mercifully not before, or Hitler's Germany might have been armed with atomic weapons.

When Planck retired as professor of theoretical physics in 1927 he was succeeded by the Austrian Erwin Schrödinger, whose papers on wave equations had caused a sensation the previous year. Schrödinger's wave theory, though different in its approach, led to similar conclusions as the quantum mechanics of Max Born, Werner Heisenberg and Pascual Jordan in Göttingen which interpreted the atom in completely different, mathematical terms. Kurt Mendelssohn, who was metaphorically cutting his teeth on the new physics as a young research graduate in the 1920s, describes the excitement and bafflement at the time of the Schrödinger/Born controversy: 'Most of the time at Heyl's [a coffee house close to the physics laboratory in Berlin] was, of course, devoted to the progress of physics, or rather to our frantic efforts to understand it . . . the subject had now reached such a state of confusion that one could ask the silliest question without being branded a fool.' After a year of calculation, correspondence and argument Schrödinger found a way out of the dilemma: both treatments were equivalent and correct, although expressed differently.

Groups of talented students and younger scientists gathered round the leading figures, who remained very much at the centre of events. At one stage during the 1920s Planck, Nernst, von Laue and Einstein regularly sat in the front row at the weekly physics seminars at Berlin University, a terrifying prospect for a young scientist presenting a paper.

Among the scientific centres of excellence outside Berlin, Munich, which was strongly Catholic, was highly influential. In particular Arnold Sommerfeld, professor of theoretical physics, was in close touch with Berlin's scientists and left his mark on a generation of physicists; he trained nearly a third of Germany's professors of physics and four of his students were awarded Nobel Prizes.

The other great cluster of scientific excellence in pre-Hitler Germany, rivalling even Berlin in physics and mathematics, was Göttingen. The ancient university city had no truck with Berlin's grandeur and showy style, cultivating instead a 'donnish provincialism'; but its academic community was world-famous. The town-and-gown atmosphere was perhaps akin to that of Cambridge; life revolved around the university in the city centre, which was small enough for people to walk everywhere, and even well-to-do houses took in scientific scholars as paying guests.

In the university close collaboration between physics and mathematics departments was encouraged by its leading mathematician, David Hilbert, and his younger colleague Richard Courant. Hilbert was also chairman of the prize committee for a curious award – a citizen of Göttingen had left a large bequest to whomever could solve the mathematical problem known as Fermat's Last Theorem. The committee was in no hurry to find the correct answer, as the interest on the fund was used to pay for lectures by visiting scientists, including Planck, Nernst, Sommerfeld and the Dane Niels Bohr. Göttingen's scholars flocked to hear guest lecturers – Bohr in particular was held in great esteem and affection, and his visit in summer 1922 became known as the Bohr Fest.

Göttingen's greatest theoretical physicist was Max Born, a man whom Bertrand Russell described, much later, as 'brilliant, humble and completely without fear in his public utterances'. At one time or another Werner Heisenberg, Wolfgang Pauli and Eugene Wigner worked with him, all of whom, including Born himself, later won Nobel Prizes.

Max Born's father was professor of anatomy at Breslau and Max grew up in comfort, surrounded by his extended Jewish family and his father's scholarly and musical friends. One of them encouraged Max towards mathematics and astronomy rather than engineering, as he had first intended, and he became an exceptional student at Breslau University. After studying in Heidelberg and Cambridge he moved to Göttingen in 1908 and rapidly proved his brilliance in mathematical physics. He was enticed away to Berlin, then to Frankfurt, before accepting the Chair of Theoretical Physics at Göttingen. There was another vacant position and he lost no time in recommending his colleague and friend, James Franck, to head a second department of experimental physics.

Born was by now mainly interested in applying the quantum theory to the structure of atoms. He met James Franck daily, whose group was working in a similar field, comparing their findings with those of Bohr in Copenhagen. The result was the theory of quantum mechanics, which fitted another piece into the confusing picture of the new physics. Born's pupil Werner Heisenberg, a boyish German genius, worked on the problem too, and before long their joint paper with Pascual Jordan appeared in *Zeitschrift für Physik* in 1926. Born later wrote: 'It was a time of hard but successful and delightful work, and there was never a quarrel between us three, no dispute, no jealousy.' The new ideas were picked up with excitement and consternation by scientists elsewhere – notably Paul Dirac, who heard Heisenberg lecture in Cambridge, and Schrödinger in Berlin. In 1933 Heisenberg, Dirac and Schrödinger were awarded Nobel Prizes for this work; Born, by then in exile in England, had to wait two decades for his. James Franck had won his Nobel Prize in 1925 for formulating the laws governing the impact of electrons on an atom, another step in understanding atomic structure.

Göttingen attracted scholars from all over the world, including the United States. In 1927 Born had to put in a special plea to the Board of Examiners and the Ministry, for an American student of his who had fallen foul of German bureaucracy when applying for a doctorate. Born's intervention enabled the student to pass with distinction. He was Robert Oppenheimer, later director of the atomic bomb project. Many years later, Oppenheimer wrote:

> Our understanding of atomic physics, of what we call the quantum theory of atomic systems, had its origins at the turn of the century and its great synthesis and resolutions in the 1920s. It was not the doing of any one man. It involved the collaboration of scores of scientists from many different lands . . . It was a period of patient work in the laboratory, of crucial experiments and daring action, of many false starts and many untenable conjectures. It was a time of earnest correspondence and hurried conferences, of debate, criticism and brilliant mathematical improvisation. For those who participated it was a time of creation. There was terror as well as innovation in their new insight.

At the start of this chapter we noted that a remarkably high proportion of Germany's Nobel Prize winners were Jewish. In 1933, within months of Hitler coming to power, the world-famous centres of learning that had flourished for 50 years, producing so many of the ideas on which modern science was founded, were attacked by racial vandalism. About 20 per cent of all physicists and mathematicians were dismissed because they were Jews, and most left the country.

Germany's Jewish scientists came in the main from a community rooted deeply in German society and confident of its stability. Unlike other central European countries and Russia, Germany had not expelled its Jewish population and the prospect of serious interruption to their way of life must have seemed almost inconceivable. After legal equality was granted in 1869 a growing minority of Jewish families believed that the only feasible solution to their acceptance in wider German society was total assimilation; they regarded their Jewish background as religious rather than racial, and converted to Christianity, considering themselves wholly German. They regarded with suspicion the Jews from the East, the Ostjuden, who had fled from pogroms across the Pale of Western Russia, in 1881 and later.

The orthodox religion, clothes and language of these refugees set them apart, and their presence in Germany and Poland was resented in their host countries.

All but a few members of Germany's Jewish upper class were excluded from the nobility; instead they formed a cultural élite. In Berlin, as in Vienna, affluent, sophisticated Jewish circles created an 'aesthetic aristocracy', forming and closely identifying with German culture – education in its widest, civilizing, sense. Literature, music and philosophy became a common heritage. In scientific circles the peculiar affinity of mathematics and physics with music was especially evident, and professional relationships were often cemented by musical friendships. Max Planck's musical evenings with Einstein and with Lise Meitner, for instance, were another aspect of the cultural fusion that underlay their scientific achievements.

In the lives of the German-Jewish scientists prejudice can be seen sometimes in the form of overt anti-Semitism, sometimes as a more shadowy presence. The physicist Rudolf Peierls described how, when making friends in childhood, he learned the delicate lesson of how and when to reveal his family background to his non-Jewish companions; this, he said in a typically positive aside, was a valuable social skill to be employed in later life.[2] Professionally, some scientific fields were more accessible to Jewish graduates than others – established disciplines were more resistant. Promotion, too, was harder to come by.

Advancement for Jewish scholars seems to have depended partly on the attitude of individual establishment figures in charge of appointments, and partly on the creation of jobs, which tended to cluster in new fields such as theoretical physics. Max Planck in Berlin and Arnold Sommerfeld in Munich were strictly unprejudiced in their appointments. Physics circles at Göttingen were also notably liberal, and an exceptionally high proportion of Jewish scientists found places in the new physics and mathematics departments.

Chemistry was apparently more difficult. Fritz Haber came from an assimilated German Jewish family yet for years after getting his doctorate he could not find a way into chemistry, despite formidable talent. He had to take work in his father's business and as assistant in the laboratory at Jena before finally landing a post from which he could rise at the technical university at Karlsruhe. As we have noted,

Haber became one of Germany's most revered scientists, first director of the new Kaiser Wilhelm Institute for Physical Chemistry (which was funded by a Jewish banker).

There was perhaps a degree to which prejudice worked as an incentive to success for outstanding talent. Fritz Stern suggests that 'the obstacles that prejudice put in their way often had a contrary effect: in general terms, anti-Semitism was the sting that spurred Jews on to over-achievement . . .'. He cites a 'pattern of success' in medicine and the natural sciences whereby the Jewish researcher, passed over for promotion, compensated by retreating into research and thus created another path to advancement.

The cross-currents of prejudice experienced by Jews in Germany were much less than the official anti-Semitism elsewhere in central Europe. Leo Szilard, whose contribution to atomic physics was so crucial in the 1930s, came to Berlin in 1920 not only because physics research was virtually non-existent in Hungary at the time, but because he had been set upon by anti-Semitic fellow students. Szilard and his fellow Hungarians Eugene Wigner and Edward Teller had all experienced open prejudice at first hand before they set foot in Germany.

The experience of some of the Jewish scientists during the Great War gives a revealing glimpse into German prejudice, and German-Jewish reactions. Anti-Semitism in the regiments barred Jews from holding regular commissions, but 100,000 Jews volunteered to fight and more than 12,000 lost their lives in action. It was a Jewish officer who recommended that Hitler should receive the Iron Cross for his wartime conduct.

The physicist Franz Simon, one of the first German victims of poison gas, was wounded twice, the second time severely, and was awarded the Iron Cross First Class. In 1933, disgusted by the Nazis, he resigned his professorship at Breslau, and sent back the medal, which carried the inscription 'The Fatherland will always be grateful'. James Franck volunteered for front-line battle early in the war, was decorated with both classes of the Iron Cross and was commissioned as an officer despite his being Jewish – despite also his inherently unmartial character: he was said to have once ordered his troops to 'Come to attention – please!'

The biochemist Otto Warburg, whose outstanding abilities had just led to his appointment at the KWI in Berlin in 1913, when he was 30, joined a smart cavalry regiment as a volunteer in 1914. A super-patriot, he was commissioned, wounded and, like the others, decorated with the Iron Cross. In March 1918, when the German High Command staged its last offensive, Einstein (an ardent pacifist and internationalist) wrote to Warburg offering to try to get him released from the army, where his 'life continually hangs on a thread'. It was madness, Einstein wrote, for Warburg as an outstanding young scientist to risk his life in this way; would he allow himself to be 'claimed' for other work? Einstein expected his suggestion to be rejected but, rather surprisingly, Warburg agreed. Einstein's initiative, taken together with other scientists, shows how high Warburg's reputation stood.

Warburg did not regard his time in the army as wasted; on the contrary he looked back on it with pride. His affinity for military life suggests features of his character that surely affected the unique direction his life took subsequently: Warburg had the doubtful distinction of being the only Jewish scientist in Germany left to continue his work unscathed throughout the Second World War.

2

The Coming of the Nazis

By appointing Hitler as . . . Chancellor of the
Reich, you have delivered our holy German
fatherland into the hands of one of the greatest
demagogues of all time. I solemnly prophesy to you
that this unholy man will cast our country into the
abyss, and bring our nation into immeasurable
misery. Future generations will curse you in your
grave for what you have done.

*Letter from General Ludendorff to
President Hindenburg, 1933*

The First World War ended suddenly – so suddenly that Germany's defeat seemed inconceivable to its people. In March 1918 the Treaty of Brest-Litovsk with the new Soviet Russia sealed Germany's victory on the Eastern front. On the Western front in none of the four terrible years of trench warfare had the battle been fought on German soil, and in March 1918 a German attack pushed almost to the Channel coast.

Yet within a few days of an Allied assault on the Western front on 8 August 1918 the German military leaders, left with no reserves, knew they were defeated. By November their forces had been pushed back to the Belgian border; only months after apparently being poised for victory they had lost the war. The Kaiser abdicated and was replaced by new politicians who sued for peace. This fuelled the widespread belief in Germany that the nation had been 'betrayed' by its new leaders.

The turbulent postwar decade began with sporadic revolts by sailors and soldiers. The honest politicians of the new liberal-democratic Weimar Republic attempted to establish a democratic political system. But the government was never popular: it alienated both Left and Right.

Nor did the Weimar politicians find sympathy abroad from the Allies. The Treaty of Versailles, which forced them to agree to unspecified war reparations and to cut back the German army, was humiliating to a nation which before the war had been an apparently unstoppable world power. In 1923 the French occupied the Ruhr, heartland of Germany's industrial wealth; the currency crisis that followed, partly self-inflicted by the Treasury to scupper reparations, led to fantastic inflation. By November the mark's value had fallen to 130,000 million to the dollar; middle-class savings were wiped out, working-class earnings were worthless.

Amid hardship and social disintegration, Corporal Adolf Hitler pinned the blame on the Bolsheviks and the Jews. He magnetized audiences desperate to find a saviour. The Fatherland had been 'stabbed in the back' by the 'criminals of Versailles . . . Down with the perpetrators of the November crime'. By 1923 Hitler had helped Captain Ernst Röhm of the Weimar Republic's District Command to organize a parallel army of 15,000 uniformed stormtroopers, many recruited from the Freikorps (ex-service groups).

The Austrian corporal had imported a racism that was pervasive in the Austro-Hungarian empire. Moving to Munich in 1913 to avoid conscription into the Habsburg army, Hitler encountered a brew of extreme pan-nationalism mixed with the new 'science' of eugenics. By 1919, after Germany's defeat, this had been transmuted into Hitler's obsession with Jews; it was not based on religious prejudice or envy of Jewish wealth or success, which had fuelled earlier waves of violent anti-Semitism in Russia and Poland, but on race. The nationalist cause of restoring German greatness was, for him, now fused with the need to destroy a 'conspiracy of Jewish power' which threatened Germany from without and within. His diatribes against the Jews found eager listeners as early as 1920.

The economic chaos fomented the Munich putsch in November 1923, led by Hitler with the support of General Erich Ludendorff, who had been second in command of the German army. After its failure, at the trial Ludendorff was acquitted and Hitler sentenced to five years, which was later commuted to nine months, giving him just enough time to write *Mein Kampf* in prison. From then on Hitler publicly renounced direct action in favour of the constitutional route to power.

After 1923 the government of Gustav Stresemann inaugurated a period which brought six years of relative political and economic stability, and an atmosphere of intellectual experiment. In the aftermath of war Berlin became the new social and artistic capital of Europe. By 1929 German industry was surging ahead, stronger than it had been in 1913. But it was shattered by the collapse of the Wall Street Stock Exchange in October 1929, which set off world economic depression. Companies cut back production and unemployment soared to 7 million by 1932, more than double the British figure. Britain's democracy was under strain; in Germany, where there was no democratic tradition to sustain a moderate minority government, the centre could not hold. A coalition formed in 1928 collapsed in March 1930, and Field Marshal Paul von Hindenburg, its octogenarian President, appointed the Centre Party leader Heinrich Brüning as Chancellor. From then on the Weimar Republic was ruled by Presidential Decree, and ceased to operate as a parliamentary democracy.

In the 1930 election Hitler's National Socialist Party (Nazis) won 18 per cent of the total with 6 million votes. A succession of further elections, intended to create a stable government, had the reverse effect. Politics had become dangerously polarized; riots and street battles became commonplace, increasing the nation's desperate yearning for order.

How could the German people have allowed the Nazis' 'gutter élite' to seize power? The first thing to remember is that the National Socialists never achieved a majority vote. In 1932, in the last free elections before Hitler became Chancellor, their highest-ever vote of 37 per cent in the July election fell to 32 per cent in the final November poll. After that all elections and plebiscites were arranged to produce figures of near-unanimous support and are meaningless.

Very soon non-supporters had no way of showing their opposition or even lack of enthusiasm. The Nazis' pioneering use of propaganda on one hand, and the efficiency of their political police and systematic use of terror on the other, were enough to deter all but the most determined opponents.

Verbal and physical violence had been part of the Nazi cult throughout the 1920s; but so it was with other parties, especially the Communists. They too had organized riots and violent street demonstrations and threatened their opponents. At one stage they even followed a Comintern-dictated policy of collaboration with the Nazis against the Social Democrats – 'social fascists', as they labelled them. Nazis and Communists fed on each other; for each party, the opposition was crucial to its own success. Weimar politics became increasingly compressed between the two extremes; fear of Bolshevism was perhaps the Nazis' most powerful weapon.

Watching documentary footage today of Hitler in the 1930s, his appeal is a mystery. Biographers have struggled with a 'black hole' at the core of the man, an absence of personality, with his limp handshake and banal conversation. But there were many who found him mesmerizing; and as a public speaker he knew exactly how to manipulate his audience. With the Nazi publicity machine focused on him as Führer after 1926 he came to personify the magnetism of power. In the discordant, shifting political arena of the Weimar Republic his pathological fixations came across as determination and sense of purpose. The indecision and mutual distrust of Weimar politicians and surly aloofness of the army made any consistent and far-sighted policies almost impossible. Hitler offered a clear programme to restore the power of Germany at home and abroad, couched in lofty ideals that transcended politics and seemed to offer something for everyone. Germany, degraded by defeat, was looking for a saviour; and Hitler's boundless egomania made him ready to seize the role.

Hitler always insisted that he would succeed to power by legitimate means, and that he would meet no serious resistance. The workers would be persuaded by his rhetoric and his programme – his party was, after all, the National Socialist German Workers' Party, the NSDAP. As for the middle classes, supposedly the brains and bastion of the State, Hitler said in 1931: 'Do you think perhaps that, in the event of a successful revolution along the lines of my party, we would not inherit the brains in droves? . . . Do you believe that the German middle class, this flower of the intelligentsia, would refuse to serve us and place their minds at our disposal? The German middle class would take its stand on the famed ground of the accomplished fact; we will do what we like with the middle class.'

Indeed, Nazi campaigns against Germany's 'common enemies' fell on fertile ground in the years of the Great Depression, massive unemployment and social unrest. In fact the National Socialists found more support in the universities, including the surgeon Ferdinand Sauerbruch, the philosopher Martin Heidegger and poets and writers, but few scientists, than in the State as a whole. Heidegger even said: 'The much praised academic freedom will be rooted out of the German university.' The Nazi movement's calls to restore traditional values to education appealed to the conservative academic establishment, which trained Germany's civil servants. To these people, who saw themselves as guardians of the nation's scholarship, the ferment of scientific and artistic experiment in Germany during the Weimar years was threatening rather than exciting. Hitler seemed to promise a return to the order of a past era.

Meanwhile Nazism was enormously popular among students, who eagerly responded to appeals to join the common cause of rebuilding Germany's greatness. Hitler, as Führer, answered an emotional need among German youth for a new leader who would erase the past generation's failures and inspire them with new ideals. 'Nowadays the task of the university is to cultivate not objective science but soldier-like military science; another foremost task is to form the will and character of the students.' Or, as the Nazi newspaper *Völkischer Beobachter* put it: 'The very best thoughts are those inculcated by marching; in them reverberates the secret German spirit, the spirit of centuries.'

Moderates who were alarmed by the Nazis' strident anti–Semitism could console themselves that the army and industrial magnates would not let Hitler go too far. These two pillars of the State were greatly respected and were trusted to control the Nazi government as they had controlled others in the past. It seemed inconceivable that the army itself would surrender its independence in exchange for rearmament with hardly a protest.

How did they so misread the signs? 'National Socialism,' in Joachim Fest's phrase, 'represented a politically organized contempt for the mind.' Hitler had already declared that the idea of free-thinking scientific research was 'absurd', that its rationality was suspect because 'it leads away from instinct'. His idea of a good education was one that produced a sound physique and 'a good firm character'; scholarship and research produced pacifist weaklings. Yet after years of unrest and insecurity people ignored the philistinism and looked for the best in the movement. The Nazis' wilder threats and boasts seemed scarcely believable; extremist elements had risen to the surface before, only to be eclipsed. As the young Jewish protagonist observes in *Reunion*, Fred Uhlman's moving book about a boy's friendship with his aristocratic classmate in Hitler's Germany:[1] 'When the Zionist mentioned Hitler and asked my father if this would not shake his confidence, my father said: "Not in the least. I know my Germany. This is a temporary illness, something like measles, which will pass as soon as the economic situation improves. Do you really believe the compatriots of Goethe and Schiller, Kant and Beethoven will fall for this rubbish? How dare you insult the memory of twelve thousand Jews who died for our country?"'

The language of prejudice was common currency; the virulent new strain was expected to die down soon enough. Victor Klemperer, a Jewish professor of Romance languages at Dresden University, expressed current thinking in his diaries at the time, *I Shall Bear Witness*:[2] 'There is no German or Western European Jewish question. Whoever recognizes one only adopts or confirms the false thesis of the NSDAP and serves its cause. Until 1933, and for at least a good century before that, the German Jews were entirely German and nothing else. Proof: the thousands upon thousands of half and quarter etc. Jews and of Jewish descent.'

Long-standing prejudice was not evidence against this: 'the friction between Jews and Aryans was not half as great as that between Protestants and Catholics, or . . . between East Prussians, for example, and Southern Bavarians . . . the German Jews were part of the German nation.'

The legality of the Nazi takeover of the German government gave Hitler a crucial psychological advantage. Law-respecting middle Germany was used to obeying constitutional authority. Despite his revolutionary designs on the state Hitler was well aware of this. In 1932 his followers urged him to seize power, but he waited until at last on 30 January 1933 President Hindenburg invited him to become Chancellor. For all his incendiary rhetoric and threatening behaviour Hitler had taken over the German house of state not by smashing it to pieces but by walking in through the front door at the invitation of its owner.

It is bitterly ironic that General Ludendorff, Hindenburg's second in command in the First World War, much the cleverer of the two, who had supported Hitler at the time of the Munich putsch in 1923, now wrote to Hindenburg: 'By appointing Hitler as Chancellor of the Reich, you have delivered our holy German fatherland into the hands of one of the greatest demagogues of all time. I solemnly prophesy to you that this unholy man will cast our nation into the abyss ... Future generations will curse you in your grave for what you have done.'

Despite their initial minority in the Cabinet the Nazis moved to consolidate their power with astonishing speed. The delusion of Franz von Papen, former German Chancellor, that Hitler could be held in check by Germany's traditional ruling classes merely gave 'a murderous enterprise ... an honourable veneer'. It was von Papen who actually persuaded his friend Hindenburg to appoint Hitler Chancellor, one of the most disastrous acts in the history of the world. (Von Papen never fell out with Hitler, survived him by 24 years and died in his bed. Behind von Papen was General Kurt von Schleicher. When challenged that von Papen did not have a head for administration, he replied, 'He does not need a head. His job is to be a hat.' Von Papen was to be the 'stirrup-holder' of the new regime. Schleicher and his wife were shot on the 'Night of the Long Knives', 30 June 1934.)

The Reichstag fire on 27 February 1933 was used to create the spectre of a communist threat to the state, so that the moderates were frightened into voting for an Enabling Bill. This was passed on 23 March, giving Hitler the right to pass laws simply by signing the documents. There were no more restraints. Hitler had seen off his conservative opponents without their realizing what had happened.

The Nazis' anti-Semitic programme was put into action immediately. Hitler's anti-Semitism, one of the central drives of his life, was at first widely underestimated. Winston Churchill was one to the first to recognize its force. He wrote in 1935:

The Jews, supposed to have contributed, by a loyal and pacifist influence, to the collapse of Germany at the end of the First World War, were also deemed to be the main prop of communism and the authors of defeatist doctrines in every form. Therefore, the Jews of Germany, a community numbered by many hundreds of thousands, were to be stripped of all power, driven from every position in public and social life, expelled from the professions, silenced in the Press, and declared a foul and odious race.

The twentieth century has witnessed with surprise, not merely the promulgation of these ferocious doctrines, but their enforcement with brutal vigour by the Government and by the populace. No past services, no proved patriotism, even wounds sustained in war, could procure immunity for persons whose only crime was that their parents had brought them into the world. Every kind of persecution, grave or petty, upon the world-famous scientists, writers and composers at the top down to the wretched little Jewish children in the national schools, was practised, was glorified, and is still being practised and glorified.

A similar persecution fell upon socialists and Communists of every hue. The trade unionists and liberal intelligentsia were equally smitten. The slightest criticism was an offence against the State.

Hitler was an aggressive paranoiac, the essential feature of a tyrant. His hatred could focus on anybody or anything. A small episode late in the war illustrates his state of mind perfectly. Ferdinand Sauerbruch, the most famous surgeon in Germany, who was serving as an army general, was sent for to come urgently to Hitler's headquarters in Vinnitsa in Russia. He was shown into a waiting room which was empty:[3]

Suddenly a door opened, just enough to admit an enormous dog who bounded towards me, all teeth and snarls, and prepared to spring at my throat. Fortunately, I am used to dogs and know how to handle them. Keeping perfectly still, I spoke some meaningless but soothing words to the animal, 'Steady, old boy! What's all this nonsense?'

I put out my hand gently and patted the brute. The change was startling. He sat down on his haunches and held out a paw. I sat down on the chair beside me and the dog rested his front paws in my lap, begging to be stroked, and bending on me an adoring gaze. At that moment, Hitler walked in.

And then followed one of the most sinister scenes I have ever witnessed. For an instant he stood stock-still, taking in the dog's fawning behaviour. His eyes filled with rage and, clenching his fists, he hurled himself towards me.

'What have you done to my dog?'

I did not know what to say. The dog was now licking my hand and importuning me for more caresses. Hitler bellowed in anguished fury,

'The only creature in the world who is utterly faithful to me and now you've stolen him from me. I'll have him shot. I'm the only one he comes to. He obeys only me. He's the only creature in the whole world who loves me, and you've enticed him away.'

His voice rose to a shrill scream that must have been audible all over the shelter. I was completely taken aback. The dog had stretched himself at my feet and was rubbing his head against my leg. The Führer went on raving, if possible louder than before. His vituperations now embraced all and sundry. 'I can't win the war, he screamed, 'if the army gives in and generals and officers betray me.'

On 31 March 1933 all Jewish judges in Prussia were dismissed, and the next day the Nazis organized widespread anti-Jewish demonstrations in a national boycott. Jewish shops and businesses were daubed with Nazi slogans and guarded by stormtroopers who prevented anyone from entering; posters threatened reprisals against those who used Jewish businesses and sporadic violence broke out. Hitler's Propaganda Minister, Joseph Goebbels, reported in his diary for 1 April: 'Boycott fully effective in Berlin and the whole Reich . . . All Jewish shops are closed, each guarded by the SA. The people support us with exemplary discipline. An imposing spectacle . . .'

The lack of opposition in Germany to this first consolidated initiative against the Jewish community must have encouraged the Nazis to make their next move. On 7 April 1933, less than three months after Hitler became Chancellor, a new law for 'the reconstruction of the civil service' was passed. Political appointees since 1918, and employees with a doubtful political background or of 'non-Aryan descent', were forbidden to work in any branch of the civil service, the only exceptions being those who had served in the German army or lost a close relative during the First World War (even these exceptions were abolished by the Nuremberg laws of 1935). Germany's state-run universities were entirely subservient to the government, so that appointments and dismissals were handled by the Ministry of Education and few other sources of employment were open to academics.

The new directive was announced during the spring vacation when many academics were away on holiday; some learned they had been dismissed by seeing their names included in lists published by the newspapers. Rank was no protection; heads of department, professors, lecturers and instructors were placed 'on permanent leave' with pay. Dismissals were instant and brutal. The rector, dean or head of department would summon the person in question and order him or her to leave, in most cases without the customary courtesy of giving a period of notice.

Wilhelm Feldberg worked in the Institute of Physiology at Berlin University. One April morning he was summoned by the director, Professor Paul Trendelenburg, who, showing him the text of the new civil service statute, simply said, 'Feldberg, you must be out of here by midday, because you are a Jew.' Feldberg, who was not a man to take anything too seriously, protested that he had just started a new experiment. 'Well then,' the director said, 'you must leave by midnight.'

Dismissals were as inconsistent as they were abrupt. In December 1932, for instance, the young biochemist Hans Krebs had been recommended for a lectureship by the dean of the Medical Faculty at Freiburg, who had described him as 'of outstanding scientific ability . . . unusual human qualities . . . loyal and reliable'.[4] Four months later Krebs received a letter from the same dean, Professor Rehn: 'I hereby inform you, with reference to Ministerial Order A No. 7642, that you have been placed on leave until further notice.' On 11 April Krebs wrote his last entry in his Freiburg laboratory notebook: 'I could not settle the question of which nitrogenous substances are formed from the added ammonia and glutamate because I was forced to break off my research.'

The speed of events took most people in Germany by surprise. Within weeks hundreds were forced to leave their jobs. Others resigned and left the country, or resigned while they were on foreign leave and did not return. Science departments all over Germany, like other academic faculties, were decimated by expulsion and emigration and news of the extraordinary developments spread abroad.

Göttingen University was devastated. James Franck, head of the Second Physical Institute, and Max Born, director of the Institute for Theoretical Physics, were both Jewish, as was Richard Courant, director of the Mathematical Institute. Of 33 staff of the four physics and mathematics institutes, only 11 remained.

Academics placed 'on leave' continued to receive a salary, but it could not be transferred abroad. Born, for instance, used the money paid into his account in Germany to help Jewish friends and relatives who were still there, and for family trips to Germany until these became too dangerous.

Unlike most of his colleagues he had no illusions that the regime might be short-lived. In June he wrote to his old friend Einstein:[5] 'Franck is resolutely determined not to go abroad while he has the slightest prospect of finding work in Germany (though not as a civil servant). Although there is, of course, no chance of this, he remains in Göttingen and waits. I would not have the nerve to do it, nor can I see the point of it. But both he and Courant are, in spite of their Jewishness, which is far more pronounced than in my case, Germans at heart.' When they did leave, Courant and other academics took refuge first in Britain or countries neighbouring Germany, staying close to home in the forlorn hope that the political tide would soon change and allow them to return to their former lives.

Franck held out in Göttingen until late November 1933. In the early days colleagues took courage from unofficial seminars at his home, where they talked about physics and (increasingly) exchanged news about jobs abroad. In September Niels Bohr, on a visit to Lübeck, invited him to Copenhagen. The day Franck left by train so many supporters came to the station to see him off that they almost overflowed from the platform, standing in silence as the train drew out.

In some cases resignations pre-empted dismissals. Two resignations which transfixed Berlin's scientific community and particularly enraged the National Socialists were those of Albert Einstein from the Prussian Academy of Sciences and Fritz Haber from the Kaiser Wilhelm Institute for Physical Chemistry and Electrochemistry.

Non-Jewish scientists who might have protested or emigrated could well have been deterred from doing so by the example shown by Planck and Heisenberg, who decided to stay although their attitude to the Nazis was unsympathetic. Emigration was viewed not as a laudable protest but as a desertion of the State. Public protest might lead to dismissal followed by a Nazi-appointed replacement. To some extent the ranks of scientists who were left were drawn together by a common concern to maintain and teach the values of science, which had no protectors in the government.

Meanwhile anti-intellectual fever gripped Germany. Many book-burning incidents were staged in May, not by Nazi thugs but by students, urged on by Goebbels; 20,000 books by Jewish authors were destroyed in Berlin's Unter den Linden alone. Nothing showed more strikingly the barbarian nature of the new regime. Yet in early 1933 teachers, doctors and lawyers headed an opportunistic rush to join the Nazi party after Hitler became Chancellor. The Party had 850,000 members in January; that spring some 1.5 million more applied to join, 20 per cent of them civil servants, presumably hopeful that signing up would help them avoid dismissal – or bring promotion. So many applications came in that offices had to close temporarily to process them all.

The display of anti-reason dismayed many in Germany and abroad, convincing doubters of how life would be under the Nazis. The fragmented working-class movement which was Hitler's strongest opposition was quickly wiped out after the Nazis seized power, its members arrested and held without trial, sent to concentration camps or forced into exile for political 'crimes'.

Others were slow to understand the implications of the unprecedented Nazi phenomenon. The new regime was still feeling the extent of its power. Its citizens failed to recognize the spreading threat, believing that such ferocious persecution could not last: 'Nothing is eaten as hot as it is cooked,' as the saying went.

At the time most people were astonished, even incredulous, at the speed and intensity of the National Socialists' anti-Jewish measures after January 1933. The course of events was so bizarre and irrational that intelligent people could not comprehend it. Leaving their homeland seemed inconceivable to academics and their families whose entire lives had been spent in Germany. They had been productive and successful even during the difficult years of the Weimar Republic and were proud to have contributed to the phenomenal success of German science. Going into exile meant abandoning their posts and, perhaps even more telling, their staff and students. Most had collected promising teams of younger scientists, who looked to them for help and guidance and afforded them the pride and pleasure that a teacher takes in his successful students.

Their position was no more clear to those who recognized the risks. A professor was apparently in a strong position while he stayed in his post. The alternative, resignation, would bring vilification on himself and his family. He would have to emigrate, perhaps learn a new language, adjust to new ways and probably suffer financial hardship.

Whatever their response, Jewish scientists were forced out. Some senior figures of high repute hung on for a few years; finally they, too, had to leave. By the late 1930s life had become hard and few continued to be productive. Younger colleagues, with their lives ahead of them, found moving easier; these, like Hans Krebs, Otto Frisch, Rudolf Peierls, Hans Bethe and Ernst Chain, were among the scientists who succeeded so spectacularly. Fleeing from Germany's anti-Semitism, they found the less authoritarian, more informal intellectual atmosphere in Britain and the United States much more congenial and receptive to new ideas.

Some 2600 scientists and other scholars left Germany within the first year, the vast majority of them Jewish. Twenty-five per cent of all physicists were lost from German universities in an insane squandering of talent. Faced with a gifted scientist who was also Jewish, the government allowed its anti-Semitism to take priority, regardless of the loss of the individual to science and the applied knowledge he could offer the nation.

After their exodus the great mathematician David Hilbert was asked by a government minister, 'And how is mathematics in Göttingen now that it is free of Jews?' 'Mathematics in Göttingen?' Hilbert repeated. 'There is really none any more.'

3

Einstein

The greatest Jew since Jesus.

J. B. S. Haldane

Einstein is such a towering figure in the history of science that it is difficult to realize now that he was once opposed, even reviled, long before Hitler came to power.

We start his story at the end of the First World War. Einstein was already famous, for his special theory of relativity produced in 1905 and his general theory published in 1917. However, they were still theories and not everyone was convinced. Then in 1919 an expedition, under the British physicist Sir Arthur Eddington, went to tropical Africa to photograph a total eclipse of the sun. This confirmed Einstein's prediction, made in 1917, by showing that light was bent by gravity. Almost universal acceptance followed and Einstein was hailed as a genius.

In London, the discovery was announced by J. J. Thomson, President of the Royal Society, as 'one of the greatest achievements in the history of human thought'. Introducing the findings based on the expedition's photographs, Thomson continued: 'It is not the discovery of an outlying island but of a whole continent of new ideas. It is the greatest discovery in connection with gravity since Newton enunciated his principles.'

Einstein became world-famous not only among scientists but also to the public. He was modest and of a tentative demeanour but that did not dampen the interest in everything he said and did. Mockingly, he compared himself with Midas: everything he touched turned not to gold but to publicity. He was honoured and fêted everywhere as the embodiment of science and the cleverest man in the world. No scientist had then, nor has since, been so admired or so famous. He was still only 40 and had not yet won the Nobel Prize, which came in 1921 (for his discovery of the law of photoelectric effect, not for relativity).

The profound originality of Einstein's work lay in his way of thinking about inconsistencies in natural laws that were already known and finding ways to reconcile them. The questions he asked were almost closer to the realms of philosophy than physics; for instance: What would happen if you followed a beam of light at its own speed? His conclusion that light could behave like a stream of quanta, or packets of energy, and could also have a wave nature, baffled even Max Planck, whose quantum theory had served as a catalyst for Einstein's Gedanken or 'thought' experiments. While other scientists were working on the microscopic structure of matter, Einstein's first theory of relativity was concerned with large-scale concepts of space, time and speed, and appeared so odd that it was noticed only gradually by leading physicists. Max Born did not hear of it until 1907, when he was told about Einstein's paper at a conference; he went to the library and looked up the work, which 'had a stronger influence on my thinking than any other scientific experience'.

The speed and greatness of Einstein's fame was liable to lead to jealousy. Among non-scientists that was not likely to be a problem. Few of them, and not all scientists, understood his theories of relativity, nor do most people understand them now. His ideas were extraordinary and, above all, difficult – they seemed to be non-sensical. The very scope, originality and incomprehensibility of Einstein's theories ensured their fame. He had overthrown Newton, it was said. He was on that level. Perhaps it is remarkable how little jealousy he seemed to arouse among scientists. The great majority immediately understood his significance and therefore his greatness. His theories were not proved by the Eddington expedition but they were powerfully supported and certainly could no longer be written off as mere speculation or hypothesis.

In Germany, their impact was different from elsewhere. At first Einstein and his work were accepted but gradually they were attacked. There were several reasons. Einstein was a pacifist and an internationalist. He did not like the rigidity of German academic life and he had turned down a chair in Berlin in 1913. A few months after the war started in 1914 he had also refused to sign an 'Appeal to the Cultured World', which was a hypocritical exculpation of German aggression. Einstein was a theoretical physicist and some practical physicists in Germany found this preference for pencil, paper and speculation irritating and even impertinent. Furthermore, he worked in Berlin, which so dominated the physics scene that it was natural that some of those in other excellent centres, such as Munich, Breslau and Göttingen, might resent the dominance of the capital. Finally, Einstein was a Jew, and this became an increasingly important irritant to a few leading, but disgruntled, physicists more than a decade before Hitler came to power.

The most important of the Einstein-hating physicists was Philipp Lenard. He was a man full of resentment, despite having achieved success beyond the reach of most scientists. He had won the Nobel Prize in 1905, when only 43, for work with cathode rays. But this did not soften him. He particularly disliked British physicists, especially J. J. Thomson, the discoverer of the electron, with whom he had worked, unhappily, for two years. Also, in 1895, Röntgen had discovered X-rays and Lenard felt that he would have made the discovery if his laboratory facilities had been better (he might have been right in this). He had given Röntgen technical advice which he thought had not been properly acknowledged. Gradually, and in part because of his suspicion of theoretical work, he fell behind in the increasingly rapid advances of physics. During the First World War Lenard's feeling of alienation got worse; he hated Britain and felt that the war was between the heroes (Germany) and the merchants (Britain). He even wrote a letter attacking the British 'because they had never quoted him decently'. He became infected by the racial theories of Houston Stewart Chamberlain (Wagner's son-in-law) and *völkisch* ideas which extolled German or Aryan or Nordic superiority over other 'races'.

Lenard's emotions spilled over into his science. His hatred of Einstein, the Jew, worsened when in 1921 Einstein was awarded the Nobel Prize. Lenard actually wrote a letter of protest to the Nobel committee and gave it to the press. Relativity, he said, was 'a Jewish fraud'. In his anti-Semitism he was a leader in the German scientific community; others followed him later. He advocated the removal of Walther Rathenau, the Foreign Minister, who was a Jew. When Rathenau was assassinated he would not respect the national day of mourning, refusing to fly the flag of his Heidelberg physics institute at half mast. This enraged the students, who organized a march on the institute which ended with Lenard being jostled at a meeting and taken into protective custody for a few hours. His next public move towards the right and fierce anti-Semitism came when Hitler was imprisoned after his failed putsch in Munich in 1923. Lenard publicly declared his support for Nazism, together with another Nobel Prize-winning physicist, Johannes Stark. Hitler and his comrades, he said, 'appear to us as gifts of God'.

Lenard's final parting from the majority of his colleagues came when he resigned from the German Physical Society because they had published a paper in English without a German translation. It was therefore hardly surprising that when Hitler came to power and expelled the Jewish scientists, including Nobel Prize winners, Lenard was not in the least disturbed: the Nobel Prize had 'become of increasingly contestable spiritual value', he said.

The other anti-Semitic Nobel Prize winner, Johannes Stark, was professor at Göttingen, Hanover, Aachen and then Würzburg. His isolation from his colleagues resulted from frustrated personal ambition and absurd rows about priority and credit. He was, of course, highly intelligent and, as a young man, had collaborated with Einstein, but he gradually became involved in quarrels with him and others. James Franck, a professor at Göttingen, described Stark as 'in every respect a pain in the neck'. Stark moved steadily towards the Nazis and joined them in 1930. He could not refute Einstein's discovery of the relation between energy and mass, $E=mc^2$, but, as so often in similar situations where Jews had made a discovery, he said that it had been made before and by someone who was not Jewish.

These critical views were made by Lenard and Stark at a distance, in articles and speeches, not directly to Einstein or in his presence. The opportunity for this came at a meeting of the German Physical Society in Bad Nauheim in September 1920. The preliminary rumbles had been menacing. The trouble came not because the ideas were wrong but because it was Einstein who had proclaimed them.

While Einstein was speaking there were organized interruptions so that, in spite of himself, Einstein became angry, quite unlike his usual character. Max Planck, the chairman, closed the meeting to stop it from becoming even more rowdy, but the anti-Einstein faction remained as resentful as ever, concluding that as the Physical Society would not allow an open discussion of relativity, other means would have to be found. A threatening air hung over the world of physics. It persisted until Hitler came to power, when it became only too manifest in the dismissals, expulsions and imprisonment of the Jews.

This air of menace was very clear to Einstein. He knew he had antagonized many Germans in almost every way he could, and in some he could not help. He was a Jew, and he was widely known to be a pacifist and politically on the left. He took the threats to himself so seriously that, in November 1923 at the time of the Hitler-Ludendorff putsch in Munich, he fled to Leiden in the Netherlands. Max Planck, knowing that Einstein would receive offers from abroad and concerned as ever with the preservation of German science, implored Einstein to come back to Germany. The reason for his return was the Berlin physics environment, which he valued above all else and which, so long as it lasted, was a magnet to him. The ability to get on with his work was the overriding consideration for him, nothing else mattered. This is what had taken him back to Berlin in 1914 when he was offered a professorship at the Kaiser Wilhelm Institute and this is what brought him back in 1923. He and his work prospered there until 1933. When Hitler came to power that year, while Einstein was in California, nothing could have persuaded him to go back. Everyone who reveres Einstein should remember what he had to contend with both personally and politically in the atmosphere in Germany during the 1920s and early 1930s. For more than two thirds of his life he had lived there, and for a large part of that time was under threat, personally as well as professionally,

But Einstein's fame had spread all over the world and he was invited to lecture in many places. He was like a modern footballer or baseball player, selling himself to the highest bidder, only in his case money was not the coinage. Einstein never cared about money. Two universities especially vied for him: the California Institute of Technology at Pasadena (Caltech), where Robert Millikan, himself a Nobel Prize winner, was the prime mover; and Christ Church, Oxford, where Frederick Lindemann wanted to catch him.

Millikan's idea was to entice Einstein to Caltech for three months each winter. He did not have to teach, beyond giving an occasional lecture: he just had to be around. His presence would stimulate the other physicists and create a buzz throughout the institute. This suited Einstein to perfection. So lacking was he in financial greed that in negotiating his salary he suggested that it should be reduced. What he wanted was seclusion to do his work, which was thinking, and a pencil and paper; otherwise he had no demands. He dreaded being shown off as a trophy – he loathed social occasions and the only people he wanted to talk to were fellow scientists, scientists of all grades. He was not, as so many German professors were, concerned only with his peers. He loved the company and the questions of younger colleagues.

His first visit was in 1931. American universities were not as wealthy then as they are now and Millikan had to persuade the authorities to give the money for Einstein and his wife to travel to California and stay there for a term. He succeeded and Caltech's success in netting Einstein caused some suspicion and jealousy in other quarters. Any university that could catch him would be triumphant and Caltech protected their prize catch – although not for long.

Things were not always easy for the hosts. Einstein himself behaved perfectly. He was quiet, unassertive and lacking in any urge for self-aggrandizement (there was never any need for that). He did not want to play any political role either in America or Germany. But, of course, he had done so. In Germany he was seen as left-wing and a pacifist, which he was. He was never a communist but in the eyes of some he was not sufficiently anti-communist. He never made any secret of his views, so they were known in the United States as well as in Germany. And he was a Jew. This weighed with some Americans and they were not enthusiastic about welcoming this German 'communist' Jew. Anti-Semitism in the West, though infinitely more subtle than in Germany, was still a potent force and it was worse in the early 1930s during the Great Depression. Many scientists were not inclined to welcome foreigners to their country to compete with them. The American job market in science was tight then, hard though this may be to imagine today when there are two million scientists. This understandable suspicion was more powerful in the case of other, lesser-known scientists than with Einstein, but it still existed for him.

The right wing in American politics was as bad as the 'Aryan' physicists in Germany in its hostility to Einstein and his work. The National Patriotic Council called him a German Bolshevik and said that his theory 'was of no scientific value or purpose, not understandable because there is nothing to understand'; and the American Women's League formally claimed that the State Department should not let in Einstein, who was a member of the War Resisters International and a communist. The American horror of supposed (or real) communists has a long history, although one would think that no country in the world has less reason for it. In fact, Einstein was never refused entry to the United States, he loved his visits there and his hosts loved having him.

His other enthusiastic foreign host was Frederick Lindemann (later Lord Cherwell), Professor of Physics at Oxford, who knew all the world's physicists and was himself of their company. Lindemann was not a great physicist in his own right, though he played a crucial role in Oxford physics. Seeing Einstein's quality very clearly, he wanted to get him for Oxford. He arranged for him to come to his college, Christ Church, where Einstein could be a research Fellow enjoying the hospitality of the college and the university with no duties to perform. As an added inducement Lindemann told Einstein, who was a passionate sailor, that he could sail in Oxford, so he would not be 'wasting his time here altogether'. It worked, for Einstein also visited Oxford in 1931. He gave a few lectures, not understood by all his audience because they were on relativity and in German. He was highly popular for himself and his eccentricities, which were almost the rule in Oxford (if eccentricity can be the rule). Einstein returned to Oxford in 1932 and the hope was that he would spend about a month each year there. Everyone was delighted, he loved Oxford and Oxford loved him. Because of developments in Germany he did not come back in later years and asked that his outstanding salary should go to help other German Jews.

It has been suggested that Einstein found Oxford stuffy and England too formal. This does not seem to be the impression he gave at the time. Roy Harrod, the economist, who was also a 'student' (Fellow) of Christ Church, found him charming and relations with him were of 'easy intimacy'. Einstein often dined in College, played the violin in his rooms and made Harrod feel that he, Einstein, was 'a very good man, a simple soul and rather naïve about worldly matters'. Although Einstein was a gentle, sweet man with a general love for mankind, he had difficulty in loving men or women personally. He could not form a close relationship with any individual, not even his wives. Lise Meitner commented on his elusive coldness towards colleagues, including those he knew well.

While Einstein was at Oxford the seeds were sown for the eventual decision over where he should spend the rest of his working life. It was largely made for him by events in Germany; certainly they made it impossible for him to return there.

When Hitler was made Chancellor of Germany on 30 January 1933 Einstein was at Caltech. Immediately he cancelled a lecture at the Prussian Academy of Sciences that he had been due to give when he got back. In the midst of the outpouring of anti-Jewish hate in the German press, Einstein was specifically singled out, accused of 'cultural internationalism', 'international treason' and 'pacifist excesses'. After the Reichstag fire on 27 February, which gave a clear sign that the Nazis were not just another German political party which would rule briefly and then be gone, Einstein knew he could not return to Germany. In a press statement he gave to the *New York World Telegraph* when he heard that Hitler had been made Chancellor, he declared: 'As long as I have any choice in the matter, I shall live only in a country where civil liberty, tolerance and equality of all citizens before the law prevail. Civil liberty implies freedom to express one's political convictions, in speech and in writing; tolerance implies respect for the convictions of others whatever they may be. These conditions do not exist in Germany at the present time.' Next day he left California with his wife Elsa for New York, where he spoke out about the danger in Germany. Not surprisingly, his public criticism stirred a response in Germany. One Berlin newspaper wrote: 'Good news from Einstein – he is not coming back.' Under one photograph of Einstein appeared the words 'not yet hanged'. He returned with his wife to Europe that month. While they were on board they heard that their summer home at Caputh, near Berlin, had been searched and the garden dug up under the pretext of looking for an arms cache. Clearly it was impossible for them to return to Germany. When their ship docked at Antwerp on 28 March on the way to Hamburg, Einstein disembarked, to be met by the Mayor of Antwerp and a group of Dutch professors who offered him temporary hospitality. He had been officially told by the German consul in New York that it would be safe for him to return, but privately he advised him not to.

He formally surrendered his German citizenship but kept his Swiss nationality. This infuriated the German authorities, who did not know how to deal with such a voluntary action – they were more used to depriving people of their rights, not having them surrendered. They were inhibited by the effect abroad of Einstein's expulsion, particularly fear of Great Britain and the chance that he would be given British citizenship. For a time they could not decide what to do about him. They did not want to create too much hostility abroad because he was by far the most famous of all the Jewish scientists but, on the other hand, they did not want to issue a list of those to be expelled which did not include his name. One can get some wry amusement from seeing the Nazis in political and bureaucratic doubt when their image and intention was always to appear quick and decisive.

The Nazis had no power to decide what Einstein did. He stayed in Belgium, where he received many offers of help and hospitality. One step he did take on the day he landed: he resigned from the Prussian Academy of Science. When he was elected to the Academy 20 years earlier, he had said that it was 'the greatest benefit . . . which you could confer on me'. It had been one of the main attractions in coming to Berlin, which was the world centre of physics. Now he left the Academy because it had always been closely associated with the Prussian State and because he knew that he would be expelled from it, thus embarrassing his friends, who would be in danger if they protested.

The Academy was craven in its response. It spoke of its indignation at Einstein's 'participation in atrocity mongering' and his 'activities as an agitator in foreign countries', adding that it had 'no reason to regret Einstein's withdrawal'. The Academy behaved as an organ of the Prussian State, and its attitude was mirrored in other academic institutions.

A few Academicians did protest, notably Max von Laue, the bravest of all the German scientists who remained in the country. He objected that no member had been consulted about the letter which spoke of 'no reason to regret Einstein's withdrawal', though the letter was nonetheless approved at a general meeting. Even Max Planck, the great conciliator, who had been on holiday at the time of the crucial meeting of the Academy, said that Einstein's press statement had made it impossible to retain him, while making it clear that Academicians realized Einstein's greatness, adding: 'the Einstein affair ... will not be counted among the Academy's pages of glory'. Returning six weeks later, he tried to mend fences. On the one hand he spoke of Einstein's greatness, comparing him to Kepler and Newton; on the other, he added that Einstein's own actions had made it impossible for him to remain in the Academy.

Many foreign invitations came to Einstein as he waited at Coq-sur-Mer, Belgium. The French government rushed through an Act of Parliament to create a new chair for him at the Collège de France. Madrid University offered him a chair, but Einstein withdrew when he was attacked in the Catholic press – a reminder of the forces outside Germany which hated him for his pacifism and left-wing views, not merely for being a Jew. He also received an offer from Chaim Weizmann, later founder of the State of Israel and himself a scientist, who tried to entice him to the Hebrew University in Tel Aviv. Einstein was reluctant. Weizmann naturally wanted to get great scientists to go to his new university, but Einstein thought that established scholars would have little difficulty in finding places and that the young and promising refugees should be given preference.

Einstein considered the plight of all the Jewish academics forced to leave Germany. There were also very many non-academic refugees, of course, but the academics were particularly hard hit because nearly all universities were State-run and thus their staff were civil servants and greatly affected by the law for 'reconstructing' the civil service passed in April 1933. He thought of starting a university for refugee professors and wrote to Leo Szilard, his former student and colleague in Berlin, and they met in Belgium on 14 May. Szilard had already started his own rescue operation but quickly realized that rather than start a new university for refugees it was better to support the efforts already being made in Britain to find new appointments for the refugees there and elsewhere. Einstein gave all the encouragement he could to the efforts of the Academic Assistance Council in London but did not take part in the organization of these efforts – perhaps just as well, as he was no organizer.

After some weeks in Belgium Einstein went back to Oxford at the invitation of Lindemann and stayed in Christ Church. The day after his arrival he gave the vote of thanks after a lecture to the undergraduates by Lord Rutherford. The two men were a complete contrast: Rutherford large, self-confident and extrovert; Einstein small, quiet and timid, especially on this occasion, his first visit to England since the coming of the Nazis.

'I can almost see Einstein now,' wrote one of the undergraduates who attended the meeting:

> a poor forlorn little figure, obviously disappointed at the way in which he had just been expelled from Germany by the Nazis. As he delivered his speech, it seemed to me that he was more than a little doubtful about the way in which he would be received in a British university. However, the moment he sat down he was greeted by a thunderous outburst of applause from us all. Never in my life shall I forget the wonderful change which took place in Einstein's face at that moment. The light came back into his eyes, and his whole face seemed transfigured with joy and delight when it came home to him in this way that, no matter how badly he had been treated by the Nazis, both he himself and his undoubted genius were at any rate greatly appreciated at Oxford.

Einstein stayed in Britain for several months, and everywhere people clamoured to have him to speak. He gave two named lectures in Oxford, then another in Glasgow in English and German, often without a script. Usually his audience was enthusiastic, sometimes it was baffled. In one series of lectures, the first was packed, the second was half full and the third attended by only a handful.

He was besieged not only for lectures but for support for the efforts being made in Britain to rescue the refugee academics from Germany. His most dramatic gesture was to speak at a meeting in the Albert Hall in London organized by a swashbuckling MP, Oliver Locker-Lampson, on 3 October 1933. The MP had done everything he could to help Einstein, offering him a cottage in Norfolk as a retreat. Fearing possible trouble, he arranged for Einstein to be 'protected' by his two young female secretaries armed with shotguns. It was Locker-Lampson's bold idea to take the Albert Hall, the largest in London, for the meeting; others doubted if there would be enough of a crowd to fill it, but it was packed. In addition to Einstein, there were many other stars: Rutherford chaired it, and other speakers included William Beveridge, head of the London School of Economics and Secretary of the Academic Assistance Council, and Austen Chamberlain, the former Foreign Secretary. Locker-Lampson himself spoke of the pride of the British people in welcoming the refugees, in flight from a 'pogrom of the intellect'. The public atmosphere at the time was thought to be so tense that the organizers, thinking there might be trouble, alerted the police, who searched everyone going into the meeting. In fact, there was no disturbance and the mood was one of enthusiasm for Einstein and for the whole rescue effort.

Among the people Einstein had met while staying in Norfolk was the sculptor Jacob Epstein. In his autobiography Epstein remembered Einstein vividly: 'His glance contained a mixture of the humane, the humorous and the profound', and he compared him to 'the ageing Rembrandt'. Einstein told Epstein that a hundred Nazi professors had publicly condemned his theory of relativity, adding: 'Were I wrong, one professor would have been quite enough.'

Einstein's arrival in Britain, perhaps inevitably, led to some controversy. He was accused of naivety in having supported pacifist movements which were really communist-front organizations. He wrote to *The Times* and the *New York Times* dissociating himself from the communist International. He also came to a painful decision. All his life he had been a pacifist, for pacifism completely reflected his own character and inclinations. But now, with the rise of Hitler, he realized that pacifism would no longer do. The world would soon face a threat more deadly and more powerful than any other, which could be defeated only by military power. It is easy to agree with this view now, but there were good people in the mid-1930s who, while far from left-wing, had still not come to that conclusion. In 1933 Germany was still militarily weak and many people in other countries did not see the danger, or preferred not to see it.

When Einstein made a public statement of his change of view in the summer of that year many of his old friends and allies were disappointed, even rejecting his idea of some kind of international force to keep the peace. The disappointed became articulate when Einstein declined to support two Belgians who had refused military service on conscientious grounds. This was a long way from his earlier statement that he 'would rather be hacked in pieces than take part in such an abominable business as war'. Now he said that if he were a Belgian he would cheerfully accept military service.

Einstein was uncertain of his future, especially as to where he should live, but his destination was finally settled. Oxford wanted him, Caltech wanted him, but they were eventually disappointed when Abraham Flexner enticed him to the new Institute for Advanced Study at Princeton. The place was to be what its title described: a place for study. There would be no teaching or administrative duties – in fact, no duties other than thinking. This suited Einstein perfectly. Anything that distracted him from thinking about physics was in his view a waste of time. The Institute would remain small, its staff a dozen or so of the greatest mathematical and other scholars. Einstein could have as much or as little to do with them as he liked. The world knew that, having made this decision, he would not go back to Germany, where things were getting worse.

The effect was immediate: refugees left Germany in large numbers, seeking shelter and employment abroad, many in Britain and America. The anti-intellectual atmosphere being fostered by the Nazis was hideously exemplified by the burning of the books on 10 May 1933. Large crowds watched as students – not Nazi thugs, but university students whose studies depended on books – carried piles of books by both German and foreign authors to the flames, to the cheers of the crowds. This happened not only in Berlin but in many towns all over Germany. Nothing showed more strikingly the essentially barbarian nature of the new order than the book burnings. It was, or should have been, a sign to everybody outside as well as inside Germany of what sort of regime was in power. The Nazis made no pretence that they were interested in the life of the mind: 'Nowadays the task of the universities is not to cultivate objective science but soldier-like military science, and their foremost task is to form the will and character of their students.'

The organized bodies of science went along with this travesty of learning. Max Planck, President of the Kaiser Wilhelm Institute, even said that no one could stand aside 'rifle at rest'. The Kaiser Wilhelm Society sent Hitler a telegram tendering 'reverential greetings' and pledging German science 'to cooperate joyously in the reconstruction of the new national state'.

In this atmosphere the personal attacks on Einstein increased. His bank account was seized, his flat and country house closed and his sailing boat smashed. Not long afterwards right-wing organizations offered a monetary reward for killing Einstein. Typically, Einstein took this threat lightly, saying that he did not know his life was 'worth so much'.

Einstein finally sailed for America and his lasting home at Princeton. Perhaps it is paradoxical that, in those ideal surroundings, he was unproductive. That may sound harsh. Of course, this stage of Einstein's career does not detract from the glory of his achievements in relativity and his discovery of the relationship of energy and mass, but those great events had occurred a quarter of a century earlier, when he was in his twenties and early thirties. They were the achievements of a young mind and nothing comparable could now be expected from a man in his fifties, even Einstein. Furthermore, he had turned to a search for a general field theory: the mathematical relationship between electromagnetism and gravitation. His colleagues, who loved and admired him for his great achievements and sweet nature, thought he was on a hopeless quest and promptly and politely told him so. The waggish comment of Wolfgang Pauli, another Nobel laureate, was: 'No man shall join what God has put asunder.' To no effect: Einstein went on. Max Born, his old friend and admirer as well as a great physicist, said: 'many of us regard this as a tragedy, both for him as he gropes his way in loneliness, and for us who miss our leader and standard-bearer.'

If the last third of Einstein's life was, in the scientific sense, a decline, that perhaps was not surprising, for generally the peak of intellectual output in science comes – if at all – early in life. The main effect of the Nazi persecution of the Jewish scientists was not so much in the expulsion of the famous but in the expulsion of the younger men – such as Krebs, Perutz and Chain – who themselves grew up to be great. They were the real harvest of Hitler's insanity.

(We refer throughout this book to scientists, and others, being 'expelled' or 'ejected' or 'thrown out' of Germany. In most but not all cases the refugees were not physically forced out of the country, but they lost their jobs – often without any notice – their salaries and their opportunities. They were in effect thrown out of Germany. Later the expulsions, especially among non-professionals, became even more brutal and abrupt.)

Einstein remained as a symbol to the world of opposition and contempt for Nazism and support for decency and humanity. Max Born called Einstein a standard-bearer, meaning the leader of the scientific endeavour, but he was also a standard-bearer for humanity in the fight against evil.

While Einstein played no part in the creation of the atomic bomb, his famous letter to President Roosevelt of August 1939, actually drafted by Szilard, Wigner and Teller (all European refugees), alerted the President to the need for a bomb-building programme. Einstein called this 'the greatest mistake of my life'. He could have spared himself such criticism: the bomb would surely have been made if the letter had never been sent. In fact, little happened until seven months later, when the work of Peierls and Frisch showed that a bomb was indeed a practical possibility. Einstein did not learn of the existence of the bomb until the public announcement on 8 August 1945. He was as horrified as anyone else and he joined in the movement of scientists to control and restrict atomic energy to peaceful purposes.

After the victory of 1945, Einstein was even more anti-German than most of his colleagues. The only man who had stayed in Germany whom he still respected was Max von Laue; for the nation as a whole he was as full of hatred as anyone on the Allied side. He refused invitations to travel to Germany and speak; he even refused to rejoin German scientific academies. He also refused to become an honorary citizen of Ulm, where he had been born. When Max Born retired in 1952 and went to live in Germany, Einstein criticized him for going back to the country of mass-murderers. Einstein had always been out of sympathy with the general view of the Prussian character. Now he laid the blame on all Germans. This hardness of attitude, seemingly so at variance with his character, came, we must remember, after the discovery of the Holocaust, a crime of unparalleled wickedness. So forcefully had the horrors of most of recent German history imprinted themselves on Einstein that, in his middle years, he could not soften his attitudes.

Viewing Einstein from this distance in time it is clear that the actual loss to Germany of his departure was not significant. His great scientific work had been done much earlier. His contribution to science thereafter was not in itself important. Symbolically, however, his rejection of and by Germany was hugely important. He stood for reason, tolerance and gentleness against a regime of anger, hatred and aggression.

4

Rescuers

First they came for the Socialists, and I did not speak out – because I was not a Socialist. Then they came for the trades unionists and I did not speak out – because I was not a trades unionist. Then they came for the Jews and I did not speak out – because I was not a Jew. Then they came for me – and there was not one left to speak for me.

Pastor Niemöller

Within weeks of Hitler's coming to power efforts to rescue German academics began. Sir William Beveridge, Director of the London School of Economics, was on holiday in Vienna in March 1933. He was talking with friends in a café when the evening paper was brought in. It listed the names of professors in Germany known to Beveridge who had been dismissed from their posts solely because they were Jews – intimidation and sackings of Jewish scholars and professionals had begun well before the law reconstructing the civil service was passed on 7 April that year. Beveridge and his friends read the names with growing indignation. He immediately decided to do what he could to help them. He cut the article from the newspaper and posted it to his office in London.

Shortly afterwards Beveridge was visited at his hotel by the Hungarian Jewish physicist Leo Szilard. Szilard clearly foresaw how Nazism would develop in Germany and guessed that the logical process of German thinking would largely prevent resistance: 'If I protest,' the reasoning went, 'I shall be removed from my post where I have influence, then I'll have none. So I had better be quiet and see what happens.'

Szilard had left Berlin the day before the anti-Jewish national boycott. Fearing for his life, he picked up his ready-packed suitcase and took the train to Vienna. Through economist friends he took the opportunity to meet Beveridge to discuss his own plan for helping the dismissed scholars: a university in exile in Switzerland. The project was ambitious but, as it emerged, impracticable. Instead Beveridge invited Szilard to London to 'prod' him about rescue initiatives.

The story of Leo Szilard runs through the refugees' histories during the 1930s. Even as the enormous forces of international events interrupted and redirected his own life, he managed to help shape history. Szilard was a good example of an escaper who left Germany on his own initiative and then put all his energies into rescuing others. He came from a comfortable background in Budapest, living in an enormous house filled with extended family. He had graduated from the Budapest Technical University with a degree in civil engineering, largely because there were no openings in Hungary for a career in physics. In later life he wrote: 'I cannot say that I regret it because whatever I learned while I was studying engineering stood me in good stead later after the discovery of the fission of uranium.' During the First World War he joined the Austro-Hungarian army as a one-year volunteer in 1917, and after the armistice in November 1918 he returned to the Technical University.

By then Hungary was in a state of collapse, with anti-Semitism feeding on an economy wrecked by the war and galloping inflation. Leo and his younger brother Bela had joined a group of freethinking students involved in socialist politics. In autumn 1919, when the brothers tried to enter the Technical University, a group of students barred their way and beat them up because they were Jews. First the Communists and then counter-revolutionary forces gained power, and Romania seized the opportunity to invade Hungary.

Szilard had already renounced his Jewish religion (he and his family were not practising Jews) to become a Calvinist. He began to limit his possessions to a packed suitcase and, after the incident at the Technical University, using whatever influence he could muster, he acquired a passport and visa. With banknotes hidden in his shoes and carrying his suitcase containing his possessions, he took a train to Vienna on a one-day excursion ticket. By a roundabout route he arrived in Berlin in January 1920, registered at the Technical University and arranged for Bela to join him.

He was soon drawn into the orbit of the University Physics Institute's galaxy of physicists and, with typical chutzpah, had talked his way into the KWI. Before long he asked Einstein to teach him statistical mechanics with a few friends, including fellow Hungarians Eugene Wigner and Dennis Gabor (later inventor of holography), both future Nobel Prize winners, and John von Neumann, who developed games theory and economic theory. Einstein, at 41, soon became friendly with the 22-year-old Szilard and by 1922 they were working together on the design of an electromagnetic pump to propel refrigerator coolants. Nearly three decades later the system was used in the cooling systems of nuclear reactors.

Despite taking courses in calculus, applied mathematics, theory of temperature and electrotechnical experiments, Szilard did not seem overworked. In the evenings he passed his engineering sketches to Bela to complete while he sat thinking – a process of allowing intriguing ideas to flow into his mind which he called 'botching'. During these botching sessions and long walks Szilard's fertile imagination devised solutions to problems others might not even consider. Noticing, for instance, that women in Berlin constantly hitched up their stocking tops, he concluded that if iron threads were woven into the stocking tops a couple of strong magnets in a jacket or coat's lower pockets could hold them up.

Szilard's doctoral thesis was accepted by Max von Laue, whose assistant he became in 1925; his paper on thermodynamic equilibrium is now thought of as the forerunner of Information Theory, developed 30 years later. He became an unpaid lecturer at the Technical Institute. Galvanized by ideas, living an impoverished life in paper-strewn rented rooms, Szilard was a true intellectual wanderer, forever flitting from one subject to another, preoccupied with understanding life itself and devising solutions to the world's problems.

In 1933 the coming of the Nazis provoked Szilard's reverse flight from Berlin to Vienna. Depositing some money in a bank in Geneva, he took up Beveridge's offer and went to London, where he immediately threw his energies into making contacts with people who could help the refugees.

As the Nazi regime's political and racial persecution began to take effect, the British government was forced to consider its policy in relation to the sudden influx of 'visitors' arriving at its ports from Germany, many of whom admitted that they were refugees. On 12

April the British Cabinet met to consider what could be done for the Jewish exiles. Reaching a cautious decision, it resolved to: 'Try and secure for this country prominent Jews who were being expelled from Germany and who had achieved distinction whether in pure science, applied science, such as medicine or technical industry, music or art.' This, the Cabinet considered, would 'not only obtain for this country the advantage of their knowledge and experience, but would also create a very favourable impression in the world, particularly if our hospitality were offered with some warmth'.[1]

The Cabinet's mixture of cautious compassion and opportunism was characteristic of a country which, at that time, was not a multiracial community and had comparatively few immigrants. The early 1930s were marked by widespread unemployment and insecurity in the labour market and immigrants were seen as competitors for jobs. The government was acutely conscious that, only 15 years after the end of the First World War, an influx of large numbers of refugees could spark off a wave of anti-German feelings, as well as open anti-Semitism. Jewish immigration to Palestine was also problematic, with strong objections being raised by the Arab populations there and in neighbouring countries. The British government, which had a mandate from the League of Nations to administer Palestine, had to tread a fine line between conflicting demands of Arabs and Jews. Above all, if Britain and other European countries opened their doors to the Reich's refugees, the insoluble problem loomed of millions of penniless Jews from Poland and elsewhere in Eastern Europe who might be expelled in their wake.

The Home Office, Foreign Office, Treasury and Colonial Office wrestled with different aspects of the problems posed by Germany's measures against the citizens it classed as 'undesirables'. The Home Secretary responded to questions about the refugees with a stock parliamentary response: 'The interests of this country must predominate over all other considerations but, subject to this guiding principle, each case will be carefully considered on its individual merits . . . in accordance with the time-honoured tradition of this country no unnecessary obstacles are placed in the way of foreigners seeking admission.'

There the matter seems to have rested. In the 1930s the government intervened far less in public and private life than its successors have done since the Second World War; it was content to pass the initiative to voluntary associations and committees bent on the rescue and relief of the victims of the Nazi regime.

A crucial aspect of the admissions policy was that no refugee was to become a charge on the government; if the public purse was unaffected there could be no accusation that the refugees were a drain on the nation. The Jewish community in Britain acted promptly to rescue the Jews exiled from Germany under the Nazis' first racial statutes. The Jewish Board of Deputies met on 3 April and agreed to support whatever initiatives were taken in aid of the refugees. Several Anglo-Jewish organizations in association created the Central British Fund for German Jewry, later the Council for German Jewry, which launched an appeal in May that raised many thousands of pounds. This was spent on helping refugees in Britain, on setting up Jewish schools in Germany (after Jewish children were banned from taking up more than 5 per cent of places in German schools) and assisting pioneering work in Palestine. A Jewish Refugee Committee, later the German Jewish Aid Committee, was launched to cover admissions, as well as maintenance, training and employment of further emigration of refugees. The Committee was largely organized by Otto M. Schiff, a banker who had contacts with the Home Office and other ministries. In effect the Committee undertook either to find work for each of its charges as they arrived in Britain or to maintain them while here.

William Beveridge had meanwhile returned to London from Vienna for the start of the new academic term and quickly persuaded the Professorial Council of the London School of Economics to launch an Academic Assistance Fund to support the displaced scholars. The staff of the LSE donated between 1 and 3 per cent of their salaries, the initial target being to raise £1000 a year for three years. However, it soon became obvious that funding on this scale would be nowhere near enough.

During the weekend of 6–8 May 1933 Beveridge was invited to stay with the historian G. M. Trevelyan, Master of Trinity College, Cambridge. He warned his host beforehand that he would probably be able to talk of nothing but the displaced German professors, and proceeded to do so. During the weekend the Trevelyans, Sir Frederick Gowland Hopkins, professor of biochemistry and discoverer of vitamins, and Lord Rutherford, President of the Royal Society, drew up a scheme for an Academic Assistance Council (AAC) to help the refugees. Lord Rutherford became its President, and Professor A. V. Hill, Biological Secretary of the Royal Society, its Vice President. An appeal was drafted and signed by 42 eminent academics, scientists and public figures; this was published in *The Times* and sent on 10 May to The Royal Society. The AAC approved the appeal the following day, and the Royal Society offered the use of two rooms in the attic of its premises at Burlington House, Piccadilly. These were only a bedroom and a bathroom but at least the address was good; they were soon occupied by Leo Szilard, who was already exploiting every contact on behalf of the refugees.

The Royal Society suggested that in order to avoid the risk that the appeal might look like a crusade by Jews for their own people, the officers and signatories should not be of Jewish origin. Only one signatory was a Jew, Professor S. Alexander OM, one of Britain's foremost philosophers. The appeal, in the form of a letter, made it clear that although Jews were the immediate target of the Nazis, the rise of Fascism would also displace many others, and that the refugee problem was not exclusively a Jewish one.

The news about the displaced academics was taken up by the press. The *Manchester Guardian* played a leading role, publishing on 19 May the names and appointments of 195 professors who had been dismissed during the previous three weeks. Late in May all Britain's major newspapers carried the AAC's appeal. The purpose of the AAC, this explained, was 'to raise a fund to be used primarily, though not exclusively, to provide maintenance for displaced teachers and research workers, and find them the chance to work in universities and scientific institutions . . . We ask for means to prevent the waste of exceptional abilities exceptionally trained . . . Our only aims are the relief of suffering and the defence of learning and science.'

By the time the AAC held its first meeting on 1 June, the appeal had already raised £10,000. Beveridge and C. S. Gibson, Professor of Chemistry at Guy's Hospital, were appointed joint secretaries, and shortly after the initial meeting Walter Adams left a lectureship at University College, London to become the AAC's full-time Secretary. An Assistant Secretary was appointed at a salary of £2 10s. (£2.50) a week: Esther (Tess) Simpson, who had been working in

Vienna for the International Fellowship of Reconciliation and then as assistant to the Director of the YMCA in Geneva. The salary was about a third of what Tess Simpson had been paid in Geneva, but she took the job at once. For 19 out of the 25 years of the AAC (which in 1936 became the Society for the Protection of Science and Learning, or SPSL) she worked tirelessly and effectively to help the 2600 exiled scholars who received its assistance in starting a new life. When she retired in 1966 she was presented with a cheque and hundreds of letters. 'Our Miss Simpson,' read one, 'was always there . . . she helped each of us most efficiently, yet without a trace of the immense trouble to which she went.'

During her years working abroad Tess Simpson had got to know a number of scholars and academics through what she called her 'two passports . . . one was being English – and that was a very great plus – and the other, music'. She played the violin and was in regular demand to play chamber music with friends, acquaintances and colleagues. Musicianship ran like a freemasonry through Viennese society in the late 1920s, and was a meeting point with a striking number of refugee scholars whom she helped through the AAC.

Tess Simpson arrived at Burlington House on 17 July 1933, to find Szilard already ensconced – in fact he had been instrumental in getting her the job. They had met in Geneva when he went to deposit his money there, through a mutual friend, the economist Karl Polanyi, who hoped that she could arrange contacts who might help Szilard with his university in exile. At Burlington House Szilard turned his hand to anything that required doing, especially the business of bringing together those in need and organizations capable of providing help. While Tess Simpson ran the office, he flitted between London and Europe, travelling light as usual, supplying the AAC with lists of contacts. He continued to work with Tess Simpson until he left for America in 1937.

Other British and German scientists also gave their time, among them Hermann (later Hugh) Blaschko, who escaped from Germany in May 1933. He immediately went to work putting refugees in touch with the AAC and helping them to find jobs. The AAC's small staff often worked late in the evenings until they were forced to leave because the gates of the Royal Society at Burlington House were locked at ten. Their task was to act as a kind of labour exchange, matching refugee scholars to academic institutions that could use their particular expertise. At first nearly all the refugees were Jews who had been dismissed or had already reached Britain. Those most likely to succeed in finding a place were academics between 30 and 40 who had made a name for themselves, and promising younger PhD graduates. An annual grant of £250 was made to a married couple and £180 to a single person, to keep them going while they learned the language and made their own contacts. The AAC gave grants only to academics. Applicants who were unlikely to succeed in finding a university post were encouraged to teach, or to go into industry, where they often earned more than those who found academic work.

Beveridge spoke everywhere he could about the need for the AAC's work, using his contacts with the press, the BBC, government ministries and foundations to raise money. He also approached bankers, trusts and trades unions, although the cause did not attract widespread attention until the late 1930s. 'Whatever you give is valuable,' he said in his appeals. 'Whatever you give will be too little.'

In June the AAC appealed to the vice chancellors of every university to find places for the refugee scholars and, if possible, funds to maintain them. Oxford was perhaps typical in offering no concerted university response and insisting that no financial charge must be made on the university. But it encouraged colleges and departments to help with temporary hospitality for the displaced scientists. By May 1934 London University had found places for 67 scholars, Cambridge 31 and Oxford 17.

In its first three years the AAC helped 1300 displaced university teachers as well as being instrumental in finding permanent jobs for many others. It also gave temporary assistance while refugees looked for permanent positions. Its efforts raised £46,000 and while this was a small sum compared with that raised by the Jewish Board of Deputies, the AAC's remit was restricted to academics, and its role as a facilitator was invaluable to people for whom a job was their passport to a new life.

Others besides Beveridge initiated rescues. Einstein's host at Christ Church, Frederick Lindemann, had close connections with Germany and German science, and this made him uniquely qualified both to help its refugee scholars and to exploit their skills. As Professor of Physics at Oxford (there called Experimental Philosophy), he presided over the Clarendon Laboratory, which was small, outdated and old-fashioned; no match for the Cavendish Laboratory at Cambridge under Lord Rutherford. Lindemann's aim was to raise the Clarendon's standing to rival that of the Cavendish.

He quickly seized the opportunity to import scientific talent from Germany to Oxford. In May 1933 he was driven by his chauffeur in his Rolls-Royce to Breslau to meet Professor Nernst. 'Have you got anyone for me?' he asked. Nernst had.

Lindemann was a complex and, to many people, daunting figure. His happiest years were spent in Germany, and he regarded Walther Nernst as his mentor. Lindemann's father was from Alsace and both Lindemann and his brother were sent to study for their doctorate in Nernst's laboratory in Breslau. In 1911 Lindemann had been co-secretary with the Duc de Broglie of the first Solvay Congress. However, he did not become a great physicist. Nernst, ever caustic, once remarked that his favourite pupil might have been a better physicist if his father had not been so rich. Those early years of privilege, studying under Nernst and competing in tennis tournaments with European royalty, ended abruptly when the First World War was declared.

In Britain, Lindemann's German connections were suspect and he was refused an army commission. Working instead in aircraft research at Farnborough, he took a plane up to a great height and then put it into a nosedive to show how it could come out of a 'tail spin' and land safely. This potentially suicidal test was almost certainly undertaken to defy the supposed dishonour attached to his German name.

On taking up his professorship at Oxford in 1919, Lindemann had found that his ambitions to improve the Clarendon Laboratory's reputation by building on his low-temperature research in Germany were frustrated by lack of funds from the university as well as the Clarendon's reputation as a place for 'gentleman scientists'. This, on top of his wartime experiences, made him withdrawn and uncommunicative and he was often disliked for his apparent arrogance. A meeting with Winston Churchill in 1921 led to a close friendship and, during the Second World War, by which time Lindemann was

Viscount Cherwell, he wielded considerable power as Churchill's scientific adviser.

Nernst had several candidates at Breslau for Lindemann's shopping list. They were young, bright and Jewish. Kurt Mendelssohn had already moved back to the Clarendon Laboratory in late April 1933, only months after he had returned from working there setting up a helium liquefier – thus enabling Lindemann to steal a march on the Cavendish. Franz Simon gave up his professorship at Breslau in July, followed by Nicholas Kurti and Heinz London and then Heinz's brother Fritz, who worked with Erwin Schrödinger.

With his excellent connections, Lindemann persuaded ICI to put up the money to fund the new scientists and the equipment they needed at the Clarendon. Thus he was able to bring them all to Oxford, giving its physics department a huge boost as well as an identity in its research. The Clarendon acquired an international reputation in cryogenics (low-temperature research) and also became a centre of high-resolution spectroscopy under Heinrich Kuhn with Derek Jackson. By 1939 a new laboratory had been built to house a staff which had increased from two to 20. Lindemann had good reason to be pleased with his shopping trip.

The geneticist Professor J. B. S. Haldane also took action. As celebrated for his reckless disregard for convention as for his outstanding intellect, Haldane was in 1933 Professor of Biometry at University College, London, having previously been attached to the biochemistry department at Cambridge. Among the refugees he befriended was Hans Grüneberg, a young geneticist from Heidelberg, for whom he managed to find a place in the zoology department. Grüneberg arrived promptly at the department at eight o'clock on his first morning and had to wait more than two hours for Haldane. When he turned up Haldane proceeded to make Grüneberg welcome, taking him first to the zoo and later to lunch. Grüneberg recalled that soon after his arrival in London he was touched to see a policeman in Whitehall stoop to stroke a cat, not a gesture he had seen in Nazi Germany. Despite his background in genetics, during the Second World War he and Hans Kalmus, another refugee geneticist, helped Haldane with war work, including practical experiments on escaping from submarines in which (as often with Haldane) they took part themselves. Both men stayed all their working lives at University College, where Grüneberg said he 'felt at home from the very beginning'.

The great physiologist A. V. Hill, as Vice President of the AAC, was actively involved in the rescue of many German scientists. In one case he played an unusual role, that of beacon rather than lifeboat. In an article in *Nature* on the international status and obligations of science, he roundly condemned the Nazis' treatment of German scientists. His statement provoked a reply from the pro-Nazi Nobel laureate Johannes Stark, who was effectively Gauleiter of Science in the Third Reich. Stark replied that Hill was quite wrong: the German government was entitled to protect itself against disloyal citizens and any other government would have taken similar action. By the time Stark's letter appeared in *Nature*, Hill had already raised money in aid of the refugee scientists. His letter in response, also published in *Nature*, conceded that he did not know whether his fund-raising success was due to his own advocacy or to Stark's, but at any rate he thanked Stark for his help. This light-hearted riposte to a deadly viewpoint so delighted Bernard Katz, a young medical graduate at Leipzig, that he made his way from Germany to University College with little else but his degree. He stayed for most of his working life, becoming Hill's successor and winning a Nobel Prize in 1970 for his work on the biochemistry of muscle.

William Beveridge's efforts on behalf of the refugee scholars included approaching the Rockefeller Foundation in New York, to suggest that it might set up an international office to coordinate the efforts of different countries to find positions and funds for the refugees. The Foundation had funded the research of many bright young German scientists and also helped with other scientific projects in Germany up to the late 1930s – it partly funded a new home for the Kaiser Wilhelm Institute for Physics in Berlin, built in 1937. Although it did not set up a coordinating office, the Foundation did at once raise a special fund for use by American universities in support of academic refugees. By the end of 1934 it had assisted 31 scholars in Britain and 9 in Europe; by the end of the war $1 million had been spent and 300 individuals rescued.

The American effort was started by the Emergency Committee for Aid to Displaced German Scholars, and by 1935 the total American contribution, led by the Rockefeller Foundation, equalled the rest of the world's. Otherwise known as the American Emergency Committee (AEC), the agency ultimately managed to assist half of the 1700 academic refugees in America. The AEC did not ask the universities for financial aid for the refugees, as the AAC had done in Britain, because the universities themselves were at that time starved of funds. Almost all the money for the AEC came from Jewish foundations. American society was in the main resistant to the problems of European refugees; Ed Murrow of the AEC (the foreign correspondent who later did so much in the United States to foster sympathy for the British war effort by his wartime broadcasts from London) wrote to Walter Adams in London complaining about the 'general indifference of the [American] university world' and the 'complacency in the face of what has happened to Germany. There is a tendency to consider the matter as a Jewish problem and a failure to recognize that it represents a threat to academic freedom in this country as well as Europe.'

The Royal Society had been wise to recommend that neither the secretaries nor members of the AAC should be 'of Jewish origin', thus avoiding the presentation of the problem as relating only to Jewish refugees. It was, of course, much easier for people in Britain to recognize Hitler's threat to academic freedom, because he was virtually at the door of every European nation. In the United States, refugee academics found themselves competing for places and funds with American scholars, a situation which created resentment on the campuses. In 1935 the AEC, acutely nervous of the possibility of an anti-Semitic backlash, sent a delegate to Britain with the message that American universities had no more room for refugees. The AAC, unconvinced, continued to supply applicants with funds for return tickets to the United States, advising them to seek places in smaller universities there. Almost all returned with jobs confirmed.

By the summer of 1935 any hopes the AAC might have had that the flow of refugees would recede were dashed by the passing of the so-called Nuremberg laws, which deemed that having one Jewish grandparent made a person Jewish.

In September, Goering announced a new law of citizenship with two categories: the Reichsburger of pure German blood, and the *Staatsangehöriger*, now classed as a subject but not a citizen. The new legislation decreed that the two categories could no longer cohabit, in or out of marriage; and also dealt with hereditary health – enforcing abortion if a parent carried an hereditary disease. Other clauses banned Jews from all professions, schools and colleges, from owning factories, publishing houses, theatres and large stores. Jewish doctors could treat only Jewish patients; Jewish musicians could no longer play in orchestras or theatres. From that autumn every passport belonging to a Jew was stamped with a 'J'. Deprived of their citizenship and political rights, Jews and 'non-Aryans' alike were driven out of the State economy by relentless segregation.

Far from there being less need to help the persecuted, there was more. In March 1936 the AAC accordingly changed its name to the Society for the Protection of Science and Learning. The SPSL was formally launched with a document signed by William Beveridge called 'A Defence of Free Learning', and its stated aim was 'to assist scholars who are victims of political or religious persecution'.[2] The organization was, to borrow the words that Sir Francis Bacon used to describe the founding of the Bodleian Library in 1544, 'an Ark, built to save learning from deluge'.

There was one remarkable character who was both rescuer and rescued. He was the 'Great Dane', Niels Bohr. Everyone with ambition in physics went to Copenhagen to work with him or sit at his feet. He was a magnet professionally and personally: professionally as the leader in quantum mechanics and a winner of the Nobel Prize in 1922 while still in his thirties; personally as a supremely friendly and helpful man, especially to young physicists.

Bohr was an inspiration to everyone he met, not only scientists. He was his country's most famous man, 'the uncrowned king of Denmark', open and friendly to all, as is illustrated by a charming story told by the young Austro-American scientist Victor Weisskopf:[3]

One evening at six o'clock, my usual quitting time, Bohr and I were still deep in discussion. I had an appointment that night and had to leave promptly, so Bohr walked me to the streetcar stop, about five minutes from his house. We walked and he talked. When we got there, the streetcar was approaching. It stopped and I climbed on to the steps. But Bohr was not finished. Oblivious to the people sitting in the car, he went right on with what he had been saying while I stood on the steps. Everyone knew who Bohr was, even the motorman, who made no move to start the car. He was listening with what seemed like rapt attention while Bohr talked for several minutes about certain subtle properties of the electron. Finally Bohr was through and the streetcar started. I walked to my seat under the eyes of the passengers, who looked at me as if I were a messenger from a special world, a person chosen to work with the great Niels Bohr.

Bohr had lived in Denmark all his life and was not a Jew (though his mother was) so his interest in the Nazi persecution was not at first direct. But every part of his nature was out of sympathy with the Nazis. He sheltered many German physicists in his institute in Copenhagen until they could find, or have found for them, permanent jobs; he also sought out threatened scientists within Germany and found institutions which would receive them. By 1933, when the Nazis came to power, although he was only in his forties, Bohr was a father figure to young and not-so-young physicists. When the Germans occupied Denmark in 1940 he was able to continue with his work but he could not travel and he was cut off from his friends and colleagues in the West.

There was a bizarre episode in August 1941 when Heisenberg visited Copenhagen from Germany to see Bohr. (This episode forms the subject of an interesting play by Michael Frayn, *Copenhagen*, first staged in London in 1998.) Even now no one knows why he went. To offer not to make an atomic bomb if America did not? To warn Bohr that Germany was making one? To say that he would prevent a bomb being made in Germany? The visit was a disaster. It destroyed for ever Bohr's trust in Heisenberg, and later many other people's.

From early in 1943 the British government, realizing Bohr's potential importance in atomic-fission research, wanted to get him to Britain. In the autumn of that year things got worse in Denmark. King Christian X, who had insisted on wearing the yellow star that Jews were compelled to wear, was interned, others were also interned and Jews were deported. Although he was not yet personally threatened, Bohr saw the danger. With others he was smuggled across the narrow straits to Sweden. Thence he was flown in an RAF Mosquito to Britain, an uncomfortable journey. The plane had to fly high; Bohr did not hear the instruction to put on his oxygen mask and fell unconscious halfway across the North Sea, although when they dropped to a lower level he recovered consciousness. (A bizarre episode! Should a Nobel Prize winner need to be told to put on his oxygen mask?) Soon afterwards he was flown to the United States, where at Los Alamos he was amazed to discover the progress in building an atomic bomb – something he had thought impracticable. His presence was immensely helpful to the research team.

Bohr saw the danger of the weapon. He tried – unsuccessfully – to persuade Churchill and Roosevelt to confide in the Russians in order to reduce their suspicions of the West (probably impossible, but the extent of Stalin's paranoia was not yet fully realized). Bohr spent years trying to persuade statesmen of the need for control of the atomic bomb. He met Churchill, who was completely out of sympathy with his actions and even suspected him of treachery. Churchill persuaded Roosevelt, who described himself as 'worried to death' about the problem, to maintain absolute secrecy. The existence of the weapon was finally disclosed to Stalin at the Potsdam Conference in July 1945; he seemed quite uninterested because, as we now know, he already knew all about it through the activities of Klaus Fuchs and others.

Although he won every honour imaginable, Bohr remained utterly open and modest. Not only was he one of the greatest scientists of the century but he was universally beloved. Perhaps the feelings of those who knew him are best shown by Otto Frisch. In 1933 Frisch had gone to Hamburg; his Rockefeller fellowship to work with Fermi in Rome had been withdrawn, which meant he had no appointment to return to. Bohr was travelling through Germany to see who needed help, and Frisch recalled:

> To me it was a great experience to be suddenly confronted with Niels Bohr, an almost legendary name for me, to see him smile at me like a kindly father. He took me by my waistcoat button and said, 'I hope you will come and work with us sometime; we like people who can carry out "thought experiments"' . . . That night I wrote to my mother . . . and told her not to worry. The Good Lord himself had taken me by the waistcoat button and smiled at me. That was exactly how I felt.

Frisch also described Bohr 'drawing wisdom out of us which we didn't know we had and which of course we hadn't'.[4]

Bohr not only inspired reverence in others but he felt the same himself. He worshipped his own physics mentor, Ernest Rutherford, the man who 'split the atom'. Bohr worked with him when Rutherford was still at Manchester and later when he moved to the chair in Cambridge, where Rutherford tried to get a chair for Bohr. 'Rutherford showed a kind of sympathy for my youthful enthusiasm and became till the end of his life almost a second father to me,' Bohr said. As for his own greatness and method of work in the 1920s and 1930s, Victor Weisskopf wrote:

> Here was Bohr's influence at its best. Here it was that he created his style, the 'Kopenhagener Geist', the style which he has imposed on physics – the style of a very special character. We see him, the greatest among his peers, acting, talking, living as an equal in a group of young, optimistic, jocular, enthusiastic people, approaching the deepest riddles of nature with a spirit of attack, a spirit of freedom from conventional bonds and a spirit of joy which can hardly be described.

Bohr was such a great and pervasive figure in the world of physics for over 40 years before he died in 1962 that it is difficult to categorize him. We have briefly described his life here in the group of rescuers because he helped so many of the refugees. Later we shall include him in the discussion of the atomic bomb (see Chapter 10).

Britain and America were not the only countries to rescue displaced academics. Efforts were made in Switzerland, Turkey and France. Professor Philip Schwartz was a Hungarian Jew who became Professor of Pathology in Frankfurt-am-Main. Ousted by the racial laws in 1933, he fled to Zurich and there founded the Emergency Society of German Scholars Abroad, the *Notgemeinschaft*. At the end of 1933 the Turkish government invited Schwartz to set up a university in Istanbul. He helped to found a medical school there and served for 20 years as head of its Institute of Pathology, recruiting some 250 first-class scientists. When Schwartz left Zurich, Dr Demuth, the former administrator of the College of Commerce in Berlin, became chairman of the *Notgemeinschaft* and moved the office to London. There the SPSL found room for it and the two organizations began to work closely together.

In France a movement to assist refugee scholars started at the same time as the AAC in Britain, but it was poorly organized and foundered a year later. It also ran up against traditional French anti-Semitism. The dramatist Jean Giraudoux, head of the Commission of Information, was not alone in complaining that Jewish refugees were swamping the 'noble French artisan'. His declaration that he was in full agreement with Hitler's policies in respect of the Jews pandered to widespread fears of unemployment and poverty after the Great Depression.

Later another French organization was launched by Louis Rapkine, a Russian-born Jewish biochemist who had emigrated to Canada as a child. He had returned to France, to the Pasteur Institute in Paris. He went to London to consult Tess Simpson and Walter Adams at the AAC on the French situation. The new French agency involved Irène Joliot-Curie and other leading academics, who were anxious to keep in regular contact with the AAC. Rapkine had practical plans for coordinating the work of the various international rescue agencies, but Hitler's invasion of Austria in 1938 prevented this.

When war broke out Rapkine, who was in London with a French scientific mission, stayed in Britain. Determined to rescue some 80 Jewish scholars stranded in France at risk from Nazi persecution, he went to Washington to ask the Americans to help. Somehow he contrived to get word back to the scholars, and to his own wife and small daughter, to travel by certain dates to several French ports, where they would be picked up by American ships and taken across the Atlantic to safety. In the event the scholars were unhappy in the United States, where they were not allowed to work unless they took out American nationality. Rapkine eventually managed to bring them to England, where they joined either de Gaulle's Free French or the British forces.

Rapkine became a close friend of Tess Simpson. Aside from being a brilliant biochemist, he had a matchless talent for persuasion, organization and avoiding American red tape. Brave and humorous, he saved many lives. After his death in 1948 at the age of 44, friends set up a memorial fund for the exchange of young French scientists to study in Britain and young British scientists to work in France. In an address to a memorial meeting for Rapkine in 1949, A. V. Hill said: 'Rapkine's attitude to refugee scholars was precisely that of the SPSL. For him – as for the SPSL – they were not so many "cases" but valuable individuals whose knowledge and experience must be saved and whose dignity must be upheld for the benefit of the learned world and who, as persons, must be made as comfortable as possible in alien circumstances.'

In 1958 Lord Beveridge decided to find out from scholars who had been assisted by the SPSL how they had fared in their places of resettlement.[5] Of 1170 letters and questionnaires posted worldwide, 561 replies were received – a sizeable number, considering how many of the academics had moved or died. Their answers were appreciative: several mentioned in particular the way the help had been given 'with no strings whatever attached to it and without the slightest psychological pressure on the recipient in order to make him or her feel they had received help'. Surprisingly, the majority responded that they had no regrets at having been forced to emigrate. Dr J. Rzoska, a Polish biologist, wrote: 'Being forced to change my life at least three times in the last twenty years has proved to be difficult, but on the whole salutary ... the exigencies have broadened my ideas and judgements on human and scientific problems.'

Inevitably some refugees found it difficult to adjust to life and work in a foreign country, but the answers showed that it was the scientists who found it easiest to adapt, probably because they had had more contact with overseas colleagues before they were exiled.

Many of the refugees brought intellectual riches to Britain. Of the 2600 rescued by the AAC and the SPSL, 20 became Nobel laureates, 54 were elected Fellows of the Royal Society, 34 became Fellows of the British Academy, and ten received knighthoods. Lord Beveridge wrote: 'No study that I have made in my life has ever seemed so worthwhile.'

5

Refugees to Britain – Physicists

Croydon Airport, 1933. The Customs official
looked at Heinz's bandaged hand and asked:
'Where do you come from?' 'From the
concentration camp.' The official went silently
from one of our many cases to the next and passed
them without a further word.

Thea Lachmann

The effects of Hitler's arrival in power on 30 January 1933 was so quick and intense that many German Jews took steps to leave the country, even before they were dismissed. Hundreds left within weeks. This applied to Jews in all occupations, but academics were particularly hard-hit because they nearly all worked in universities, which were run by the State. They had no choice.

Although at a disadvantage because they were State employees, they had the advantage that their profession was international and that, in some cases, they had already travelled abroad. For example, physicists, biologists and chemists were often known to their opposite numbers in Britain directly or through their scientific publications. Thus it was that Schrödinger, Peierls and Simon were well known and, as a result, prompt and strenuous efforts were made to rescue and receive them. These efforts were in general highly successful, with beneficial effects on the Allies before, during and after the war.

In this chapter we consider those scientists who had the greatest effect on British science, those we knew previously or have met in the course of writing this book. The result cannot be comprehensive, and it may be that we have left out some who should have been included; we do not think the reverse is true.

We tell the stories of 21 scientists who came to Britain and stayed here for the rest of their lives. We have separated the physicists from the rest, as the movement of German physicists in the half-dozen years before the Second World War probably had a bigger effect on the countries they left and went to than that of any other group of refugees. As some of the physicists – Simon, Peierls and Frisch – played such a large part in the early stages of the creation of the atomic bomb, we have also included that aspect of their stories in a separate chapter (see Chapter 10).

ERWIN SCHRÖDINGER

Erwin Schrödinger was unique in that he left, returned and left again. He was an Austrian physicist and one of the greatest scientists. He was not a Jew, so did not have to leave when Hitler came to power; yet he left at once. His main studies were on statistical problems of the quantum theory, on magnetism, on the general theory of relativity and on X-ray diffraction. His four classic papers on wave mechanics established the subject in its final form and gave birth to the subject of wave mechanics. In 1927, when he was only 40, Schrödinger was invited to succeed Max Planck as head of physics at the Kaiser Wilhelm Institute in Berlin. As a result of this appointment he became a German citizen.

Since the 1920s he had followed the turmoil of the Weimar Republic and the alarming rise of the Nazi Party. He loathed the Nazis, their violence, their anti-intellectualism and their anti-Semitism. He did nothing to conceal his feelings – which, before Hitler became Chancellor in 1933, was not dangerous.

Two months after they came to power the Nazis staged a 'national boycott of the Jews'. Jews were forced to scrub the streets while onlookers jeered, windows of Jewish shops were smashed and anyone who tried to help was beaten up while the police did nothing. This was too much for Schrödinger. When he came upon such a scene he went up to a stormtrooper to protest. The stormtrooper responded in the usual way of his kind and was about to hit him when a young physicist, who was a Nazi, recognized Schrödinger and got him away to safety.

By the time Professor Frederick Lindemann arrived in Berlin on the lookout for bright young scientists expelled from their jobs, Schrödinger was thoroughly alienated from Nazi Germany.

Lindemann visited Schrödinger's house for tea and told him that he had invited Fritz London, an assistant of Schrödinger's, to come to England. 'Naturally he accepted?' said Schrödinger. Lindemann replied that he had asked for time to think it over. 'That I cannot understand,' said Schrödinger. 'Offer it to me; if he does not go, I'll take the position.'[1] Lindemann was amazed and delighted – he knew what Schrödinger thought of the Nazis but had not realized that he was prepared to take the risk of giving up his secure and splendid position in Berlin for the uncertainties of emigration to England. Once back in England, Lindemann got a promise of funds from ICI and set about arranging a fellowship at Magdalen College, Oxford, for Schrödinger. He did this with the help of the College's President, George Gordon, the Professor of Poetry. By 21 July Gordon had made arrangements for Schrödinger to be elected as a Fellow at the next College meeting on 3 October. Many Englishmen would have given much to achieve such a delectable appointment – rooms in one of the loveliest colleges anywhere, superb food and wine, no teaching duties, highly agreeable company; an ideal position.

Schrödinger asked Lindemann if he could also secure an appointment for his assistant, Arthur March, another non-Jew. Schrödinger wanted to take March with him to Oxford because he was in love with March's wife. While the two families were in the Austrian Tyrol on their slow and roundabout journey to England, Schrödinger and Hilda March became lovers and by the time they reached England she was pregnant by him. Lindemann, a stiff man even at his most genial, later resented having to make arrangements not only for Schrödinger but for his mistress as well.

By the time Schrödinger arrived in Oxford in November a splendid house awaited him, and there was another for the Marches. He was formally admitted as a fellow of Magdalen at exactly the same moment as it was announced that he had won the Nobel Prize (with Paul Dirac). This was well timed for Schrödinger, covering with glory what might have been a difficult time in his career. For those in Germany who still cared about such things it must have been galling that a scientist who had left, not because he was a Jew but because he abhorred the Nazis, had so soon afterwards won such an award.

Schrödinger and Werner Heisenberg – the discoverer of the

Uncertainty Principle – had received nominations for the Nobel Prize before 1933. Albert Einstein was among those who had supported Schrödinger; he wrote that if forced to choose he would put Schrödinger just ahead of Heisenberg. In the event Heisenberg won the prize, which had been held over from 1932, and Schrödinger and Dirac took the prize for 1933; on 10 December 1933 all three received their awards together.

At about the same time Schrödinger was invited to Princeton. There was a vacancy for the professorship of mathematical physics, an ideal appointment for him in that it involved no formal teaching. Schrödinger travelled to the United States to consider the job and while there gave some greatly appreciated lectures. He returned to Oxford, where, after a couple of months, he decided to turn down Princeton's offer. His first objection was that the salary and pension were 'not sufficiently agreeable'. The salary was $10,000, as high as that of almost any other American academic at that time. At Princeton the only higher salary was Einstein's $15,000. Typically, Einstein had suggested a salary of $3000 and added, 'Could I live on less?' The $10,000 Schrödinger declined was about twice his salary in Oxford, which itself was regarded as good. On top of his salary he had his Nobel Prize money safely lodged in a Swedish bank.

There may have been another reason for refusing the Princeton offer. Schrödinger's domestic arrangements were unconventional, even for today. Professor March's wife was Schrödinger's mistress. She and Schrödinger went on trips together with the acceptance of March and of Schrödinger's wife, Anny, and in Oxford they went everywhere together as man and wife. When Hilda's baby was born March was registered as the father. Schrödinger had considered it quite natural to have several lovers; he said of his wife, 'I like Anny as a friend, but I detest her sexually.' Perhaps fortunately Anny had her own lover, Peter Weyl. The relevance of these relationships is that they are thought to have contributed to a certain unease on the part of the President of Princeton about having Schrödinger on the staff. Schrödinger himself may not have been too sad about the outcome. He had reservations about the American way of life ever since being served iced water with his oysters and he referred to Princeton as 'a quaint ceremonious village of puny demi-gods on stilts'.

Even Oxford did not wholly appeal to him. He, a lover of women, found the all-male atmosphere of college life irksome and did not like the formality of dining in hall. He remained unsettled in spite of circumstances which many of his refugee (and English) colleagues might envy.

Schrödinger grumbled: 'You never know who your neighbour at dinner might be. You talk to him in your natural manner, and then it turns out that he is an archbishop or a general – huh.' This situation, which Schrödinger resented, is precisely what Francis (formerly Franz) Simon in Balliol, and many others, found such a congenial feature of a college attachment. After visiting Schrödinger in Oxford, von Laue described him as 'not at all happy'.

In the summer of 1934 Schrödinger asked for formal retirement from his Berlin professorship and to be made emeritus. This was granted and was accompanied by a letter of thanks from Hitler, possibly the only creditable thing Hitler ever did.

Whatever his dissatisfaction with his life in England, his lack of a permanent appointment and his inferior status compared with his position in Berlin, Schrödinger showed some appreciation of the help the academic refugees from Germany had received in England; with Albert Einstein and V. Tschernavin he wrote a letter to *The Times* on 25 March 1936 giving formal thanks to the Academic Assistance Council.

Late in 1935 the Chair in Physics became vacant at Edinburgh. Although this post, like most professorships in Scottish universities, carried a heavy teaching and administrative load, Schrödinger was interested and the appointment was offered to him. He would probably have taken it but British bureaucracy intervened. The Home Office took so long to give permission for him to take it that he eventually lost interest. The chair was then offered to another German, Max Born, and this time the Principal of the University explained to the Home Office that as their dilatoriness had lost them one great opportunity, would they please not let this chance go. The permit came immediately.

At about the same time, 1936, Schrödinger was attracted by an offer from the University of Graz in Austria. He yearned for his homeland and he accepted it. Leaving Oxford proved not to be quite as simple as he expected. Schrödinger managed to have a row over a seemingly trivial matter which caused offence to his generous supporters. ICI, who had paid his salary while he was in Oxford, now deducted some of the money for plumbing fixtures and to cover the cost of resurrecting his neglected garden. Schrödinger was furious at what he called ICI's 'insolence' and wrote angry letters to Lindemann and George Gordon. Considering how generously he had been treated in Oxford, all this left a sour taste in some mouths, especially Lindemann's.

Schrödinger should have realized that it was crazy to go back to Austria in October 1936. Hitler was clearly on the move. When he had occupied the Rhineland in March, Britain and France had done nothing. There was already talk of an Anschluss whereby Germany would annex Austria, and the Nazis in Austria were starting to create trouble, especially in Graz, where they were strong. It is astonishing that Schrödinger should have preferred the turbulence of Austria to the peace of Oxford, apart from any consideration of scientific ambience.

By the middle of 1937 there were reports in the press that Mussolini, previously a strong backer of Austria's independence, would take no action if Hitler took over. In March 1938 Hitler entered Vienna. The Austrian population received him ecstatically. The Austrian Nazis behaved worse than the German Nazis had done and were even more anti-Semitic. The old scenes of helpless Jews being made to scrub the streets were repeated and Jewish civil servants were immediately dismissed. A professor of physical chemistry, Hermann Mark, was arrested but managed to bribe his way out of the country. He converted his wealth into platinum wire, which he shaped into coat hangers, and got away to Switzerland. There was no opposition to the Anschluss from the political establishment or the Catholic Church in Austria nor any protest from Britain or France. The USSR suggested the formation of a united front against the Nazis, but nothing happened.

Three weeks after the Anschluss Schrödinger wrote a fawning letter to Hitler entitled 'Confession to the Führer':[2]

In the midst of the exultant joy which is pervading our country, there also stand today those who indeed partake fully of this joy, but not without deep shame, because until the end they had not understood the right course. Thankfully we hear the true German word of peace: the

1. Hitler and General Ludendorff
after the unsuccessful
Munich Putsch, April 1924

2. Hitler, President Hindenburg
and Goering, 1933

3. Solvay Congress, Brussels 1927
Left to right, first row: I. Langmuir, M. Planck, Mme Curie, H. A. Lorentz,
A. Einstein, P. Langevin, C. E. Guye, C. T. R. Wilson, O. W. Richardson
Second row: P. Debye, M. Knudsen, W. L. Bragg, H. A. Kramers, P. A. M. Dirac,
A. H. Compton, L. de Broglie, M. Born, N. Bohr

Third row: A. Piccard, E. Henriot, P. Ehrenfest, E. Herzen,
T. De Donder, E. Schrödinger, E. Verschaffelt, W. Pauli, W. Heisenberg,
R. H. Fowler, L. Brillouin

4. Tess Simpson, Secretary of the Academic Assistance Council, 1994

5. A.V. Hill, Vice President of the Academic Assistance Council, *c.* 1940

6. Sir William Beveridge,
c. 1960

7. Max Planck presenting
Albert Einstein with a medal,
1929

8. Burning the books, 10 May 1933

9. Werner Heisenberg receiving the Nobel Prize
from King Gustav V of Sweden, 1933

hand to everyone willing, you wish to gladly clasp the generously outstretched hand while you pledge that you will be very happy, if in true cooperation and in accord with the will of the Führer you may be allowed to support the decision of his now united people with all your strength.

It really goes without saying, that for an old Austrian who loves his homeland, no other standpoint can come into question; that – to express it quite crudely – every 'no' in the ballot box is equivalent to a national [*völkisch*] suicide.

There ought no longer – we ask all to agree – to be as before in this land victors and vanquished, but a united people [*Volk*], that puts forth its entire undivided strength for the common goal of all Germans.

Well-meaning friends, who overestimate the importance of my person, consider it right that the repentant confession that I made to them should be made public. I also belong to those who grasp the outstretched hand of peace, because, at my writing desk, I had misjudged up to the last the true will and the true destiny of my country. I make this confession willingly and joyfully. I believe it is spoken from the hearts of many, and I hope thereby to serve my homeland.

News of Schrödinger's letter was published in *Nature*. It was generally assumed that it must have been written under duress and that he was in jail. British friends were surprised to hear that he and his wife were on a skiing holiday. Despite the letter Schrödinger was unsure what would happen to him. He had not been dismissed, and expected to continue his teaching, but did not think he would be allowed to leave Austria to return to Oxford. Although he disliked the anti-Semitism he wanted to make his peace with the regime. He apparently hoped to be appointed to the vacant chair in Vienna. This was not how things were arranged by the Nazis: such vacancies were filled by enthusiastic Party members.

Besides his appointment at Graz Schrödinger had another at the University of Vienna. On 23 April he was dismissed from that appointment in terms always used in such situations: 'You are therefore to refrain from any professional duties falling within the scope of your former appointment.' It was signed by the dean.

People outside Austria were trying to help Schrödinger. Lindemann, even though he later refused to see him, wrote to the

Foreign Secretary, Lord Halifax, who declared himself unable to do anything. However, he did write to von Ribbentrop, the German Foreign Minister, who of course refused to let Schrödinger leave. Eamon de Valera, Prime Minister of Eire, a former mathematician, was trying to set up an Institute for Advanced Study in Dublin and was keen to capture Schrödinger.

The help from his British colleagues was, however, hedged by a natural caution. As Francis Simon put it, Schrödinger's letter to Hitler had 'made an awful impression' and he talked of the need to 'restore his reputation – and in a certain sense of all the emigrants', of whom Simon was one. If Schrödinger did come out of Austria he would have to give the best explanation he could of his conduct, and would certainly never be able to go back. Simon said that the remark of the King of Hanover was being much quoted: 'professors can be bought like whores'.

After his dismissal from Vienna University in April, Schrödinger was abruptly dismissed from Graz University on 26 August for 'political unreliability'. He at last got the point. The Nazis hated him for this 'political unreliability' and for leaving Germany in 1933. The first wonder is that he did not realize this much earlier, the second that he was not dismissed from his Graz appointment until four months after losing the Vienna chair. Now he became frightened. He and his wife got away by train to Rome, taking almost no money or possessions so as not to attract attention. He was helped by the Vatican (he was a member of the Papal Academy) and by de Valera, then at a congress in Geneva. Eventually the couple made their way to Oxford. Schrödinger's reception by his former colleagues, especially Lindemann, who had done so much for him, was cool. 'Is he mad?' asked Lindemann. 'Doesn't he realize after this letter he has published what people think of him?'[3]

Max Born said: 'How are you supposed to believe a man who has published that pretty letter?' Francis Simon wrote to Born: 'he does not have it in his heart to confess that what he has done is wrong (which does not surprise me in someone who so loves himself to the exclusion of all others) ... he behaves like a spoiled boy.' Schrödinger was unabashed. 'What I have written, I have written. Nobody forced me to do anything. This is supposed to be a land of freedom and what I do is nobody's concern.'

It is not surprising that the Nazis were hostile to Schrödinger, but it was stupid of them. If they had welcomed him back to the Reich and rewarded him handsomely they would have scored an enormous propaganda coup. After his letter to Hitler and his political naivety he would probably have cooperated willingly, at least until it was too late.

De Valera had set up his Institute for Advanced Study, and invited Schrödinger to come to Dublin to be its leading light. On his way there Schrödinger was invited to Belgium, where he was given university appointments for a few months at Brussels, Louvain, Liège and Ghent. He made important contributions, including support for the theory of an expanding universe, then very uncertain but now generally accepted. On 1 September 1939 war at last broke out and a few weeks later the Schrödingers left for Ireland. Schrödinger might have had difficulty in getting the necessary transit visa for Britain but again his friends helped. The man who arranged it was Lindemann.

Schrödinger stayed in Dublin for 18 years, continuing to work on general relativity and quantum mechanics. The relative quietness of Dublin – Eire remained neutral throughout the war – suited him; he was very much a lone worker.

In 1944 Schrödinger published a book entitled *What is Life? Mind and Matter*,[4] which became immensely popular. Its central theme was that the transmission of the genetic message laid down in the chromosomes cannot be explained by the known laws of physics. That proved to be nonsense, but it drew many young physicists, eager to take up the challenge, into biology. One of them was Maurice Wilkins, who shared the Nobel Prize with Watson and Crick for the discovery of the double helical structure of DNA.

Schrödinger's book took its cue from a paper by Delbrück, Timofeeff-Ressovsky and Zimmer, who showed experimentally that the gene is a molecule and gave a rough estimate of its size. One of Schrödinger's chapters is essentially a transcript of part of that paper. He knew no chemistry and chemists and biochemists realized that his book did not make chemical sense, but that did not diminish its popular appeal. In Dublin Schrödinger made no more significant contributions to physics, but he became a successful popularizer of science.

Schrödinger returned to Austria in 1956, dying there in 1961. In the years since his death he stands out as a talented man even in this gallery of geniuses. He was one of the ablest theoreticians of his time and was also a philosopher and classical scholar. His papers on wave mechanics, written in the mid-twenties, form the theoretical basis for much of modern chemistry and physics. But as a man he is puzzling. He was one of the small number of scientists in Germany in 1933 who, though not Jewish, left at once. Yet, having taken that brave and decisive step, he seems to have shown little appreciation of the great efforts made in Britain to help him. He was treated as generously as any of the refugees but grumbled about minor matters, particularly money. He was the opposite of the modest, tentative Einstein in this respect. Having the unique honour of election to a fellowship at Magdalen College, Oxford, he complained within days about the need to dine in hall at seven-thirty. He did not shrink from securing an appointment at Oxford for Professor Arthur March, the husband of his mistress. He was fortunate in loving women whose husbands were complaisant, but this irritated some of his hosts, Lindemann especially, who had exerted themselves to help those husbands for what they thought were scientific reasons.

However much he missed his home country, Schrödinger was foolish to go back to Austria in October 1936, 17 months before Hitler invaded. He was even more foolish to have written that letter to Hitler and, when challenged, to have apparently seen nothing wrong in it. He could not see why Lindemann and others in Oxford were vexed with him, yet they continued to help him. Erwin Schrödinger was gifted with a great scientific mind set in a character of almost complete self-absorption.

SIR FRANCIS SIMON

Sir Francis Simon was born Franz Simon in Berlin in 1893 into a Jewish family. He became a physicist, studying under Professor Walther Nernst at the Kaiser Wilhelm Institute for Physical Chemistry in Berlin. In 1922 he married Charlotte Münchhausen and they had two daughters.

By 1927 he was a Professor Extraordinarius, concentrating on metallurgy and low-temperature research. That year he and his wife were invited to a conference at Odessa in Russia. They were appalled by the poverty and political servitude there.

In 1931 Simon was appointed Professor of Physical Chemistry at Breslau. While it was difficult for him to leave Berlin, one of the most famous scientific centres in the world, Breslau offered him the prospect of building a large and better-equipped low-temperature laboratory than he had in Berlin. He was also invited to spend the spring term the following year at the chemistry department of the University of California at Berkeley. He accepted but, because of his forebodings, he insisted that his wife and children move to Switzerland and remain there until he returned. In April he telephoned his wife from Berkeley to advise her not to venture back as he considered Nazism 'inevitable'. Nonetheless, she returned and Simon joined her in Breslau in January 1933. With the Nazis in power, they soon realized they would have to leave Germany.

Fortunately for Oxford and low-temperature research, as well as for the Simons, Professor Lindemann was on his 'shopping' trip for the Clarendon Laboratory when he and Simon met in Nernst's laboratory at Easter. As soon as he realized that Simon was planning to leave Germany, he invited him to the Clarendon to help develop the low-temperature research programme already begun there. He backed the offer with a two-year grant of £800 from ICI. However, there was no long-term security. When he got home, Simon asked Charlotte, 'How would you like to go to England?' 'Rather today than tomorrow,' she replied.

Simon handed in his notice on 1 July but before he and his wife could leave, an official demanded they should surrender their passports to the police. As he did so, Simon flung his Iron Cross and other medals on to the table, scornfully repeating the words the Kaiser had used when decorating him in the Great War: 'The Fatherland will be forever grateful to you.' The passports were later returned, though the Simons never knew why.

When Simon left Germany he was, thanks to a corrupt Customs official, able to leave with his apparatus. Charlotte followed two months later with the girls, a friend and an enormous amount of luggage. She left the children in Bournemouth to go house-hunting in Oxford with her husband. The house agent soon had to point out to her that the house she wanted – large and with central heating –

was not to be found on an annual income of £800. Finally they settled at 10 Belbroughton Road in north Oxford. It cost them nearly every penny they had, but they were safe and the house became their home as well as a haven for other Jewish exiles in Oxford.

The family may have been safe in Oxford, but as Simon's ICI grant was for only two years he could not afford to ignore any offer of a permanent position. Later a letter came from Professor James Franck suggesting the possibility that Simon might become Professor of Physical Chemistry in Istanbul on a ten-year contract and an annual salary of £2000. In spite of the poor facilities at the Clarendon – he did not even have a secretary – he turned down the offer. He was producing good work, his grant had been extended until 1938, his salary increased to £1000 per annum, and his family were settling down and becoming fond of England. He went on hoping for a new laboratory and more money for equipment but, on the whole, his attitude towards money was casual. Once, when he had completed his income-tax returns, he announced, 'Ah well, now we cannot afford to live.'

In 1936 he applied for the Chair of Physics at Birmingham University, supported by a galaxy of referees, including Rutherford, Nernst, Planck and Einstein. He did not get it: the Australian Mark Oliphant was appointed instead. Simon was then offered a professorship in Jerusalem but turned it down because he did not want to learn a new language. He made enquiries about jobs in the United States but prospects were discouraging because of the lack of funds. However, his position had improved, as he had been appointed University Reader in Thermodynamics and elected a member of the Senior Common Room at Balliol.

After Simon and his colleagues Kurti, Kuhn, Mendelssohn and London, all refugees, arrived at the Clarendon, the low-temperature research programme made rapid progress. The laboratory, which looked more like a monastery than a laboratory (when Simon's five-year-old daughter first saw it she commented, 'Is this filthy church a laboratory?'), was badly equipped and always short of money – electricity was supplied from the electrical laboratory next door. Work went on in cramped, subdivided rooms in an informal, untidy way, from late morning – no one ever arrived before ten – until long after midnight. Fortunately, Simon was used to improvising. Luckily he had brought some equipment from Germany, including copper vessels for liquefying helium which he had invented in Breslau and Berkeley; these enabled him to study the properties of matter at very low temperatures. Despite the poor conditions, his low-temperature work was 'quite satisfactory'. He was a popular figure and his students were devoted to him, delighting in his informality and friendliness, which encouraged them to share any sort of problem with him.

Simon began to be recognized internationally. In 1935 he gave one of the Royal Institution's Friday evening lectures, for which he received much approval. He was also elected a member of the Physical Society. As he had no strong electromagnet at the Clarendon he took to visiting the laboratories at Bellevue near Paris, where the Director, Professor Cotton, welcomed him and his team for month-long visits. It was there in the spring of 1936 that they produced the first liquid helium by magnetic cooling, which gave a temperature of 0.01° above absolute zero.

The growing reputation of Simon and his team helped Lindemann to win his long battle for better conditions for physics at Oxford. *Nature*'s leading article on 20 September 1937 called for a new physics institute for Professor Lindemann to replace the now 70-year-old Gothic 'church'. Work started on the new Clarendon Laboratory the following year.

The refugee scientists who staffed the Clarendon were not yet all naturalized. When war broke out Simon and Rudolf Peierls were prevented from working on the most secret work then in progress – radar. Instead they worked on the possibility of an atomic bomb.

All through this time of his greatest scientific output, Simon lectured and travelled to Paris, Amsterdam and the United States. He and his wife also looked after the welfare of other refugees in Oxford and during their first year in England there was only one fortnight in which they did not have guests. They also worried endlessly about the political situation in Europe and the English people's lack of reaction to it, finding the majority almost as ready as the Germans had been to bury their heads in the sand. England seemed to doze uneasily under politicians whom Hitler could easily fool. Simon thought that only Churchill and Low, the political cartoonist, saw what was coming and tried to waken the nation to the dangers ahead.

After the Fall of France in June 1940 the universities of Yale and

Toronto offered hospitality to the children of senior members of Oxford University. The Simons were torn between losing their children and fear of the future, particularly as Simon was on the Nazis' black list of those in England selected for retribution. They decided to let their daughters, Kathrin and Dorothee, go to the care of friends who promised to look after them should anything happen to Francis and Charlotte. However, Charlotte was persuaded to follow the girls, though Simon himself stayed in England despite generous offers.

In May, shortly before France fell, England had adopted its drastic policy of internment. Simon, who was by then naturalized, spent all his spare time working for the release of the Jewish refugees. He wrote almost daily to Tess Simpson at the Society for the Protection of Science and Learning. His personal knowledge of their work and importance helped to release many from internment. Simon believed that the government's policy on internment was wrong. 'They don't realize,' he said, 'that we are greater and older enemies of the Nazis than most of the natural-born ones.'

Then Simon was invited to the United States to work on the building of the atomic bomb. His highly important contribution is discussed in Chapter 10.

After the war he came back from Los Alamos to Oxford, where he continued to work on low temperatures, particularly with Kurti. They got to within a minute fraction of a degree to absolute zero (-273°C), the point at which atoms stop moving altogether.

Simon was particularly proud to be elected a Fellow of the Royal Society in March 1941 at the height of the Blitz; he could hardly have expected a comparable honour had he stayed in Germany. The FRS, and the knighthood he received in 1955, he thoroughly deserved from a country he had served so splendidly.

When Lord Cherwell retired in 1956, Simon was chosen to succeed him as the Dr Lee's Professor of Experimental Philosophy. He took over a large and flourishing department which he had done so much to convert into a world-class department. All seemed well, until he suddenly had a recurrence of his coronary disease and died on 31 October, four weeks after his appointment.

As this book goes to press, Lady Simon is flourishing at the age of 102, 66 years after moving to the house in Belbroughton Road which had been so well used as a staging post for refugees and where she still lives.

Simon's English never became idiomatic. With typical self-mockery he described himself as 'vice-president of the Broken English-Speaking Union'.

MAX BORN

When the Nazis came to power there were four professors in the physics department at Göttingen, three of them Jews. Their reaction to the threat varied from defiance (James Franck) to submission (Max Born) – whatever they did the result was the same: all left.

Max Born, a quiet and gentle man, went to a small house in the Italian Tyrol. While on the way there by train he actually saw the burning of the books (on 10 May 1933) and became furious. He was restrained by his wife, Heidi, who was frightened of a man sitting opposite them who looked like a typical Nazi.

As they waited in their mountain home at Selva, Born began to get job invitations from several universities – the best came from Patrick Blackett, then at Cambridge. They hesitated – Heidi had never been to England and was rather doubtful – but Max had studied in Cambridge and loved the place and wanted to return to the physics department.

Before he left for England he received an unexpected visitor, Frederick Lindemann, whose chauffeur had driven him in his Rolls-Royce the 400 miles from Göttingen, where he was staying. He tried to entice Born to Oxford but it was too late.

Born, his wife and family left for Cambridge. Fortunately for him, he was already very well known in the physics world, both in his own right and because those he had taught or worked with were famous, in particular Werner Heisenberg. Born had been Professor of Theoretical Physics at Göttingen for 12 years; while there he had reformulated the law of conservation of energy (the first law of thermodynamics). He was also closely involved with the quantum theory and with Erwin Schrödinger's wave equation. He had also done much other fundamental work on atomic particles.

On arriving at Cambridge in 1933 Born dropped from full professor, head of a department, to a research student with one room, but soon learned, like so many other refugees, that change of atmosphere and status (not to mention language) could be a stimulating experience, personally and professionally. He was made thoroughly welcome in Cambridge but after only two years he was invited to Edinburgh. He was perhaps a little lucky to get the Chair of Physics there. Originally it had been offered to Schrödinger, but the British Home Office was so dilatory that he lost patience. After this the University's Principal urged the Home Office to be quicker in approving Born's appointment, which it was.

Born was happy in Edinburgh: teaching, travelling, writing and continuing his research. Perhaps it is symptomatic of the rising interest of physicists in biological problems that he often attended the discussion group at the Institute of Animal Genetics.

By the time war broke out he had been naturalized, so he was not interned in 1940. He refused to take any part in the work on the atomic bomb – the only scientist to do so. From the first he thought it was a wicked enterprise, and indeed from the beginning of the war he had disapproved of the Allied air attacks with conventional bombs. Yet he was not a pacifist – at least not after Hitler's appearance – and in this his attitude was very similar to Einstein's. He thought the Nazi regime the greatest evil that had ever befallen the human race and, in an apparent contradiction, he realized that only crude power could destroy it. After the war his beliefs led him to be active in the movement of physicists and others to ban the use of atomic weapons.

Klaus Fuchs worked with Born for several years. He did first-class scientific work and behaved very creditably when he was interned, taking care of the other, less robust, internees. Fuchs was released from internment in Canada within months and was back with Born by summer 1941. While there he was invited by Peierls, in Birmingham, to do secret work with him. Fuchs was known to be a communist, but in the amazement and horror that many people have expressed about his appointment to work on the atomic bomb project it is often forgotten that in those days the Nazis, not the Russians, were the enemy.

When Fuchs was arrested as a spy five years after the end of the war Born was amazed. He thought he knew Fuchs well, he certainly knew his political attitude, yet never anticipated that he would turn out to be a spy. Today it seems remarkable that, despite intense public interest at the time, no journalist tried to interview Born about Fuchs. That reticence had already lessened a few months later when another refugee physicist, Bruno Pontecorvo, was exposed as a spy.

Born retired from Edinburgh in 1953 and, after much thought and anxiety, he decided to return to Germany, to live in a town near Göttingen. He was much criticized for going back to Germany, especially by Einstein, but among other considerations was the fact that his pension from Edinburgh University was small, whereas in Germany he could live comfortably on restitution money from the State.

At last in 1954 Born got the Nobel Prize – 'at last' because many physicists thought he should have got it when Heisenberg did in 1932/3. Heisenberg himself thought so and wrote Born a charming letter at the time. Born received the prize (with Walther Bothe, another German) for work on statistical studies on wave functions.

Max Born was an outstanding figure by any measurement. He was, among other things, modest. In 1961 he was asked to rate his achievements in physics, especially in comparison with Einstein, Bohr, Heisenberg and Dirac. He replied: 'If I have advanced now in the opinion of the world into this class, it is solely due to my luck in working in a period when fundamental results were lying about, waiting to be picked up, to my industry in picking them up and to my reaching a considerable age.'

FRITZ HABER

Fritz Haber may have expected to be spared from Nazi persecution even though he was Jewish. He was a famous chemist who had almost single-handedly saved Germany in the early months of the First World War. He was an assimilated Jew and a fervently patriotic German. To him the anti-Semitic policies of Hitler were unbelievable. He was as loyal to the State as anyone else.

The reason for Haber's confidence was that but for him Germany would have lost the Great War within a year. The Kaiser had gambled on a quick war when Germany attacked in August 1914. However, after a headlong rush in the first few weeks, the army became bogged down in trench warfare. It was then that Haber made his unique contribution, greater than any other civilian has made to the military power of his country: he discovered how to make ammonia, a step in the manufacture of the nitrates that are a vital component in explosives – no nitrates, no explosives. Previously nitrates had come from Chile but, owing to the Allied blockade, the supply was cut once the war started. Haber succeeded, where many others had failed, in making ammonia from air by compressing and heating nitrogen and hydrogen and adding a catalyst to hasten the reaction. Thus unlimited quantities of explosives could be made without the need for imports. More importantly for mankind in the long term, nitrates are the basis for fertilizers and Haber's discovery led to a huge increase in soil fertility all over the world. But for him, millions would have starved. In the play *Square Rounds* the character of Haber says of himself that he had 'saved the world that hurtled towards starvation'.

Haber is famous, or infamous, for yet another service to the German armed forces: he introduced poison gas. It had been banned by the Hague Convention, which Germany had signed. The German General Staff evaded the issue by saying that projectiles containing poison had been banned but not gas released directly from cylinders. Haber was not troubled by the issue of legality, claiming that the French had used it first, which was untrue, and overrode the objections of his junior, Otto Hahn (later the discoverer of atomic fission). He threw himself into the work, in which he was also assisted by James Franck and Gustav Hertz, both future Nobel Prize winners. Max Born refused, however. When the army commanders were instructed by the High Command to use poison gas, all but one refused. One was enough and chlorine was used at Ypres in April 1915. The effect was shattering and initially devastating. It was used to equal effect against the Italians at the Battle of Caporetto in 1917. The Allies immediately developed their own as well as gas masks and the German ascendancy did not last. It was, in any case, a capricious weapon, being dependent on the strength and direction of the wind.

Named as a war criminal by the victorious allies, Haber was forbidden by them to work on poison gas for military purposes after the end of the war. Nonetheless, he continued secretly collaborating with the Spanish and Russian governments until 1925, when poison gas was banned by the Treaty of Locarno. Thereafter he worked on its use in animals. Through the Society for Pest Control, which he founded, he carried out experiments which led directly to the production of Zyklon B, the gas used by the Nazis for the extermination of the Jews in the death camps. No wonder that, in *Square Rounds*, his stage wife says bitterly after his death: 'He'll never live to see his fellow Germans use his form of killing on his fellow Jews.'

It is hardly surprising that the Allies should have named Haber as a war criminal at the end of the First World War. What is surprising is that his work did not ensure Nazi approval. Anti-Semitism overruled any appreciation of past or future services to Germany's war efforts. He could have saved the Nazis time in developing and exploiting later techniques used to kill Jews.

When Hitler came to power, Haber was not expelled but life was made very difficult for him: his Jewish staff was dismissed and he was not allowed to exercise his own choice of replacements. So he decided to leave Germany and went to Cambridge, where he was received by the chemistry department. Despite the support he received in his application to settle in England, the process was not easy as there was still some resentment of him as the inventor of poison gas. Rutherford, while supporting Haber's application, nonetheless refused to meet him, and the new arrival also encountered hostility among the laboratory staff.

A few months later Haber died of a heart attack in Basle. He was 65. In Germany his death resulted in a further sign of Nazi disapproval. When a memorial meeting was held, the government forbade his former colleagues to attend. No publicity was allowed and Max von Laue, who had written an obituary, was reproved.

It would be fascinating to know how this ultra-nationalist German felt about his treatment by the Fatherland or, if he had lived, how he would have felt at the course his country took over the next decade.

OTTO FRISCH

Otto Frisch was famous for three important scientific breakthroughs: with Lise Meitner, recognizing and naming the phenomenon of atomic fission, proving experimentally that the energy released by fission of the uranium nucleus was as great as he and Meitner had calculated, both in 1938; and, two years later, with Rudolf Peierls, calculating that an atomic bomb could be made.

Frisch was born in 1904 and, like his aunt Lise Meitner, came from Vienna, where he had studied physics before moving to Berlin in 1927. It was in Berlin that he came into contact with some of the great physicists of the time, among them Meitner. Three years later he moved to Hamburg, where he was a research fellow. There he met the extraordinary Otto Stern, who later won a Nobel Prize for his work on molecular beams.

The last scientific paper Frisch wrote from Hamburg, on 22 August 1939, ended with the note 'the experiments had to be discontinued for external reasons'. It was not difficult to imagine what they were, ten days before the outbreak of war. Thanks to Stern, Frisch had been awarded a Rockefeller Fellowship to work with Patrick Blackett in London. One of the conditions of a Rockefeller award was that the recipient should have a job to return to. Frisch did not. Therefore in London he was supported by the Academic Assistance Council.

The previous Christmas, in 1938, Frisch had taken a holiday with Lise Meitner in Sweden, whither she had fled. During a walk they talked about the consequences of Otto Hahn and Fritz Strassman's incredible results in bombarding uranium with neutrons. They realized that what had happened was atomic fission: an atom of uranium had split into two atoms of barium with the release of energy.

In England, Frisch discussed the results with Rudolf Peierls, particularly the question of how much uranium would be needed to produce a chain reaction, an atomic explosion. They calculated that, far from being many tons as previously thought, only a few pounds would be required. A bomb was therefore possible. The result we know: the prodigious Anglo-American effort to create the atomic bomb. And the story of Frisch's part in the making of the atom bomb is told in Chapter 10.

Frisch was also an excellent pianist as well as a violinist. He was much in demand among the nuclear physicists at Los Alamos, where he entertained his fellows at evening concerts, leading one to remark:

'This guy is wasting his time doing physics.'

After the war Frisch became head of nuclear physics at the Harwell Atomic Energy Research Establishment, after which he accepted the Chair of Nuclear Physics at the Cavendish Laboratory in Cambridge. Through his broadcasts and writing he popularized physics. He died in 1979.

RUDOLF PEIERLS

Rudolf Peierls was born in Berlin in 1907 to a middle-class Jewish family. At Berlin University he met many of the famous physicists of the day: Walther Nernst, Max Planck, Hans Bethe and Wolfgang Pauli. When he moved to study in Leipzig, in 1928, he worked under Werner Heisenberg.

In 1932 he was awarded a Rockefeller Fellowship. However, he chose not to go to the United States but to Rome as Fermi, who started the first chain reaction in 1942, was there. After a period with Fermi he went on to Cambridge and he was there when Hitler came to power in January 1933. Thereafter, although he travelled a lot, England became his home. In 1937 he became Professor of Theoretical Physics at Birmingham. There he got to know Otto Frisch, and together they realized an atomic bomb was feasible.

The Maud Committee, which had been set up to examine the possibilities of making an atomic bomb, had decided it was impossible because it would be heavier than the aircraft carrying it. Now the two men realized that there were the means to create an explosion of unimaginable violence, changing the course of the world's history. They produced a memorandum on their findings, which led to the British government's go-ahead for the designing of the bomb. Later he also joined the Bomb Project at Los Alamos with Frisch (see Chapter 10 and Appendix II).

NICHOLAS KURTI

Nicholas Kurti was one of the group of scientists who worked under Franz Simon at Breslau on low temperatures.

He was born in Budapest in 1908 and lived there for the first two decades of his life. Hungary was unstable, especially after the First

World War, and cursed with anti-Semitism. It was this that drove Kurti and so many other talented Hungarian scientists from the country to Berlin, Vienna or, in Kurti's case, to Paris. From there, he later moved to Berlin, where he was stimulated by the brilliance of its physicists, among whom was Simon. When Simon was invited to Breslau in 1931, Kurti went with him and, when Simon left for Oxford in 1933, Kurti, with London, Kuhn and Mendelssohn, also went. There he worked with Simon on isotope isolation, vital for the production of the atomic bomb.

Kurti was credited in the *Guinness Book of Records* with having reached within one hundred-thousandth of a degree centigrade of absolute zero. He was as pleased by being mentioned in the book as with the achievement which merited it. This highly ebullient character's hobby was cooking and, with his wife, he edited the Royal Society cookery book *But the Crackling is Super,* and later gave popular lectures at the Royal Institution and on television on 'gastrophysics'. He died in 1998.

We include here brief accounts of the work of two émigré inventors. They were not scientists but made very important contributions.

RUDOLF STRAUSS

Rudolf Strauss was born in Augsburg. He completed his diploma thesis in physics at Dresden's Technical University in 1938. After *Kristallnacht* on 9 November 1938 Jews were forbidden even to enter academic premises. Strauss obtained his certificates confirming he had completed his university courses because three of his teachers were brave enough to sign them secretly and to smuggle them to him. He knew he had to leave Germany and did so with the help of his parents' English friends Mr and Mrs John Fry.

John Fry owned a smelting works in south London and gave Strauss a temporary job in his research laboratory. It lasted 40 years and Strauss rose to become head of research of the Fry Group of Companies. In June 1940 he was interned as an enemy alien, and shipped with 2000 others to a camp in New South Wales. He enjoyed the climate, and the company, for ten months before John Fry secured his release and he returned to England. There he resumed his work at Fry's and specialized in the uses of soldering.

He met and became friends with Paul Eisler, a refugee from Austria, who had invented the printed electrical circuit board, which revolutionized the electronics industry. Strauss invented a technique for soldering thousands of electric connections in one operation. His 'wave soldering' machine, built in 1958, is still being made in a sophisticated form all over the industrial world.

Strauss retired in 1977 and travelled widely, teaching the technology of soldering. In 1990 he collected his Engineering Diploma from Dresden, of which the events of 1938 had robbed him. Four years later he was awarded his Doctorate of Engineering in Munich.

Currently living in London, Dr Strauss is preparing a second edition of his third book on the technology of soldering electronic circuit boards.

PAUL EISLER

Dr Paul Eisler fled from Nazi Austria in 1936, settling in north-west London. Trained as an engineer but also an experienced printer, he was full of ideas. He changed the untidy bird's nest of hand-connected wires in an electronic circuit into a tidy two-dimensional pattern of conductors, producing the pattern for the circuit by a printing process which could be mass produced. This combination was to revolutionize the whole of the electrical industry. At first there was little interest and the war and internment brought a temporary stop to his work. After release and a short spell in the Pioneer Corps, he joined a firm of specialized printers and naively assigned to its owners all future patents of his printed circuit. He worked hard on its development and demonstrated the results to many engineers and Allied military personnel. No one, except the Americans, even offered him a trial. The Americans had recognized its value and used a printed circuit in the development of a proximity fuse for anti-aircraft shells. Eisler's invention played a major role in bringing down some 4000 of Germany's flying bombs, the 'doodlebugs' launched against Britain towards the end of the war.

Recognition of Eisler's work took years. In late 1957 Lord Hailsham told the Royal Society that he rated the printed electric circuit as important an invention as penicillin or atomic fission.

France gave him a high award, the Pour le Mérite for invention, and the Institute of Electrical Engineers honoured him with the Nuffield Silver Medal.

On the morning he died, in October 1991, he was still inventing. He rang a friend to tell him of his new idea: how to make a microscopic electric motor.

6

Refugees to Britain – Biologists and Chemists

The helping hand which the scholars of Britain, and later also the United States, extended to the Jewish exiles has often been represented as a shrewd move on the part of those countries to secure for themselves first-rate scientists at low cost. Nothing could be further from the true facts and it is the duty of those who benefited from this manifestation of academic solidarity to repudiate this explanation emphatically . . . The great majority of the scientific emigrants were young, unknown people. Those who later made worthwhile contributions were able to do so because their host countries generously gave them the chance that Germany denied them.

The World of Walther Nernst by K. Mendelssohn

The second group of scientists forced out of Germany between 1933 and 1939 were the biologists and chemists. The number of doctors was greater but we have not, with very few exceptions, included them in this book.

A contest as to which group is the more important, physicists or biologists and chemists, is futile. The biologists included people who had an enormous effect on science and society. They were often almost unknown when they arrived in Britain, especially outside their specialities, but that soon changed. Among them were the co-discoverer of penicillin, one of the creators of molecular biology (the dominant science of modern biology and medicine) and one of the greatest biochemists of our times.

This chapter includes only eight biologists, four of them Nobel Prize winners – a fraction of all the biological talent which came to Britain. We knew nearly all of them, at least slightly, and liked and admired them all. One, Max Perutz, has written the Foreword to this book.

WILHELM FELDBERG

Wilhelm Feldberg's story is like that of many of the other scientific refugees: he was born and lived in Germany until the age of 32, then moved to England, made good there, becoming a world leader in his field; he died full of honour and of years.

Feldberg came from a prosperous family which owned shops selling women's clothes. They were disappointed when he decided not to go into the business, nor even into clinical medicine but into research, which in his case was unpaid. His older brother said scathingly: 'He isn't even good enough to go into general practice.'

His family's commercial background had a lasting influence on Feldberg. Even in later life, whenever he came to a new place in a town he would find himself sizing up the values of the various buildings. This seemed to be out of pattern with the rest of his character: a quiet, gentle scientist interested in music, art and literature.

Feldberg trained in Berlin and when medically qualified turned to neurophysiology. In 1925 he went to England to work, first in Cambridge with J. N. Langley, Professor of Neurophysiology, and, when Langley died, with Sir Henry Dale at the National Institute for Medical Research in London; both men were outstanding in their field. After his stay in England he returned to the Institute of Physiology in Berlin.

After being dismissed from his post in 1933, Feldberg went to see the representative of the Rockefeller Foundation in Berlin, who was besieged by anxious enquiries. He did not know Feldberg but a memory stirred. 'Feldberg? I seem to have heard that name.' Then he found a letter from Henry Dale saying: 'If Feldberg comes to you in trouble tell him to come to London, I have a job for him.'

The situation in Germany was so menacing that Feldberg went at once, leaving his wife and two children to follow. A few weeks later Feldberg went to meet them at Harwich. He got there very early to meet the overnight boat, but it was late and Feldberg, a solitary figure in the dark, paced up and down in an agony of anxiety, imagining all the frightful things that might have befallen the family before they finally got out. When they arrived an immigration officer, having seen Feldberg's state, said: 'Mrs Feldberg, you must never leave your husband again.' She didn't.

Feldberg soon picked up his research, working directly with Dale at the National Institute for Medical Research for three highly productive years. His interest was to find how nerve impulses pass from one fibre to the next. Was it by a minute electric impulse or was there a chemical messenger? Feldberg's main contribution to the work was based on his discovery that the muscle of a leech was extremely sensitive to a chemical, acetylcholine, which turned out to be the transmitter in a wide variety of the nerves in the body, especially those controlling unconscious functions such as heartbeat, gut movement and blood pressure. The field of neurotransmission developed rapidly and proved to be one of the most productive in physiology at that time.

Feldberg's research interests were wide. They all started from studies of nerve transmission, especially, in later years, *within* the brain, but spread to include work on brain mechanisms controlling blood sugar concentrations, possibly relevant to such disorders as diabetes.

Money was not unlimited in Dale's laboratory, partly because of the needs of other refugees. In 1936 Feldberg accepted an appointment with the cancer researcher C. H. Kellaway in Melbourne. He enjoyed the work and Australia too, and would gladly have stayed, but Kellaway's funds were too limited. In 1938 E. D. Adrian, Professor of Physiology at Cambridge, obtained a Readership in Physiology for Feldberg. Staying in Cambridge for eleven years, Feldberg taught large numbers of medical students – including David Pyke – who were captivated by the charm and approachability which made him such a great teacher. His sense of personal friendliness and lack of any hint of authoritarianism were the basis of his popularity.

In 1949 Feldberg returned to London to be head of a division at the National Institute. His teaching there, now exclusively of postgraduates, was just as successful as in Cambridge and his own research with a succession of colleagues from all over the world made him famous. He collected a string of honorary degrees and lectureships as well as a Fellowship of the Royal Society.

It was typical of Feldberg that, after the war when he got a considerable sum of money as restitution from the German government, he used it to create a foundation to support an annual exchange professorship between the British and German pharmacological societies. This scheme has been a great success and made a major contribution to the reconciliation of British and German scientists.

Everything seemed to go well for Feldberg but this appearance was deceptive, thanks to his courage and optimism. He had lost his job and his country, thanks to the Nazis. His son died. So did his wife, after 52 years of marriage. He married again and his second wife died after four years. In his retirement, when he went on working at the National Institute, he was moved to a much smaller lab. When asked how he felt about his life, he said he had been 'incredibly lucky'. This comment perfectly reflects his attitude to life. But it is also true. Thanks to taking every chance that came his way, even remotely, to unceasing energy and to having many friends and no enemies, he had led a highly productive professional life of 65 years surrounded by people who honoured his work and loved him. He died in 1993.

HERMANN (HUGH) BLASCHKO

In 1932 when he was at a physiology conference in Rome Wilhelm Feldberg got into a lift with a man he did not know and when they got out at the third floor they were 'friends' and remained so for the rest of their lives. This sounds absurd but the story is true. The man Feldberg met in the lift was Hermann Blaschko and two friendlier men it would be hard to imagine. They were both born in 1900, left Germany within weeks of each other in 1933, went into the same work – neurophysiology – and died in the same year, 1993.

Blaschko should be more famous than he is. His professional career did not take off until he was in his forties, at about the time he moved from Cambridge to Oxford. There he started studying a group of compounds called monoamines, of which adrenalin is the best known. He found out how they were made, stored and broken down in the body and what their effects were. In the course of this work, in particular what drugs affected them in the body, he discovered the monoamine oxidase inhibitors which came to play a very large part in the treatment of depression and were the first real advance in the drug treatment of the disorder. Blaschko spent the rest of his professional life studying the physiology and chemistry of the amines, often sharing his ideas with Feldberg.

He was the middle of three children of a famous dermatologist. His family was extremely well connected, especially with academic life in Britain and America. Hermann – or Hugh as he was later known – knew many famous people as a youngster in Germany: among them Albert Einstein, Max Born and Osbert Neisser, the discoverer of the bacterium which causes gonorrhoea. Despite being Jewish by birth Blaschko had little or no feeling for the Jewish religion, as was so often the case among the scientific refugees.

His health was poor. In 1927 he developed pulmonary tuberculosis which recurred on several occasions, although that did not stop him living to be 93. On one occasion in 1932 he was admitted to hospital at Freiburg under the care of Hans Krebs, who was still doing clinical work as well as biochemistry.

Blaschko's first visit to England was in 1926, his interest in biochemistry having been encouraged by Otto Meyerhof in Berlin. Meyerhof, knowing that Blaschko, who was working with him, might see A. V. Hill at University College, London, asked him to pass on his greetings. Hill was a famously friendly and welcoming man and he immediately took to Blaschko, inviting him to visit again whenever he liked. Blaschko did, in 1929 to work for a year in Hill's laboratory and in 1933, when he had to leave Germany in a hurry.

By getting to England in 1933 he was at a great disadvantage – he had no regular job in Germany (he was in hospital when the Nazis came) nor in England, where he was one of the earliest scientists to be helped by the Academic Assistance Council (AAC). In fact, he spent much of his first year in England working for the AAC in placing and helping other refugees.

Blaschko moved to Cambridge in 1934, still without a regular job but earning some money from tutoring undergraduates of St John's College. The undergraduates had no idea that his status was so uncertain. He gave no hint of anxiety: he was just one of the famous scientists who taught so effortlessly and interestingly. His contemporaries did not know either. His move to Oxford and professional security came about quite casually. One Saturday morning in 1944 he happened to mention to Harold Burn, the professor of pharmacology at Oxford and a leading figure, that he was thinking of applying for a job in New Zealand. What did Burn think? Burn said nothing other than that Blaschko should apply for all the jobs that were going. But when Blaschko got back to Cambridge on Monday morning he found a letter from Burn offering him a permanent place in his department in Oxford. Blaschko stayed there for the rest of his life, marrying an English girl in 1944 and still attending lectures and seminars right up to his death.

From 1943 he was highly productive and he became widely known and honoured, being elected to the Royal Society in 1962, at a relatively late age for such a productive scientist.

He had an exceptional number of assistants from Britain and abroad and became heavily dependent on them as he still had to spend considerable periods in hospital for treatment of his recurrent tuberculosis. It is all the more extraordinary that, despite his ill health, forced emigration and uncertain career, Blaschko should have been so productive in terms of both basic neurochemistry and clinical pharmacology. One is tempted to think that his sunny yet determined temperament, as with Feldberg and others, enabled him to achieve so much more than might have seemed possible. His charm, wit, universal enthusiasm and friendliness were overwhelming advantages.

HANS KREBS

In 1965 the Association of Jewish Refugees in Britain raised £90,000 in thanks for the help the refugees had been given 32 years earlier, and offered it to the British Academy 'for the furtherance of scholarship'. The man they chose to present the cheque was Hans Krebs, a short, unremarkable-looking German Jew. In fact he was very remarkable: an honorary admiral in the Texan Navy – this navy had 1000 admirals and only one old battleship moored in a creek; an English knight and Nobel Prize winner, as well as a freeman of Hildesheim.

Krebs, the son of a widely respected surgeon, was born in Hildesheim, near Hanover, at the turn of the century and from an early age wanted to follow in his father's footsteps. His father was a democrat, keenly interested in politics, who believed that the only course for Jews in Germany was assimilation: so the children went to Protestant scripture classes at school. Self-conscious and solitary as a child, Krebs had a classical education with only a smattering of science, spending more hours on music practice than anything else. Briefly conscripted in 1918, he enrolled as a medical student after his discharge, counting himself lucky in getting places at Göttingen and Freiburg despite anti-Semitism in the universities.

As a research assistant under the anatomist Wilhelm von

Möllendorf, Krebs learned how to stain and examine slices of tissue. He began to realize the importance of physical chemistry for biology, and first glimpsed the cycles of breakdown and build-up of foodstuffs in the body. After more studies and hospital experience in Munich and Berlin, he was taken on as research assistant to Otto Warburg at the Kaiser Wilhelm Institute for Biology in Berlin – the best position he could have imagined.

Warburg, a biochemist with outstanding gifts of intellectual insight, had told Krebs that, if he wanted a university career, 'You had better attach yourself to some old ass of a professor.' Krebs wisely attached himself to Warburg for four years, during which he published 16 papers on biochemical subjects.

In the vacations he combined learning a language with having a holiday and in 1928 he stayed on the Isle of Wight in a modest boarding house. A couple and their teenage daughter at the next dining table started to help Krebs with his English in a friendly and unobtrusive way. Krebs was so impressed by their warmth and helpfulness to a stranger that when he was exiled from Germany five years later he knew where he wanted to go.

In 1929 he had to decide whether to specialize in biochemistry or medicine. At that time biochemistry could not provide a living. Warburg advised him to go for medicine. Warned by Warburg that anti-Semitism might prevent him from getting a university post, Krebs looked for work in a university hospital where research was encouraged. After a year at Altona, near Hamburg, he moved in April 1931 to the medical department in Freiburg, where he had fewer patients, an excellent laboratory, plenty of help and a Rockefeller grant for his own research.

In order to study how the waste product urea is made in the liver from the breakdown of proteins, Krebs adapted Warburg's technique of bathing thin slices of living tissue in a fluid from which the cells take up oxygen and nutrients. Within a year he discovered how urea is formed in a cyclical process. This discovery of an endless cycle was completely new, and fundamentally important in understanding the body's chemistry. Its medical significance was not yet recognized – but, 30 years later, Krebs's hope that his work might be useful in medicine was fulfilled when five diseases were discovered to depend on the failure of the enzymes which build urea in the liver. As it was, in 1932, the fortuitous timing of his discovery about the formation of the urea brought him international recognition the year before Hitler's regime forced him to leave Germany. Thus his work was known to Professor Frederick Gowland Hopkins in Cambridge.

In 1933 the atmosphere in Freiburg was openly anti-Semitic. In June hysterically anti-Jewish manifestos addressed to university students appeared all over the city. 'The Jew can think only as a Jew. If he writes German he lies . . . our most dangerous adversary is the Jew and he who is his vassal . . . we demand from the German student the determination and ability to overcome Jewish intellectualism and the threat it contains – the decay of the spirit of the German people through liberalism.'

Von Möllendorf, the Rector of Freiburg University, courageously ordered the removal of the posters. He was immediately removed himself and replaced by Martin Heidegger, the well-known philosopher and Hitler supporter.

Krebs's dismissal from his post in Freiburg had been confirmed on 18 April 1933. The news reached a young German acquaintance, Walter Henkel, who was working in Cambridge. Henkel wrote at once to let him know that Gowland Hopkins had said he would be delighted to offer Krebs a place in the laboratory, if money for his support could be found. Soon afterwards another letter reached Krebs from a colleague in the Netherlands, confirming Hopkins's offer. Krebs wrote back by the next post, and quickly received a reply which began: 'I admire your work so much that I am very anxious to help you.'[1]

Finding financial support was the problem. Fortunately Dr Robert Lambert of the Rockefeller Foundation had also heard of Krebs's situation. He travelled from Paris to Freiburg to see the young biochemist and held out the possibility of a grant to fund him in Cambridge. Other offers arrived from Oxford, Zurich and Tübingen, but the idea of working in Cambridge appealed most.

Krebs's departure was hurried: there was no time to visit Hildesheim to say goodbye to his father, stepmother and ten-month-old half-sister Gisela. He had no idea how long the Nazi regime would last, or that he would not see Germany again for 16 years. His father's farewell letter to him ended: 'If you do well abroad, which is my sincere wish and hope, do not forget your brother and sister in

Germany, and above all little Gisela and her mother. It may be that you will be called upon to be their shield and succour.' Krebs's father died just before the war. Some of his relatives managed to escape, but after the invasion of France in 1940 he had no contact with those left in Germany for five years.

Krebs was not allowed into his own laboratory to collect his possessions. His assistants packed his scientific apparatus – Warburg baths for the tissue slices and 24 manometers – into 20 crates. On 19 June he was seen off to England on the night train from Freiburg by an assistant, Heinz Fuld. As the train drew out he called to Fuld, 'Don't wait too long yourself.' Fuld left a few weeks later, and made his way to Scotland; later he became a successful physician in Liverpool.

The next morning Krebs was met at Victoria station by his old friend Hermann Blaschko, who had arrived in England only a few weeks before and who took him to stay with an aunt in Connaught Square, Bayswater. Krebs was almost penniless, apart from £20 in German banknotes stuck between the pages of his books, but at 32 he felt full of curiosity and optimism and confident in his training and reputation.

In Cambridge Krebs was welcomed by Gowland Hopkins, who confirmed that a Rockefeller grant of £300 had come through. He stayed with David Keilin, the great Russian-born professor of biology and parasitology, until he found lodgings; then he unpacked his crates, and within 12 weeks of his expulsion from Germany he started work in his new laboratory in England.

In 1961 he recalled this period in a memorial lecture for Hopkins at the Biochemical Society:[2]

It was in Hopkins's laboratory that I saw for the first time and at close quarters some of the characteristics of what is sometimes referred to as 'the British way of life'. The Cambridge laboratory included people of many different dispositions, connections and abilities. I saw them argue without quarrelling, quarrel without suspecting, suspect without abusing, criticize without vilifying or ridiculing, and praise without flattering. Hopkins was the central figure, beloved and respected as a natural leader ... His concern ranged far beyond biochemistry, Cambridge University and the Royal Society. What struck me, in particular contrast to the German scene, was the strong social conscience of Hopkins and his school. Between 1933 and 1935 the laboratory sheltered six refugees from central Europe: Friedman, Lemberg, Chain, Weil Malherbe, Bach and myself . . . for the acceptance of one-time strangers into the family of biochemists I shall always be grateful.

Krebs's Rockefeller grant was for one year only, and though Hopkins wanted him to stay in Cambridge, there was little laboratory space for him and no more funding. So he accepted an offer of a semi-permanent lectureship at Sheffield University at a salary of £500, and moved there in autumn 1935.

Within 18 months Krebs had discovered the citric acid cycle which bears his name. It was not a sudden breakthrough, but built upon previous knowledge about the chemical changes which occur when carbohydrates, proteins and fats are oxidized to provide the energy needed for every activity in the body. Krebs sent an outline of his paper to the editor of *Nature*, who sent a polite formal rejection regretting that he already had 'sufficient letters to fill the columns of *Nature* for seven or eight weeks'. Krebs then sent a full report of his findings to the Dutch journal *Enzymologia*, which published it within two months. This was the work that won him a Nobel Prize 16 years later.

By 1938 the refugees saw all too clearly that war was inevitable, but with the British policy of appeasement at its height they were advised to keep quiet and avoid stirring up trouble. The only personal hostility Krebs ever met in Britain came at this time, from Sir Oswald Mosley's Fascist movement. One day he found the windowsills of the staircase leading to his laboratory strewn with hundreds of red leaflets headed 'Find the refugees homes ELSEWHERE'.

Fortunately Krebs's financial supporters had different views. The same year two Rockefeller Trustees met Krebs, who was now head of the biochemistry department at Sheffield, and arranged a five-year grant for him. The Rockefeller Foundation continued to back Krebs for 30 years. He became Professor of Biochemistry at Sheffield in 1945.

Krebs applied for British citizenship in June 1938. His naturalization was accepted in August the following year, but the papers had still not arrived when war broke out in September. For Krebs the delay was maddening; for three days he was classed as an enemy alien and his car confiscated.

During the war Krebs worked for the Medical Research Council. Forty conscientious objectors volunteered to act as guinea pigs in a study on the optimum requirement of vitamins A and C. The diet was dull and the study long-term, but the volunteers stuck to it; Krebs admired them and enjoyed working with people from such diverse backgrounds.

His team published 25 papers, mainly on basic biochemical problems, on nutrition and on the way carbon dioxide is involved in the energy cycles of higher animals. His staff of up to ten people worked in a single large room, with a desk and some privacy at one end, following Warburg's example – an open-plan workplace where ideas could circulate and newcomers could learn the techniques and disciplines they needed. Krebs always discussed problems with the group before reaching a decision. So successful were his methods in welding the team together that when he moved from Sheffield to become Whitley Professor of Biochemistry at Oxford in 1954, the whole team went with him; and 13 years later the group moved with him again to his 'retirement' job at the Radcliffe Infirmary at Oxford, where he stayed until his death in 1981.

Max Perutz

Max Perutz left Austria for England as a young postgraduate student in 1936 – not because he had to leave then, but because he wanted to work in Cambridge. The university would have much to thank Perutz for in later years. Three decades of patient research produced the discoveries of first the structure and then the precise function of the haemoglobin molecule. Perutz's work also helped to inspire research leading to a series of Nobel Prizes awarded to himself and colleagues at the Laboratory of Molecular Biology in Cambridge, of which he became chairman.

Perutz's parents, prosperous textile manufacturers in Vienna, had hoped he would become a lawyer, but he dreaded the prospect, having been inspired at school to take up chemistry. His wishes prevailed, and he enrolled as a chemistry undergraduate at Vienna

University. A young lecturer, Fritz von Wessely, included in his lectures the great advances in biochemistry at Cambridge, and he hoped to study for his PhD in Gowland Hopkins's laboratory, already the first refuge of Krebs, Chain and other bright young refugee scientists. His father put a deposit of £500 with his London agent to support him; the difficulty was to find a place. Professor Mark was about to visit Cambridge, and Perutz asked him to sound out Hopkins about taking him in. 'Oh God, I forgot all about it,' Mark admitted afterwards. 'But I went to see J. D. Bernal, and saw his X-ray diffraction pictures of crystals – and Bernal is looking for a research student. Why don't you go there?' Perutz was dismayed – he knew nothing abut X-ray crystallography – but Mark told him not to worry, he would soon learn.

Bernal accepted Perutz as a research student at the Cavendish Laboratory. When instructed to join a college, he applied to King's and St John's, but was turned down by both, so he decided to visit Cambridge in person for advice. Essential inside information came from a physics lecturer who advised Perutz to choose the college which served the best food: 'Apply to Peterhouse,' he suggested. Perutz was accepted and remained there, eventually becoming one of its most distinguished scientific Fellows.

His reservations about X-ray photography were soon dispelled. He learned quickly, and Bernal encouraged him to tackle the structure of proteins by the X-ray diffraction method. So began Perutz's long quest to discover the structure and function of proteins, starting with haemoglobin; since all physiological reactions depend on enzymes, and all enzymes are proteins, successful analysis of a protein molecule held out great promise.

Protein crystals were extremely hard to obtain, but Perutz acquired some horse haemoglobin crystals and began his doctoral thesis on the analysis of its structure. His fellow laboratory students thought him mad to tackle a molecule containing so many atoms when simple sugar had not been analysed.

In March 1938 Hitler's troops marched into Austria and Perutz's family's circumstances changed drastically. His parents managed to escape from Austria to Switzerland but overnight became penniless refugees, and with no financial support his future at Cambridge seemed doubtful.

That summer was taken care of when Perutz became one of a three-man team sent to Switzerland to study the transformation of snow into glacier ice, 11,000 feet up the Jungfraujoch. A crystallographer who could ski was needed. Perutz had excelled in skiing since childhood, when his mother had encouraged him to learn after he suffered from pneumonia and TB, and he was also an experienced mountaineer. After a summer combining work with skiing and mountaineering, he wrote up the results for the *Proceedings of the Royal Society*, and became known as an expert on glaciers.

Lawrence Bragg, who took over as Cavendish Professor of Experimental Physics in October 1938, was fascinated by Perutz's X-ray pictures of haemoglobin and applied to the Rockefeller Foundation for a grant to cover Perutz's research. The Foundation duly came up with funds from January 1939, enabling Perutz to bring his parents from Switzerland in March.

By the time war was declared in September 1939 Perutz had virtually finished his thesis, which was accepted in March 1940. Two months later politics broke into his life again when he was put under police arrest as an enemy alien. Having been rejected as a Jew by his native Austria, he was now rejected as a German by his adopted country. Along with other refugee scientists he was deported to Canada and interned for several months. An entertaining account of this experience was published in the *New Yorker* on 12 August 1985, and part of this is reproduced in Appendix III.

Later released, Perutz returned to Cambridge. For some time nobody asked him to do any work except fire-watching, so with Professor Bragg's encouragement and supported by his Rockefeller grant he continued his research on protein structure.

Then in 1942 his reputation as an authority on glaciers led to another digression, which began with a mysterious summons from Geoffrey Pyke (David Pyke's father). Pyke was a friend of J. D. Bernal and one of three eccentric civilian advisers – the others being Bernal and Solly Zuckerman, Professor of Anatomy at Birmingham – on the staff of Lord Louis Mountbatten's Combined Operations Headquarters.

Perutz was called to Geoffrey Pyke's rooms in London for consultation on 'an urgent wartime project' which involved harassing the Germans in Norway. Pyke wanted to know whether a battalion of British commandos could be landed in Norway and hidden in ice shelters under the glaciers. Perutz gave his advice and returned to Cambridge. Six months later his advice was again sought, this time for 'the most important project of the war', known only to Bernal, Mountbatten and Pyke. He was to find ways of making ice freeze faster and make it stronger, never mind why. Perutz found very little help in the literature until Geoffrey Pyke gave him a report by Hermann Mark, Perutz's former professor in Vienna, who had escaped to the United States. Mark and his assistant's tests showed that stirring small amounts of either cotton wool or wood pulp into water before freezing it turned the mixture into an extremely hard substance. Thereupon Perutz and Kenneth Pascoe, an engineering student, built a big wind tunnel in a large meat storage cellar beneath Smithfield Market in London. They soon found that ice containing only 4 per cent of wood pulp was, weight for weight, as strong as concrete. They called the substance Pykcrete, in honour of the still-mysterious project's originator. Finally it was revealed that Churchill had envisaged building 'bergships' out of ice cut from ice fields in the Arctic, which were to be stationed in the Atlantic as landing bases with fuel and equipment for aircraft on transatlantic crossings.

Perutz was needed for the project in the United States, but the American Embassy refused to give him a visa on his invalid Austrian passport – upon which Mountbatten's second in command insisted that the Home Office should naturalize Perutz at once. Demands from Combined Operations Headquarters were not to be ignored, and Perutz was exceptional as an alien who was naturalized during the war.

A miniature prototype of a bergship was successfully built on Lake Patricia, Alberta, Canada, but the project eventually foundered: too much steel was needed for the refrigerating plant, and the increasing range of land-based aircraft made floating islands unnecessary.

Again Perutz returned to his work on protein structure, taking thousands of X-ray photographs of the haemoglobin molecule. In 1947 Professor Bragg asked the Medical Research Council (MRC) to support Perutz's work. After four and a half months of acute anxiety for Perutz, a reply at last arrived from Sir Edward Mellanby, secretary of the MRC: 'Rather to my surprise, your project for the establishment by the MRC of the research unit at the Cavendish

Laboratory on molecular structure of biological systems was adopted by the Council at their meeting.' Perutz was jubilant, barely realizing at the time the MRC's courage in supporting a project of such apparently doubtful promise. He was now head of the new Molecular Biology Unit of the MRC, and he could continue to study every detail of the enormously complicated atomic structure of the haemoglobin molecule and show how it takes oxygen to the brain, muscles, lungs and every other body tissue.

Perutz's new unit attracted young researchers who realized that the greatest promise for physics and chemistry probably now lay in the field of biology. Francis Crick arrived in 1949 and was toying with a thesis about protein structure. Then in 1951 James Watson, a 23-year-old zoology student from Chicago, joined the unit. Perutz remembered the electrifying effect of Watson's arrival: while English research had concentrated on the structure of proteins, the young American was more interested in the structure of genes, which were not proteins but deoxyribonucleic acid. Great questions about how genetic information is copied and passed from one generation to another were hidden in its structure.

Two years later, in March 1953, Perutz admired their famous model of the double helix made of brass rods, aluminium plates and retort clamps that won them the Nobel Prize jointly with Maurice Wilkins. Watson and Crick had got ahead of Wilkins and Rosalind Franklin at King's College, London, whose photographs of the brilliant diffraction patterns of DNA fibres moistened by water had taken them to the brink of the greatest biological discovery of the twentieth century.

Nineteen fifty-three was a good year for the unit: in July Perutz discovered how to 'read' the X-ray diffraction patterns of haemoglobin. The labour involved in Perutz's project was enormous, comparable to working out the detailed architectural structure of Notre-Dame Cathedral by taking close-up pictures with a box Brownie camera. He had found that there was no direct way of connecting the X-ray diffraction pattern of haemoglobin with the three-dimensional structure and patterns of the molecule. After years of work he believed that the molecule consisted of parallel chains all running in the same direction; Francis Crick showed that not more than a tenth of the molecules were thus arranged. Perutz naturally hated to have his theory proved wrong by a brash newcomer, but later he was glad he had been made to rethink the problem. Then he adopted the technique of attaching two heavy atoms of mercury to each molecule of haemoglobin. Comparing the X-ray diffraction picture of this molecule with the mercury-free haemoglobin molecule, he saw on the screen how the subtle changes in intensity between the pictures could be used to make a three-dimensional model. He rushed off to tell Bragg; they realized the problem that they had been working on for 16 years was finally solved in principle. Even so, another six years of experiments and calculations were needed to produce the first three-dimensional model of haemoglobin.

What Perutz described as 'the most thrilling moment of all my work' occurred one morning in September 1959:

> After I had worked hard and often fruitlessly on the problem for more than twenty years, the first three-dimensional pictures of the haemoglobin molecule emerged from the Cambridge University computer. It was an overwhelming experience to see a vital part of ourselves that is a thousand times smaller than anything visible under a light microscope, revealed in detail for the first time, like the first glimpses of a new continent after a long and hazardous voyage.

By the 1950s the laboratory had become too small for all the research workers and their apparatus. In 1957 Max Perutz applied to the MRC for accommodation with a report on the department's work; several council members told Perutz that his account of recent advances in molecular biology was the most exciting scientific document they had ever read. His proposals for new premises were approved the same day, and in March 1962 everybody moved into the new laboratories. Perutz was Chairman of the new Laboratory of Molecular Biology, which cost £385,000 and was opened by the Queen in May 1962. The visit proved educational; a lady-in-waiting shown the three-dimensional models of the haemoglobin molecule exclaimed, 'I had no idea we had all these coloured balls inside us.'

In 1991 Perutz gave a lecture to the Royal College of Physicians on 'Determining the Atomic Structure of Living Matter – What Use to Medicine?'. This was extended into a series of lectures in America and thence to a book; *Protein Structure: New Approaches to Disease and Therapy* is a bible for medical students and doctors, and much of the beautifully clear and simple text can be understood by the lay reader.

In 1992 the authors visited Max Perutz at the Laboratory of Molecular Biology. He recapitulated his life story, from Austrian childhood to mountain climber to Cambridge PhD, to internment in Canada, discovery of the structure and functions of haemoglobins and proteins, and to the Nobel Prize in 1962. Asked if he had any great regrets, he answered, 'Not to have climbed the Matterhorn.' But the problems he had solved were infinitely more demanding.

HERMANN LEHMANN

Hermann Lehmann was one of those German scientists who had a classical training but was determined to go into science or medicine. By the time he was ready to qualify there was such widespread anti-Semitism in the universities that he decided not to take the final examination but instead went to Basle in Switzerland to take an MD. Later he returned to Heidelberg to work unpaid with the great biochemist Otto Meyerhof. He did some highly productive work on muscle chemistry which pleased Meyerhof so much that he suggested Lehmann as the one student a year whom he sent to Gowland Hopkins in Cambridge. There Lehmann was warmly welcomed on personal and professional grounds; he was so popular that when he left, so it is said, he was invited to leave his white coat behind the lab door for when he returned. When two years later he did return, by this time penniless, he was befriended by Joseph and Dorothy Needham, two famous biochemists in Cambridge who got him a job, accommodation, money and English instruction. From then on he was highly successful: he became attached to Christ's College and later elected a Fellow. When he presented himself to the Aliens Tribunal, which had the duty of categorizing all refugees according to their attitude to this country, he was supported by another Christ's man, C. P. Snow.

In the panic of May 1940 he was interned but (thanks to his well-connected friends) was released in October and joined the Royal Army Medical Corps. He was sent to India as a specialist pathologist and was able to do important work on anaemia and malnutrition.

After the war he went to Makerere University in Uganda, then a flourishing medical school, probably the best in Africa outside South Africa before it was destroyed by another dictator, Idi Amin. There his interest in anaemia, particularly that due to different types of haemoglobin, flourished and dominated the rest of his life. He was dealing with adults and was surprised to find very few cases of sickle-cell anaemia among them. The reason, as he later reported ruefully, was that if babies were homozygous sickles (i.e. received the gene from both parents) they soon died. Colleagues who were studying the malnutrition disease kwashiorkor did not appreciate the significance of the finding.

After returning to England Lehmann became more and more interested in the recently discovered differences in types of haemoglobin and became a world expert: he described 81 different types. To find these varieties of haemoglobin he had to travel all over the world, which he did with such single-minded enthusiasm that when he went to China in the early days of Communist rule and his friends avidly asked him about the country he replied: 'There's an awful lot of haemoglobin E there.' He worked increasingly closely with Max Perutz (who had described the complete structure of haemoglobin). He also investigated the various ways in which adults metabolize drugs, and became one of the fathers of the fascinating subject of pharmacogenetics.

ERNST BORIS CHAIN

The geneticist and physiologist Professor J. B. S. Haldane wrote that helping Ernst Boris Chain to settle in England was 'what posterity may regard as the best and most important action of my life'. Chain was one of the three men awarded the Nobel Prize 'for the discovery of penicillin and its curative effect in various infective diseases'. Yet his name is unknown to many people, and the story is still not widely recognized of how it was discovered by Alexander Fleming in 1929, then in 1940 isolated and purified by Professor Howard Florey and Ernst Chain into the pure compound which has saved millions of lives.[3]

Chain was born in Berlin in 1906, the son of a German mother and Russian Jewish father. He was a talented musician and nearly made music his profession, but became fascinated by biological problems and chose science instead. At Berlin University he graduated in chemistry and physiology and took a doctorate at the institute of pathology, but his promising career there broke off when Hitler became Chancellor and Europe, as Chain said later, 'was temporarily plunged into a darkness in which the darkest Middle Ages now appear as a blaze of light'. He left Berlin immediately and departed for England as soon as he could, arriving at Harwich with £10 in his pocket on 2 April 1933.

In England Haldane helped him to find a place at University College Hospital, London. After working there for a few months, Chain asked Professor Gowland Hopkins for a place in his laboratory at Cambridge. Recommended by Haldane, he was accepted as a PhD student for two years, funded by a grant from a Jewish organization. There Chain identified the active constituent of a snake venom and its effect, meanwhile trying to decide whether biochemistry or music would offer him a better career – at the time his colleague Krebs thought Chain would do better in music.

In May 1935 Professor Howard Florey, newly appointed head of the Sir William Dunn School of Pathology in Oxford, asked Hopkins if N. W. Pirie of Cambridge would organize the School's biochemical section. Pirie was not available, but instead Hopkins recommended Chain, whose thesis he had just approved. Chain was surprised and delighted at Florey's invitation to join the laboratory as a departmental demonstrator and lecturer in chemical pathology, and accepted on the spot.

Chain was 29 when he arrived in Oxford. Florey's senior lab man, Jim Kent, met Chain at the station. Noticing a Soxhlet extractor in the window of the chemistry laboratory, Chain asked how many the lab had. Kent replied that they had one. 'One!' Chain exclaimed. 'I must have six, a dozen!'

Chain was extremely talented, with an artist's temperament, enormous energy and infectious enthusiasm, but was not built to be an easy colleague. Small and excitable, with a mane of long hair, he had a presence that was in marked contrast to Florey's laconic, undemonstrative manner. In the laboratory he was nicknamed Mickey Mouse, after his way of bounding about, talking and smiling as he went.

At first the two men got on very well. Florey decided that Chain should study lysozyme, an enzyme which attacks the cell walls of certain bacteria. While looking up the literature on more than 200 anti-bacterial substances, Chain came across Alexander Fleming's 1929 paper on the mould *Penicillium notatum*. Florey was also interested in the field and he and Chain decided to survey together a range of anti-microbial substances found naturally. They proposed to study microbial antagonism – war between different types of bacteria – using three varieties. Two of the bacteria turned out to be unimportant, but providentially *Penicillium notatum* was the third. When Fleming had discovered the subject in 1929 he suspected that it might be useful as an antiseptic, but was defeated by its instability – it lost its effects within two weeks.

Florey and Chain undertook the penicillin study not because they hoped the results would be clinically valuable but because of their scientific interest; years later Chain pointed out that 'the possibility that penicillin could have practical use in clinical medicine did not even enter our heads when we started our work . . .' They were brilliantly abetted by Norman Heatley, the ingenious biochemist whom Chain had invited to join the staff. He was Chain's assistant until 1939, when he joined Florey as his personal assistant.

Most of the financial support for this research came from the Rockefeller Foundation – according to Chain, after Florey had asked him to draft an application to the Foundation in 1939. Between 1940 and 1945 they received £6140, just over £1000 a year – a contrast to the starter grant of £100 which Florey had requested from the Medical Research Council. The MRC, which was supporting Chain at the time, came up with just £25 for research.

The task of extracting enough material of sufficient purity from the penicillium cultures was enormous. Penicillin was unstable, the cultures became infected and the vessels in which they were cultured were in short supply; Norman Heatley had to use sterilized bedpans.

By early 1940 the group had produced a small sample of extract containing penicillin, probably no more than 0.02 per cent pure. Chain, growing impatient with the lack of progress, persuaded a colleague to try injecting two mice with the substance; this produced no ill effect and the results encouraged both Chain and Florey. At the end of March Heatley made an important step forward in the method of extracting penicillin: he used the technique of back extraction, which depends on the fact that certain liquids do not mix when shaken together but divide into two layers which can be drawn up separately. Chain, put out because he considered himself responsible for the study's chemical aspects, was against trying out the technique, but Florey overruled him. Not only did it work, but it turned out to form the basis of the commercial production of penicillin.

Heatley's preparation was still only 3 per cent pure, but Florey began an experiment with it on the weekend of 25 May 1940. Eight mice were injected with lethal doses of virulent *Streptococcus pyogenes*, then four were injected with penicillin (in two different quantities) and four controls were not. By morning all the controls were dead, while all but one of the treated mice had survived. The story goes that when Chain saw them he broke into a dance, as well he might: they had shown that penicillin had therapeutic power against bacterial infection. Florey, typically, is supposed to have grunted and remarked, 'It looks quite promising.'

From then on most of the resources of the William Dunn School of Pathology's laboratory were devoted to producing enough penicillin for a clinical trial on human patients. No more than half a milligram of penicillin could be produced from a litre of Heatley's cultures, so Chain and a new colleague, Dr Edward Abraham, set about devising new means of isolating penicillin; its structure could then be determined and the stuff synthesized in quantity.

The first clinical trial of Heatley's preparation took place in the Radcliffe Infirmary between February and June 1941. The six patients chosen included three children and a baby in the hope that they would need less of the precious substance than an adult; all were seriously ill with streptococcal or staphylococcal infections. The first patient, a policeman who was dangerously ill, improved dramatically on doses of penicillin but then the stock ran out and he died. There was now no doubt that a new and effective chemotherapeutic agent could be safely used for man as well as mice.

With all Britain's resources and equipment diverted into the war effort, Florey turned to the United States to set up penicillin production on a large scale. He went there with Heatley in June 1941, again to the chagrin of Chain, who felt he should have gone. However, in their absence he and Abraham produced a preparation of penicillin which was later estimated as about 50 per cent pure, and they came close to discovering its molecular structure, which was finally elucidated by Dorothy Hodgkin.

Towards the end of the war Chain was active in attempts to synthesize penicillin, working with the distinguished chemists Dorothy Crowfoot (later Hodgkin) and Sir Robert Robinson, and he was associated with more than a thousand chemists in 39 major laboratories in Britain and the United States. By D-Day, 6 June 1944, in preparation for expected casualties, hospitals had been supplied with penicillin and pathologists had been trained to administer it.

Large-scale production was achieved in Britain with a process of deep fermentation of *Penicillium chrysogenum*, developed in the United States. There was considerable friction between the two countries about legal protection of manufacturing methods. Chain's wish to patent penicillin was opposed by the head of the MRC and the President of the Royal Society on the grounds that patenting the use of life-saving drugs was unethical; also the law did not cover patenting a natural product. Chain was furious: in his view it was unethical 'not to take out patents protecting the people in this country against exploitation'. Meanwhile Britain had to pay out millions of pounds to use an American method devised in 1941. After the war the National Research Development Corporation was set up to exploit penicillin for Britain's national interest.

The strangest twist in the discovery of penicillin concerns the way the discoverers' work was credited. In 1942 a friend of Alexander Fleming's was close to death in St Mary's Hospital, London, and the scientist asked Florey for a supply of the rare substance to save him. The 'wonder drug' did indeed work, and on 30 August its success was reported in *The Times*, followed next day by a letter from St Mary's which also claimed credit. The story went largely uncorrected by Florey, who, unlike Fleming, was publicity-shy, and multiplied into a shoal of wildly inaccurate reports which claimed, among other things, that the first clinical trials had been held at St Mary's using penicillin sent in churns from Oxford. Florey, Chain and the William Dunn School of Pathology had vanished from the equation; and no amount of subsequent corrections managed to revise the generally recognized version, which became a popular myth. There was some consolation in the joint award of the 1945 Nobel Prize for physiology and medicine to Fleming, Florey and Chain. 'Those boys in Stockholm know what they are about,' said Chain, who had been on tenterhooks lest his contribution might not be recognized.

Despite the tensions between Florey, Chain and Heatley, the three men had achieved what they had set out to do. Florey, the team's medical man, was an imaginative and steady leader. Chain, the biochemist, had encyclopaedic knowledge and experience of the substance they were trying to purify. Heatley was an outstandingly inventive and patient biochemist.

Chain never forgot his Jewish ancestry, and was often consulted about the establishment of the Weizmann Institute in Israel. An offer to run a department there came too late; he had already been wooed and won by an invitation from Professor Domenico Marotta to organize and direct an international research centre for chemical microbiology in Rome. In 1945 he agreed to go to Rome for a year, but after two years at the Istituto Superiore de Sanità, working with a staff of 90 biochemists, engineers, microbiologists and 40 general technicians, Chain resigned from Oxford and renewed his contract in Rome for another ten years. In 1948 he married Dr Anne Beloff, also a biochemist, who helped him develop the institute into an important scientific centre.

Although Chain's research in Rome included studies of carbohydrate metabolism, insulin and a cytotoxic substance called fusicoccin, he always kept up his interest in penicillin. In 1954 he became a consultant to the Beecham Group of pharmaceuticals to advise them on producing benzyl penicillin and other commercially available substances. By 1956 staff at Beecham were seconded to the Rome institute to learn the fermentation technique for penicillin production. A version of penicillin produced in Rome was isolated in crystalline form a year later, and it became possible to produce many new forms of the mould.

In 1953 Professor Patrick Blackett at the Imperial College of Science had the idea of inviting Chain back to London, to take up the chair of biochemistry. The proposal included plans for a large fermentation plant, a wide range of facilities, and a home for the Chain family on the top floor. The Wolfson Foundation and the Science Research Council provided large grants, but many complicated negotiations took place before Chain received his official invitation from the Senate of London University in January 1960. He accepted the next day.

In 1973, at 67, Chain retired from the biochemistry chair, but he had no intention of remaining neutral on the choice of his successor. This involved long and wearing battles to ensure that the new head of department would be a biochemist with a leaning for physiology, not molecular biology – in his view, 'as far as medicine is concerned, the contribution of molecular biology is nil'. After lengthy committee work Chain's Chair of Biochemistry was converted into two professorships, the second one for physiological biochemistry. Chain, who was keenly interested in food technology, knew Lord Rank, Chairman of Rank Hovis McDougall, and was instrumental in persuading the Rank Trustees to donate £50,000 to establish the new position.

In Britain academics tended to maintain a strict distance between themselves and the industrial world. Chain, trained in the German tradition of collaboration between academic research and commercial production, had no inhibitions about fostering such links and he eventually became involved in more than 50 pharmaceutical or food industries. He had strong views on the social responsibility of scientists: 'Science itself,' he said in 1970, 'has no ethical quality in so far as it throws light on the laws of nature. Responsibility for the use or abuse of its achievements must rest with society.' He believed that the application of scientific knowledge must be based on a code of ethical conduct, influenced by the wisdom of great spiritual leaders.

After his Nobel Prize, awarded when he was 39, Chain reaped honours round the world: in Austria, Russia, Japan. He was elected a Fellow of the Royal Society, and Honorary Fellow of the Royal College of Physicians and of his old college, Fitzwilliam in Cambridge; he was knighted in May 1969. On his seventy-fifth birthday a symposium was held in his honour at the Royal Society before a dinner in the Middle Temple Hall, when Chain and members of his family gave a musical recital.

He and his family spent many holidays in Ireland, and in 1971 built a country retreat in County Mayo, where he escaped from his relentlessly pressured life and played his old Steinway piano. He died there in 1979. Nobody who knew Ernst Chain will ever forget him; few could match his energy, or were so richly and variously talented.

BERNARD KATZ

Bernard Katz is another scientist whose career was ignited by one man; in his case A. V. Hill. Through him Katz developed the true scientist's attitude to his occupation: scientists were 'professional amateurs' – that is, people who love their work, learning to understand nature.

Katz met Hill in 1935. As we have seen earlier, Hill attracted Katz's admiration by his reply to Johannes Stark in *Nature* and wanted to work with him. Katz was then 24. He was born in Leipzig in 1911 and educated there, but he was not a German and never acquired German nationality. His father had been born in tsarist Russia but moved to Germany in 1904 just before the outbreak of the Russo-Japanese war and settled in Leipzig. Katz's father was in the fur trade and Leipzig was its centre. Being stateless did not seem to matter when Bernard Katz was young: he had no need to travel outside Germany and indeed did not even realize he was stateless until he was a teenager. At 24 it did. In 1935 Hitler was in power and Katz, being Jewish, wanted to leave Germany. He had good cause to fear the Nazis and their anti-Semitism for, when he was a schoolboy, one of the other pupils had suggested that the Jews of Leipzig should be invited to the basement of an underground hall, the door shut, and then killed with poison gas. A grim warning of what was to come. After reading Hill's reply to Stark, Katz wrote asking if he could come and work with him. In reply Hill invited him to work in his physiology department at University College, London. When Katz got to Harwich he had a terrifying time while the immigration officer questioned him long after the other passengers had left on the train for London. He was frightened not of being refused admission to Britain but of being sent back to the 'Niebelheim' (the cave in Wagner's *Das Rheingold* where dwarves spent their time hammering the walls, which Katz felt represented the atmosphere in Nazi Germany). Fortunately he got into the country on a League of Nations certificate and was safe.

Next day he went to A. V. Hill's department at University College and immediately felt a new man. Although Katz was still very inexperienced in neurophysiology, Hill was prepared to take him on his staff 'as an experiment'. Katz had qualified as a doctor only a year before. He had already become addicted to science at school, though his education, as so often in Germany at that time, was classical.

Hill was interested in Katz as a result of reading his MD thesis, which was published in Leipzig, and his winning of the Garten Prize, given for physiological research by a medical student. There was no chance of a Jew winning it but there was an odd rule: entries had to be submitted under a false name. There were only two entries. The judge, the current Professor of Physiology at Leipzig, knew who they were. When they were revealed he professed to be shocked that a Jew had won; the prize could not of course be awarded, he said. But a short time later he gave Katz his prize 'under the table', a rare act of courage.

In his first hour at University College, Katz saw various items that Hill had collected, including a toy figure of Hitler with a moveable saluting arm which, Hill said, was to make people like Katz 'feel at home'. When showing them to official visitors Hill would explain that the toy was a sign of gratitude to Hitler for the scientists he had expelled.

Katz regarded it as extraordinary good luck to be taken on by Hill, and he spent nearly all his professional life apart from the war with him. Not only was Hill a professional ideal but a personal one. As a result of all he did for the refugees and generally, Katz described him as 'the most naturally upright man I have ever known'.

During his early years at University College, Katz's interest in the physics and physiology of nerve conduction developed into his permanent life interest. In this his path crossed those of several other refugees, including Feldberg. Katz was in the pioneering group which studied single nerve cells, especially in the squid, whose isolated cells could be several feet long; this made their study by electric and oscillographic techniques feasible.

Katz was prospering at University College when in 1939 he received an invitation from the noted neurophysiologist Jack Eccles to join him in Sydney. Katz was very reluctant to go, particularly as war was imminent, but felt that it would be unbecoming for a 'guest' in Britain to decline such an offer, especially as he would perhaps be liberating a place for another refugee. On his way to Australia war started and his ship stopped in Colombo. After some doubt about what would happen, he went on to Sydney. After two successful years with Eccles he was naturalized and immediately volunteered for the Royal Australian Air Force. Now that he felt more sure of himself, he no longer needed to consider himself a guest of Britain.

In 1945, a month before he was to get married to an Australian girl, he had a cable from Hill offering him a Royal Society Research Fellowship. Katz's reputation was expanding rapidly. His work on muscle neurophysiology was fundamental and widely recognized to be so. In 1952 he was elected a Fellow of the Royal Society and in 1958 was appointed Biological Secretary of the Royal Society. Prizes, honours – he was knighted in 1969 – and lecture invitations poured in from all over the world. One nice episode was his award of the Feldberg Fellowship in 1965, created by his friend with his restitution money from the German government. In 1970 he, along with Julius Axelrod and U. S. von Euler, won the Nobel Prize.

Modest man that he is, Katz might agree that A. V. Hill's experiment in taking him on in 1935 has been a success.

LUDWIG GUTTMANN

Almost all paraplegics used to die. A man who broke his spine, even if he survived long enough to get to hospital, had only a 20 per cent chance of living for a year. When his spinal cord was broken he could not move, feel or control his natural functions below a certain level of his body. It might be that he could move his arms but not his legs; but if the break was in the neck he could move neither arms nor legs. As he could not move, his weight was continuously on the same part of his body, particularly the sacrum, hips and heels. The skin is not designed to be pressed upon all the time; normally we are always on the move and even in sleep we move and turn. But if we cannot move the skin is constantly compressed, becoming devitalized and soon breaking down into ulcers and sores, which are extremely difficult to heal. They become infected, infection spreads into devitalized tissue which is also difficult to control. Worse still, control of bladder (and rectum) is lost and urine is retained until the pressure is so great that urine spills out. There is always a full – or overfull – bladder and this is bound to become infected. This infection is hard to control. The treatment is to pass a catheter into the bladder and leave it there. It is not surprising that a paraplegic was in a desperate plight. The prospect seemed so hopeless that few doctors made any effort to change it.

All that changed with Ludwig Guttmann. Early in the Second World War it became obvious that many wounded men would be paraplegic. When the Allies invaded France, the number would increase greatly. Something needed to be done. Dr George Riddoch, head of the neurology services in the Emergency Medical Service, asked Guttmann to take charge. He did, made a triumphant success, reversed the mortality rate from 80 per cent within a year to 80 per cent survival. He also made paraplegics admired for their courage instead of avoided and feared. It was a great clinical triumph, created not by a dramatic advance in knowledge but by thorough, even merciless, application of every possible aid to sound treatment.

Ludwig Guttmann was a German Jew who came to Britain in 1939. He trained as a doctor in Breslau and then decided to specialize in neurosurgery. He worked with the best-known neurosurgeon in Europe, Otfrid Förster, and was then appointed chief of neurosurgery in Hamburg. When his first assistant died in 1929 Förster invited Guttmann back to Breslau. Although Förster's reputation stood very high in Europe, he was not so highly rated in Britain. He did not use some of the latest techniques for controlling bleeding and infection during operations, and when Guttmann came to Britain his host, Hugh Cairns of Oxford, was not happy to make him a neurosurgeon.

Guttmann did stay at his post in Breslau but refused to do so after the Nazis came to power because no Jews could be treated in 'Aryan' hospitals such as his. He moved to the city's Jewish Hospital at first as chief neurologist, and after 1937 as medical director. He was not harmed himself, although very many Jews were. In May 1933 there was an incident which shocked him greatly, as it did many people in Germany and abroad who saw the pictures: the burning of the books. Guttmann saw this and he wept as he realized that what he – and others – had thought and hoped might be a passing aberration was there to stay.

Under the Nuremberg laws of 1935 Jewish doctors were no longer allowed to treat non-Jewish patients. Guttmann might be the best neurosurgeon in Breslau, but a non-Jew could not consult him. He managed to carry on until 9 November 1938: *Kristallnacht*.

Guttmann, as hospital director, ordered that any one coming to the hospital that night should be automatically admitted. Only hours later he was summoned by the SS. As he went to meet them, thinking he would be arrested he took his winter coat but then noticed he had summer shoes on. He went back for his boots and his wife thought he had been freed. He was asked to explain all the 64 admissions. He took the Nazis round the wards. The first man had had a stroke, he said, and this was true. But in other cases he invented symptoms and diagnoses until the Nazi officers were convinced. He saved 60 of the 64, the other four, including two doctors, having unintentionally given themselves away. From then on Guttmann had to report to the police every day with lists of those admitted and discharged from the hospital.

Guttmann was a man of spirit. He reported the SS's invasion to the local Nazi Gauleiter, who was himself a skin specialist. The Gauleiter eventually ordered that Jewish hospitals be allowed to continue working. Some of the Jewish doctors who had been taken to concentration camps came back. Guttmann's passport had been taken by the Nazi authorities but he got it back when he was asked to go to Prague to operate on a woman with a brain cyst and again when he was asked to go to Lisbon to see a man with a spinal tumour. This request came through Dr Salazar, the dictator of Portugal, to von Ribbentrop, the German Foreign Minister. Guttmann got permission to go to Britain on his way back to Germany. He made contact with the Society for the Protection of Science and Learning and was offered a grant to work in Oxford. He went back to Breslau, got permission to leave the hospital and on 14 March 1939 left for England with his wife and two children. They arrived at Harwich in a high wind, rain and sleet. They were standing outside in a queue for the immigration shed when an immigration officer saw the two children and called the family in, saying that children should not be kept outside in such weather. This was not how the Guttmanns had been treated by officials in Germany. Mrs Guttmann was so moved that she burst into tears and Guttmann said it restored his faith in human nature. In Oxford they were made welcome, staying for the first few weeks in the Master's lodge at Balliol.

War came within six months. For some time Guttmann worked on nerve physiology and nerve injuries but was not fully engaged until, in 1943, Riddoch offered him the directorship of a new centre for spinal injuries. He did so well with the patients in his 24-bedded unit, which was housed in huts, that by D-Day all paraplegics were ordered to be sent to his unit at Stoke Mandeville, Buckinghamshire. Within a few weeks he had 50 patients.

Guttmann studied them and their injuries with ferocious intensity. To counter the danger of bed sores he ordered that all patients be turned every two hours, day and night, from back to front, from side to side. To make certain that his orders were precisely obeyed he was in the wards himself day and night. There was no let-up – and there never could be for the rest of the patient's life. Guttmann had many clashes in the fight to impose his standards on medical colleagues and other staff. He always knew what he wanted and why. His judgement was based on scientific observation: he measured the rate of healing of bed sores by tracing their outline on transparent paper; he measured the pressure in the tissues to see what they could endure before being damaged. He did all the bladder catheterizations himself with strict aseptic precautions to avoid the curse of the catheter, infection. It is still a serious hazard, and in order to reduce it antibiotics are given and the bladder regularly washed out.

It was during this routine procedure of bladder wash-outs that Guttmann made fundamental observations. Sometimes a patient would go red in the face, the pulse rate fall and a bad headache develop. The skin temperature would rise in the legs and feet and blood pressure double. By studying patients with spinal cord breaks at different levels Guttmann and the physiologist David Whitteridge found that the changes happened only when the break was above the middle level of the chest, the seventh thoracic vertebra; below that level there was no change. The changes had to be due to nervous reflexes, not chemical alterations in the blood, because they started within seconds. One of the impressive things about this research is how much trouble Guttmann took to spare the patients pain. He measured changes in blood flow by old-fashioned, complicated methods in order to avoid repeated blood sampling. Invasive methods – for example, insertion of needles into veins – were avoided. When research was done on patients it was always explained that it had nothing to do with the patient's own treatment but was done in the hope, perhaps remote, of helping others. They seldom refused to cooperate. It was the same compassionate, optimistic attitude that led Guttmann to get the patients out of bed and into wheelchairs whenever he could, to make them mobile and independent. He organized ward activities, Christmas pantomimes, long before the idea came to him of starting paraplegic games.

Morale of patients with paraplegia was often at rock bottom – not surprisingly. A man previously strong and active is suddenly unable to move below the waist or even neck, or to control his bladder or bowels or do any of those things for himself which he had previously taken for granted. Many gave up and simply wanted to die. Guttmann did not try to disguise anything: they would never recover, they would be chairbound for ever. But they could lead active, productive, useful lives. They could even, thanks to treatment Guttmann worked out, father children. (We say 'men' because the great majority of paraplegics were male, but not all. Sixteen para-plegic women conceived and bore children.) By being forced to take increasing responsibility for themselves the paraplegics gradually regained self-confidence, then hope. So much was this in contrast to the public attitude that one patient, a paraplegic army chaplain, said: 'The first duty of the paraplegic patient is to cheer up his visitors.'

'Occupational therapy', the term that used to conjure up endless basket-making, was a large part of Guttmann's regime. After woodwork and instrument making in the hospital workshop, patients tried working in a local factory in Aylesbury and showed that they could do a full day's work. This led to the creation of the Government Industrial Rehabilitation Centres. Paraplegics also studied: an army officer passed his law exam within a year of arriving at Stoke Mandeville. A jockey, who on arrival refused all treatment and simply wanted to die, took a correspondence course and qualified as an accountant.

The story of the paraplegic games began in 1945 when Guttmann saw some patients in their wheelchairs hitting a puck about with walking sticks. He realized what must be done at once. He and the chief physiotherapist started wheelchair polo, then, when this became too dangerous, wheelchair basketball. This led to the first Stoke Mandeville Games in 1948, when the Olympic Games were held in London. The first Olympic Games for the Paralysed took place in Rome in 1960 and included many field and track events, which varied according to the nature of the spinal lesion. A sports stadium was built at Stoke Mandeville which included a swimming pool. Guttmann was as proud when the stadium was opened by the Queen in 1965 as he was of anything in his life, and with good reason. He was knighted in 1966 and in 1976, long after he had retired and when he was 76 he was elected a Fellow of the Royal Society, a rare honour for a doctor, an extremely rare honour for a clinician and usually given long before that age.

A knight, a Fellow of the Royal Society, world-famous for his scientific and clinical work on paraplegia and for the rehabilitation of paraplegics – few people have contributed more than Guttmann. He did it because of his ruthless determination and energy, his intelligence and adaptability. His scientist's eye was always looking for clues on the ward, as his heart was. He gave himself no peace, nor did he give anybody else any. It was those qualities that we often think of, perhaps disapprovingly, as particularly German, especially his determination that he should be the sole chief, that his ideas should be carried through and his orders obeyed, that stood him – and more importantly, his patients – in such good stead.

Spinal injuries centres were set up all over the world. Stoke Mandeville became a focus of interest for doctors, physiotherapists, nurses, anyone interested in paraplegia. Guttmann travelled widely, but not always comfortably for his hosts, for he was not an easy man and quick to comment when standards fell below his own.

In 1999, years after his death, German scientists and doctors organized a scientific meeting to celebrate the centenary of his birth. The world has reason to be grateful that Ludwig Guttmann was deflected from the expected, well-worn track of neurosurgery to one of the most productive careers that any doctor has had.

EDITH BÜLBRING

Edith Bülbring's father was a professor of English at Bonn University, which must have been an advantage for her. When Karl, Edith's father, died young, his brother took over as head of the family. He contributed to the founding of the city of Tel Aviv and many schools in the Netherlands, where the family had roots. He was notably friendly to everyone; when asked by Edith during the First World

War which side he was on he said: 'I am German-friendly and also English-friendly; I am totally friendly.'

At high school Edith nearly decided to make a career in music but finally opted for medicine. After she qualified in 1924 she spent time in various physiological research centres in Germany and the Netherlands before taking a position in the infectious disease unit in Berlin's Virchow Hospital in early 1933, just before her superior, Ulrich Friedemann, and many of his junior staff, who were Jewish, were all dismissed. Only her mother was Jewish, so she had only two Jewish grandparents. This was two too many for the Nazis.

Her dismissal was particularly ironic. She was a junior doctor in the children's department of a hospital when a boy was admitted with diphtheria. The membrane was growing across his larynx and threatened to suffocate him – he needed an operation to save his life. Edith sent to the Ear, Nose and Throat department for a surgeon, to be told that there was none – they had all been dismissed. She had never done the operation but a nurse had assisted on many occasions. Between them they succeeded and the boy's life was saved.

Edith was so pleased with herself that when she was challenged by the hospital's director: 'Miss Bülbring, I have been told that you are Jewish', she burst out laughing. The director was furious: 'Miss Bülbring, this is no laughing matter. Leave the hospital at once.'

She did. She and her sister took a holiday in London, where she visited her old chief, who had fled there and was working at the Medical Research Council in Hampstead. She was surprised and delighted to be offered a job by Sir Henry Dale, and she went to work with J. H. Burn at the Pharmaceutical Society in London. Her career took off and she went on to Oxford, where she stayed for the rest of her life. She was a pioneer of the study of smooth muscle (in arterial and gut walls, as distinct from the muscles which make voluntary movements) and made important contributions to the burgeoning field of neuro-transmission. In 1958 Edith Bülbring was elected a Fellow of the Royal Society and a Fellow of Lady Margaret Hall. She died in 1990 at the age of 87.

RICHARD WILLSTÄTTER

One extraordinary episode, which is not widely known, concerns the great German chemist Richard Willstätter. We include his story here although he did not come to Britain. Willstätter had won the Nobel Prize in 1915 for describing the structure of chlorophyll, was professor of chemistry at Munich – and was a Jew. In 1924 anti-Semitism was increasing. It reached a crisis for Willstätter when three senior academic appointments in Munich became vacant. In each case the leading contender was Jewish, and in each case he was rejected because he was Jewish. Willstätter felt that this attitude of his own university colleagues made his position impossible and he must resign. This was in spite of great admiration for him – so much so that the famous surgeon Sauerbruch surprised him by taking him to a new lecture theatre where 300 students presented him with an address of loyalty and admiration. Despite this and several offers of jobs in Germany and abroad, Willstätter maintained his resolve and never set foot in the university again. However, he stayed in Germany for another 14 years, continuing research, much of it by telephone. After *Kristallnacht* (9 November 1938) the Nazis ordered him out of the country and he reluctantly went to Switzerland, where he was made welcome by colleagues. He was perhaps the first of the German Jewish refugees.

7

Refugees to the United States

I prefer to forgo this appointment, though it is
suited to my inclination and capabilities, rather than
having to betray my convictions, or that by
remaining silent I would encourage an opinion
about me that does not correspond with the facts.

*Otto Krayer, Assistant Professor of Pharmacology
in Berlin, dismissed immediately on refusing
to accept an appointment vacated by a Jewish colleague
driven out of Düsseldorf. Krayer was later appointed
full professor at Harvard.*

For the first two years of the rescue effort Britain alone nearly equalled the rest of the world in temporary appointments. But, as the threat from Germany increased during the 1930s, Britain was uncomfortably close to mainland Europe. America was wealthy, and safe.

Nevertheless, American policy towards immigrants was cautious and immigration increased in the form of a trickle not a flood. In 1933, 30 scientists were admitted, and the annual total never exceeded a hundred, the highest being 97 in 1939. The physicists in particular, with their international network of scholarship and friendship established over the previous two decades, were 'better able than most to provide for each other'.

The roles of the two countries could be described by saying that Britain rescued the refugee scientists and the United States received them. Often those who escaped to Britain first were eventually offered work in America. For example, Hans Bethe, whose career we follow in more detail later, migrated first to Britain, then to Copenhagen, and after two years there was invited to Cornell University, where he has spent the rest of his career.

It is notable how often the early rescue phase of the scientists' careers has been ignored by writers in the reference books; for example, the *Encyclopaedia Britannica* makes no mention of the year Edward Teller spent at University College, London, before he settled in the United States. Yet the short time he and other scientists spent in Britain was crucial; it was an early staging post where exiles could shelter while making arrangements to move on – waiting for their cases to be processed by the US State Department or until there was a vacancy under the American quota system. Without it many refugees would have had no career anywhere.

There were impressive gestures of generosity from American institutions and individuals. In 1933 the faculty members at Princeton gave 5 per cent of their salaries to the Academic Assistance Council in England. American foundations were traditionally open-handed in the cause of furthering science, awarding funds to institutions and to individual scientists. The Rockefeller Foundation in particular had made large contributions to the support of German universities, helping to fund departments and individuals; indeed, it continued to maintain its European office in Paris after January 1933. But an inherent problem lay in the Foundation's rule that any individual who received a grant to work abroad had to have an appointment to return to. After the dismissals of 1933 this presented a formidable difficulty to refugees who had been deprived of their jobs in Germany. However sympathetic the Foundation and its European representatives, the requirement was upheld, preventing exiled scholars – Otto Frisch for one – from taking up their grants.

The Foundation continued its endowment of leading German institutions, such as the Kaiser Wilhelm Institutes, although here the difficulty was the steep decline in standards of scientific education after the new regime passed its racist civil service laws. The loss of up to a quarter of the German universities' senior staff, often including the most able, inevitably led to a serious deterioration which was privately recognized within academic circles. Fewer students applied for university courses and the collapse in academic standards was in effect acknowledged in the government's instructions that students should not be penalized for time they spent in labour or military camps. The government's policy of replacing distinguished professors with inferior careerists who were Nazi Party supporters also resulted in a drastic fall in the quality of research.

Placement for the refugees in the United States was not always easy. The American committee corresponding to the British AAC, the Emergency Committee in Aid of Displaced German Scholars, at first took the same view as Europeans who had initially tried to set up a university in exile; but they soon realized that from every point of view it was better to scatter the refugees among the large number of American universities. Refugee scholars were provided with a small salary so that the host institutions were not financially penalized.

Some American authorities welcomed the new arrivals. For example, the Director of the Institute of Fine Arts in New York said: 'Hitler is my best friend. He shakes the tree and I collect the apples.' European art historians and archaeologists effectively founded courses in their subjects which had previously been almost unrecognized in American institutions. But 1933 was still a time of severe economic depression, and younger scientists in particular had trouble finding work. Furthermore there was considerable anti-Semitism in the United States in the 1930s and early 1940s. Polls showed that 70–80 per cent of the population opposed raising quotas for Jewish refugees and in 1935, as we have seen, an American envoy was actually sent to Britain to tell the AAC that America had no more room for academic refugees. Fortunately the AAC refused to accept this and continued to send refugees, most of whom found places in the less well-known universities.

Although the United States admitted more refugees from the Reich than any other single country, its record in relation to capacity was less generous than that of many, including Britain. One reason for this was the curiously negative attitude of the American Jewish community to the prospect of any large influx of refugees into the United States, and the resultant refusal of the community's leaders to urge more than token changes in immigration law or procedures. The Wagner-Rogers Bill of early 1939, which proposed the admission of up to 20,000 refugee children, after a bitter debate failed to reach the floor of Congress. At precisely the same time hospitality was being mobilized on a large scale to bring 10,000 child refugees rapidly into Britain.

RICHARD COURANT

Not everyone was happy with their first refuge outside Germany.

The mathematician Richard Courant, one of Göttingen's three departing institute heads, tried initially to stay close to Germany, believing that the Nazi regime could not last; he went first to Cambridge but could not settle there. He was so homesick that he actually returned to Germany before re-emigrating, this time to New York.

In Germany he was 'harder hit by the turn of events and less prepared than I should have thought. I feel so close to my work here, to the surrounding countryside, to so many people and to Germany as a whole that this "elimination" hits me with an unbearable force.' While still struggling to stay on, recruiting what outside help he could, he had written to Niels Bohr via the Danish consul in Hamburg: 'How hard it is for us to make use of your friendship in this manner, we need not assure you. I hope it will never be necessary to show you that at any time we would be prepared to do the same for you.'

Courant felt the blow of exclusion from Germany not only personally, but also at least as strongly on behalf of German science. 'It is a pity to think what treasures are going to be destroyed in this way after . . . years of work at reconstruction. It pains me most to see what senseless damage will be done to Germany. Only look at the Americans and other foreigners who are now getting ready to break off their studies and go home!' Courant gave one of the departing Americans an envelope containing money to pass on to the brother of Niels Bohr; it was used to help young Jewish mathematicians who were already seeking shelter in Denmark.

On arriving in New York in August 1934, Courant was welcomed on the docks by old friends and colleagues from Germany who had already made the same journey. A job had been created for him in the mathematics department of New York University; the resources were primitive but he soon set about improving them. He and his wife stayed at first with Donald Flanders, the young incumbent professor of mathematics at the university who was largely responsible for bringing Courant to America. Knowing that he himself was not a first-class mathematician and realizing the need to recruit one, Flanders carried out successful negotiations on Courant's behalf which brought great credit to the university and himself. This was not the characteristic behaviour of professors, however distinguished, then or now, and Courant regarded him as 'a saint'.

Sceptical at first, Courant soon came to love his adopted country; his wife Nina embraced their new circumstances even more quickly. Emigration, she said, 'was something we could never have brought ourselves to do on our own, but when it was forced upon us and there was nothing else we could do, it was wonderful – like being young all over again'. Many of the refugee scientists, even those who were middle-aged or elderly, spoke of this feeling of rejuvenation on reaching Britain or the United States. It stimulated them personally and intellectually.

Courant soon became intensely involved in his life in the United States, within science and outside it. Many years later he said: 'When I first came here I felt ... some kind of patriotic urge to do something for this country. I was deeply impressed by America and what was being done during the first years of the Roosevelt administration. I was very enthusiastic. I felt very loyal and thought very much about what was needed. The best I could imagine that I might be able to do was to bring my experience in Göttingen to bear upon the situation here.'

This is exactly what he did. Although offered Chairs elsewhere, Courant stayed in New York for the rest of his life and built up a large and flourishing mathematics department there. Three decades later his efforts were rewarded by the opening of a new institute of applied mathematics, known as the Courant Institute. The building itself, funded by large donations from the Alfred P. Sloan, Ford and National Science foundations, was named after Warren Weaver, formerly director of the division of Natural Sciences at the Rockefeller Foundation, who had played a considerable part in the Foundation's widespread efforts to help refugees from Germany after 1933. The Courant Institute was remarkable as the only one of several such institutes to become fully established and successful.

After the war the lives of Courant and James Franck, his friend and colleague from Göttingen, came full circle when both did what they could to help to resurrect German science. Reconciliation was not easy at first. Courant found it hard to make or resume natural personal contact with former friends and colleagues who had stayed in Germany, who all seemed to be holding back. Students were sometimes actually resentful, still grieving at Germany's defeat and unwilling to join in the reconstruction effort. Although Courant visited Germany nearly every year he never thought of returning there to live.

James Franck

During their emigration journey many physicists made their way first to Copenhagen, where Niels Bohr was not only the presiding genius of physics but also a committed supporter of the refugees. Bohr, 'the uncrowned king of Denmark', was an inspiration to everyone he met, in science and in the wider world. Beleaguered German scientists were invited to Bohr's Institute for Theoretical Physics and whenever an exile arrived Bohr sheltered him (or her, in the case of Lise Meitner) – meanwhile travelling to Britain and the United States to trawl for permanent placements for his 'boys' – until work could be found. This could entail staying on for a year or more, as in the case of Otto Frisch, who arrived in 1934 and remained in Copenhagen until 1939, when he found a place in England.

One of Bohr's guests was the famously affable James Franck, who always treated his assistants and postgraduate students as colleagues and equals – exceptional conduct in German universities, where full professors were treated almost as gods.

In 1933, after making his exceptional public protest against Nazi policy by sending his letter of resignation to the press for publication, Franck collaborated with Frederick Lindemann in helping dismissed colleagues of all degrees of seniority to find work abroad. He visited Baltimore later in 1933 but did not finally leave Germany until November, taking the train first to Copenhagen at the invitation of Bohr. After a year he emigrated to the United States, initially to Johns Hopkins University, but later, in 1938, he moved to Chicago, where he stayed.

Franck was an early recruit to the atomic bomb team, working on it because, though he was repelled by the prospect of its use, he feared even more that the Germans might develop atomic weapons and use them first. In June 1945, after the end of the war in Europe, Franck was chairman of a committee appointed to assess 'the political consequences of atomic energy'. The Franck Report, as it became known, pointed out that Britain, France, Germany and the Soviet

Union all had enough knowledge of atomic physics to produce nuclear weapons in the foreseeable future, and predicted with remarkable accuracy the nuclear arms race that would ensue. The report argued for an international agreement on nuclear weapons and for a demonstration of the atomic bomb over some uninhabited place instead of exploding it on defenceless citizens, which could unleash a backlash of hostile public opinion at home. But the newly installed President Truman was less open to approaches from the atomic scientists and the report's suggestion was thought impractical by the authorities.

Franck, as a number of other physicists did after the atomic bombs were dropped on Japan in August 1945, changed to a completely different field of research: in his case, photosynthesis.

Like Courant he made a point of visiting postwar Germany, where he received a warm welcome and, in 1953, the freedom of Göttingen along with Max Born and other old friends and colleagues. This gesture of atonement was much appreciated and helped to restore Germany to the mainstream of Western science.

VICTOR WEISSKOPF

The story of Victor Weisskopf illustrates the international fellowship of science in general and of physics in particular. Born into a Jewish family in Vienna, he was enthralled by physics, but had a passion for music common among physicists and was torn between a career in science and becoming a conductor. Science, he said, was his profession, music his religion – uninspired by conventional religious instruction, he 'got acquainted with the meaning of religion and the concept of God through the liturgical masterpieces of the great composers'.

Finding that because of anti-Semitism in Austria a Jew had to work 'ten times as hard' as a gentile in the same position, Weisskopf moved on to the great European centres of physics in the course of his postgraduate training during the 1920s: Göttingen, Munich, Zurich, Cambridge and Copenhagen, where he was inspired and enchanted by Niels Bohr. At that time Weisskopf was finding physics too detached from human affairs for his taste and considered giving it up; Bohr persuaded him to continue with the prophetic advice, 'Stay in physics. You will see how deeply the new physics is involved with human affairs.' This was in 1929, long before the new theories had given rise to transistors and computers, let alone the atomic bomb.

Weisskopf was working with Wolfgang Pauli, head of physics at Zurich, when the Nazi purge of Jewish academics from Germany began. In Switzerland he soon noticed limitations to his idealized view of the country as a haven of peace and reason. The Swiss were wary of allowing refugees from the Nazis into the country. Those found inside Switzerland were transported back to Germany if within 50km of the frontier, or to detention camps if further into the country. The authorities were also highly suspicious of Weisskopf because he had communist friends. All his letters since he arrived in Switzerland had been opened by the police; an invitation to lecture in the Soviet Union was considered damning evidence and he was finally told he must leave and never return. Many years later, in 1960, Weisskopf showed this letter to the police when he was appointed director-general of CERN (European Council for Nuclear Research), near Geneva.

The Swiss police even harboured suspicions about Wolfgang Pauli, who as an Austrian citizen was reclassed as German after the 1938 Anschluss merged the two states. He was refused Swiss citizenship and in 1940 left Europe for the United States; only in 1945, after he had won the Nobel Prize, was he deemed worthy to receive Swiss nationality.

As the threat from Nazi Germany spread across Europe Weisskopf returned to Copenhagen, where a clutch of physicists, including James Franck, Otto Frisch, the French physicist Hans Halban and others, were already sheltering. Weisskopf, like the other physicists, could not stay on indefinitely in Copenhagen, as Niels Bohr's Institute for Theoretical Physics was pressed for funds and space. He was offered a permanent post in the Soviet Union, working with the great physicist Peter Kapitsa, who had been a valued member of Lord Rutherford's team in Cambridge until on a visit home on leave he had been forbidden by Stalin to return to England. Rutherford had all Kapitsa's laboratory equipment packed up and shipped to him in Moscow. Although Weisskopf was tempted by the prospect of working with Kapitsa he was repelled by the political atmosphere in the Soviet Union and decided against it. Meanwhile in 1937 Bohr had organized a job for him at the University of Rochester, New York, which he quickly accepted despite the low salary of $200 a month. Weisskopf ruefully commented that immigrant scientists were often paid less than Americans of similar standing, though the warmth of their reception helped to compensate. The unsuccessful candidate for Weisskopf's position wrote to the head of department to say that though he was sorry not to have landed the job he was glad that it had been offered to Weisskopf, because he knew how much a refugee from Hitler's Germany would need the work, and secondly how much the American physics community would be enriched by Weisskopf's presence.

While Weisskopf immediately felt at home in the United States he was aware of anti-Semitism in the universities, where he found Jews had to excel to be appointed to academic posts. When Weisskopf wanted to move to Boston he was told that it was very difficult for Jewish academics to be admitted to Harvard or the Massachusetts Institute of Technology (MIT). But after the war he noted that anti-Semitism had almost disappeared from American universities.

Despite the obstacles, Weisskopf's career prospered, and he was invited to lecture everywhere. At one time he took over some of Bethe's lecturing at Cornell, and in the summer of 1940 he taught at the famous summer school at the University of Michigan. Early in 1943, on becoming an American citizen, he was invited by Oppenheimer to join the Los Alamos team working on the atomic bomb. Like his contemporaries, his doubts about the project were overcome by the greater fear that German scientists could be developing atomic weapons for Hitler – as well as by his pride in being part of such an eminent and committed team. The only colleague there with whom Weisskopf had difficulties was Edward Teller, who was as bitterly envious of Weisskopf's appointment as deputy leader of the theoretical division as he was of Bethe's as head of it.

After the war Weisskopf was appointed an associate professor at MIT, where he stayed until 1960. He enjoyed his years there and made many new friendships – he believed physicists were 'a kind of family', with a particular gift for making friends.

During the early 1950s Weisskopf did his best to support and mitigate some of the worst excesses of the McCarthy period. In one case Dirk Struik, a professor of mathematics at MIT, was indicted for attempting to overthrow the constitution of the Commonwealth of Massachusetts; he was forbidden to use MIT's premises, including the library, in a punitive gesture reminiscent of Germany in the 1930s.

His European background also continued to be important to him, and he renewed his European connections through annual visits. In 1960 he was appointed the first director of CERN; a chief reason why he accepted the appointment was that it was a Europe-wide, multinational organization. After five successful years there, during which he built up that now world-famous laboratory, he returned to MIT, where he became professor of physics, but kept a house on a mountainside close to Geneva as a base in order to maintain his European contacts.

During his seven years back at MIT, and retirement afterwards, Weisskopf contributed to research and public affairs by creating the High Energy Physics Advisory Panel, and becoming president of the American Academy of Arts and Sciences – more than repaying the debt he owed to the United States for receiving him after the war.

Max Delbrück

Between the wars the dominant science was physics; since then biology has overtaken it. The beginnings of this change of direction in research lay with two physicists.

The new science of biology owed an important debt to a third physicist, Max Delbrück. He was born in Berlin in 1906, and had started on a career in physics, during the course of which he visited Copenhagen in 1931. At this time Niels Bohr was getting interested in biology, and this led Delbrück to take a greater interest in their connection. He went to study nuclear physics with Lise Meitner in the Kaiser Wilhelm Institute for Chemistry in Berlin, which was next door to the KWI for Biology. There he encountered Timofeeff-Ressovsky, with whom he formed a group which met two or three times a week for long discussions on quantitative aspects of biology, especially genetics. His paper with Timofeeff-Ressovsky and Zimmer attracted little attention at the time, but later it gave Schrödinger his notion that the gene was a molecule.

When Delbrück applied for a permanent appointment in Germany he was sent to a Nazi indoctrination school, where he was judged to be 'politically immature'. He was not offered the job, but in 1937 by good fortune he was awarded a Rockefeller Fellowship (for which he had not even applied), to work on fruit-fly genetics with the world leader, T. H. Morgan, at Caltech. While there he happened to miss a seminar on bacteriophage, and went off to ask Emory Ellis, the lecturer, to explain it to him. This was the crucial event in Delbrück's career: he realized that the phage virus, which penetrates a bacterial cell, replicates with the production of zoo-progeny and bursts the cell in 30 minutes; it was the perfect experimental material for him.

After his Rockefeller Fellowship at Caltech lapsed, Delbrück moved to Vanderbilt University. In collaboration with Salvador Luria from Italy at Bloomington, Indiana, a refugee and another recent immigrant, he found that bacteria acquired resistance to phage by genetic mutation, which turned out to be true for almost all bacterial variations. Delbrück and Luria shared a Nobel Prize with Alfred Hershey for this work in 1969.

Interest in phage had become intense, thanks partly to the annual Phage Courses at Cold Spring Harbor on Long Island, which continued for over a quarter of a century, and phage meetings, which went on for even longer. These became 'a Mecca to which Max's followers . . . made their annual summer Hadj', attracting visitors for the pleasure of the company as much as for the work.

Immediately after the war Delbrück was offered several appointments. He was sorely tempted to accept Patrick Blackett's invitation to Manchester because of happy memories and connections in England, where he had worked from 1929 to 1932, but this offer was outfaced by another from Caltech, which he accepted. His department at Caltech became the focus for biologists and physicists interested in molecular biology, drawn by the rapidly expanding subject and its leading exponent.

By virtue of his ability, imagination and interests Delbrück should have discovered that DNA was the genetic material; that he did not may be due to the fact that he and Luria were not thinking in biochemical terms. James Watson often visited Max Delbrück in the late 1940s before he went to Cambridge, hungry for scientific success. After he and Crick had built the now-famous double-helical model of the structure of DNA, Watson wrote to his mentor with their findings. Delbrück saw at once that their solution was correct, and compared it to Rutherford's discovery of the atomic nucleus. Delbrück realized that he should have discovered the structure of DNA but he was never one to be concerned about priority. Unusually among refugee scientists, Delbrück returned to work part-time in Germany, visiting Göttingen once and Cologne several times. He helped to establish a genetics institute in 1961, and he returned to Cologne each year as a visiting lecturer on phage genetics and physics.

Wherever he went, Delbrück created his own atmosphere, modelling his style of work, as he said, directly from the time he spent with Bohr in Copenhagen. 'The first principle had to be openness. That you tell each other what you are doing and thinking. And that you don't care who has the priority.' His attitude would be equally valuable today, and more rare than ever.

OTTO LOEWI

The Austrian physiologist Otto Loewi was well into his sixties when he was forced to flee his country after Hitler's forces invaded Austria in 1938. He had been professor of pharmacology at Graz University for 29 years, and shared the Nobel Prize for medicine with Sir Henry Dale in 1936. Despite having to begin again so late in life, first in England, then in the United States, he wrote that: 'It took us almost no time to adjust to the different pattern of life. In fact, it appeared to us an almost negligible inconvenience, far outweighed by the luck we had been blessed with – every single member of the family was able to leave Hitler's part of Europe.'

It was Loewi who made the crucial discovery of how nerves bring messages to the body organs. In 1903 he and Walter Fletcher, a Cambridge colleague, guessed that the agent might be a chemical substance and not an electrical impulse, as previously believed, but they were unable to find a way to test the idea, which lay dormant in Loewi's mind for 17 years.

In 1920 he woke during the night before Easter and suddenly remembered the idea. He wrote himself a note and dropped off to sleep, only to find next morning that he could neither read the note nor remember anything about his revelation. Next night he woke with the same thought; this time he got up, dressed and started a laboratory experiment to test the notion. He set up two live frog hearts bathed in saline solution, connected together by minute glass tubes through the blood vessels which supply and drain the heart. He left the nerve supply of one heart intact and removed the nerves from the other. When he stimulated the vagus nerve of the first heart, the fluid drained from it into the second, nerveless, heart. A chemical substance had been secreted from the nerve ending of the vagus, through the tubes into the second heart, there to exert the same effect. Moreover, when he stimulated the sympathetic nerves of the first heart the beat of both hearts increased. Loewi's discovery opened up an entirely new field of nerve physiology and drug research.

Loewi's early years had been steeped in culture. The son of a wine merchant, he studied classics before learning science, a training he believed had 'widened horizons and encouraged independent thought'. Weekly readings of the classic plays of world literature with a group of schoolfriends were a lifelong inspiration. After graduating from Strasbourg University in 1891, he spent a year studying art history, and wanted to make it his career, but his parents persuaded him to take up medicine instead.

Cures had not yet been found for many common diseases, especially the scourge of tuberculosis, and Loewi found research more challenging. A teacher showed him the importance of studying the body's internal chemistry through which foodstuffs are broken down into the simple substances that supply the energy needed to maintain it. Two years after qualifying in 1900, Loewi discovered that the dog's digestive system can manufacture proteins from simple amino acids. He went to England to continue studying the physiology of digestion, and there met Sir Henry Dale, who became a lifelong friend.

Loewi's studies in England were followed by seven years in Marburg and four in Vienna – wonderful years for a music lover and art historian. In 1909 he began his long tenure of the pharmacology chair in Graz.

His successful career was abruptly halted on 12 March 1938, when a laboratory colleague interrupted him with the news that the Nazis had invaded Austria and seized power. Loewi was deep in an experiment to show that sensory nerves taking messages to the brain secrete a different transmissionary substance from those coming from the brain; he was so absorbed that he barely considered the implications and went home at the usual time.

That night stormtroopers broke into the Loewis' home, arrested Loewi at gunpoint, pushed him into a van and dumped him in the city gaol. His crime was to be a Jew. Hundreds of others, including his two younger sons, were also seized.

Besides acute anxiety for his wife Guida, under house arrest, and his two sons, Loewi was obsessed by the need to pass on the results of his research before he was murdered, as he believed the Nazis intended. Eventually he persuaded a prison guard to post his summarized findings on a postcard to the journal *Die Naturwissenschaft*, and felt 'indescribable relief' that his results would not be lost.

He was released after two months in prison through the determined intervention of members of the Physiology Congress, then meeting in Zurich. Professor Graham Cannon and Sir Henry Dale wrote to tell the Swiss Committee that if Loewi were not released before the Congress ended, all British and American contact with the Germans would cease. Their letters were shown to Nazi contacts and within a fortnight Loewi was freed; but not before he was forced to transfer his Nobel Prize money from Sweden into a Nazi-owned German bank.

Loewi left Austria on 28 September 1938, and stayed in London with his old friend Sir Henry Dale for several weeks as one of his many refugee guests. Dale wrote later of the courage and enterprise with which Loewi, and others in similar predicaments, wasted no time in futile resentment but promptly began to search for new careers to the scientific advantage of the countries which offered them refuge.

The Society for the Protection of Science and Learning found a grant for Loewi and he was soon offered a temporary appointment in Brussels. The next year, on holiday with friends in England, he was prevented from returning to Belgium when war was declared. Invited by Professor J. A. Gunn to work in the pharmacology laboratory in Oxford, he worked there, leaving only when approached by the Medical School at New York University to become research professor of pharmacology.

Loewi enjoyed telling the farcical story of his application for an American visa. The US consul in London informed him that all was arranged, but he needed formal proof of Loewi's experience as a teacher. The letter of dismissal from Loewi's professorship in Graz would not do. Loewi suggested the consul ring Sir Henry Dale, but the consul had no idea of Dale's eminence. Eventually the scientist suggested the consul inspect Dale's entry in *Who's Who?*; the tome was produced and the official was satisfied. Finally, after a medical examination, the doctor gave Loewi a sealed envelope and the consul gave him the visa. As he left, Loewi politely thanked the consul, and added: 'By the way, do you know who wrote this paragraph in *Who's Who?* I did. Goodbye, Mr Consul.'

By way of a postscript, as he was passing through immigration in New York Loewi got a glimpse of the doctor's note on the medical certificate. It read: 'Senile, not able to earn his living.' Fortunately the immigration officer ignored this observation, and Loewi worked as an active member of the College of Medicine at New York University for the next 15 years.

His wife managed to escape from Austria in 1941, again virtually penniless, and they became settled American citizens. Summers were spent at Woods Hole, the marine biological station on the coast of Massachusetts – a place, he told Dale, that he loved 'more than any other in the world known to me, except the Engadine in Switzerland'. He received honorary degrees from Yale and New York and, after the war, from Frankfurt and Graz. He was also elected to foreign membership of the Royal Society in London.

Loewi continued to enjoy the good things in life. On Christmas Eve 1961, when he was 89, a friend sent him a fine lobster, which he enjoyed with a bottle of wine in shared company. The next morning, talking animatedly, he stopped in mid-sentence and never regained consciousness. He was buried in the churchyard at Woods Hole. Of his expulsion from his homeland, this eminent scientist and impressively modest individual wrote: 'I am happy and deeply grateful to the fate that transported me to this country – where I continue to enjoy the stimulating, almost rejuvenating effect of new friendships and the wealth of new impressions and experiences.'

Apart from Leo Szilard, among the refugee Hungarian scholars who made their way to the United States were Edward Teller and Eugene Wigner. A hugely talented trio of Hungarian scientists who, as we shall see, played a crucial part in America's development of the atomic bomb.

EDWARD TELLER

Edward Teller, later known as the 'father of the H-bomb', like almost all Hungarian scientists migrated to Germany not only because it was the centre of activity in physics but also because of Hungary's poor academic record and blatant anti-Semitism in the universities. He had studied with Niels Bohr in Copenhagen but was at Göttingen when Hitler came to power. He left Germany, first paying a brief but momentous visit to Copenhagen to see Bohr and then travelling on to London, where he was made welcome at University College by Professor F. G. Donnan.

Teller settled in with enthusiasm, became engaged, and bought a flat in the expectation that he would stay permanently in England. A few months after starting work at University College, however, he received from George Gamow, a Russian refugee at Princeton, an offer of a full professorship. It was irresistible to the 26-year-old Teller, but he did not want to let down Donnan, who had been very good to him. With characteristic understanding Donnan told him, 'I'd like you to stay but, you know, we have invited more of the refugees than England can really absorb, so if you really want to accept you should feel perfectly free.'

Teller's entry permit to the United States added a final note of farce. He had been teaching in England for little more than a year, but to qualify for a 'non-quota' US visa he needed to have lived there for at least two years; so the visa was refused. Then it was realized that the Tellers needed no special treatment since the quota for Hungarians was not full, so they could walk in through the front door.

In 1939 the knowledge that his former friend Carl Friedrich von Weizsäcker, who had been an admirer of Hitler in the early 1930s, was in Germany's 'uranium club' strengthened Teller's conviction that America must develop nuclear weapons as quickly as possible to keep ahead of Germany. Von Weizsäcker was mentioned in

Einstein's famous letter to President Roosevelt urging America to develop an atomic bomb ahead of Germany. Teller's contribution to the development of atomic weapons, particularly the hydrogen bomb, is famous. Unlike many of his colleagues in nuclear physics research, he had no reservations about building an atomic bomb. Indeed, so ferociously anti-communist was he, and so sure that the Russians would catch up in nuclear research and technology, that he pressed ruthlessly for the development of the H-bomb. In the atmosphere of the early 1950s America was obsessed with the Cold War, which led to Teller's notorious remarks doubting Oppenheimer's political integrity when Oppenheimer's security clearance was being questioned. Teller's evident lack of trust in Oppenheimer lost him the respect of most of his scientific colleagues; but he achieved his purpose in disposing of Oppenheimer, whose doubts about the merits of H-bomb research hindered progress on the project. Oppenheimer's security clearance was suspended and work on the H-bomb could continue.

EUGENE WIGNER

Eugene Wigner was another of the extraordinary group of scientific geniuses born in Hungary about 1900. Others were John von Neumann, Michael Polanyi, Leo Szilard and Edward Teller. From the beginning Wigner was committed to theoretical physics and mathematics. He worked first in Berlin, as so many Hungarians did, and then Göttingen. In 1929, at the age of 27, he was enticed to Princeton, it is said to provide companionship for his great friend von Neumann, the father of computers, whom Princeton was determined to capture. Wigner stayed there, on and off, for the rest of his life. He saw early the political dangers in Europe, particularly of the Nazis' anti-Semitism and the military consequences of atomic fission.

Wigner, with two other European refugees, Teller and Szilard, devised a letter which Einstein sent to President Roosevelt in August 1939 warning of the possibility of an atomic bomb and he played an important part in its development at the University of Chicago. Like most of the atomic scientists, he was strongly against dropping the bomb, and threw himself into producing civil defence against it, as well as adapting nuclear reactors for peaceful purposes.

He lived for 50 years after the bomb was dropped, dying at Princeton aged 92.

HANS BETHE

Even in the biography of Hans Bethe by Jeremy Bernstein, the 18 months from 1933 to 1935 that Bethe spent in England are only touched upon. Realizing that he must leave Germany in 1933, Bethe accepted an invitation to Manchester, presumably from Rudolf Peierls, an old friend. Lodging with Peierls and his formidably energetic Russian wife Genia, he took up a temporary replacement of a scientist who was on leave. He was then invited to a fellowship at Bristol by Nevill Mott (later a Nobel Prize winner and Master of Caius College, Cambridge), but again this was for only a year. In 1934, when, at the instigation of Lloyd Smith, a former American post-doctoral fellow at Munich, Cornell University offered him an acting assistant professorship with potentially permanent status in its newly developing physics department, he quickly accepted.

Although at first Bethe had reservations about going to a department of little status, he soon felt entirely at home. 'In America,' he said, 'people made me feel at once that I was going to be an American – that I was one already. In fact, after going home for the summer to see my mother I felt that Germany was much stranger than America – that it was a weird country.' Thanks to Bethe and his colleagues Cornell's physics department soon prospered, as did Bethe's career – and his personal life. In 1939 he married Rose Ewald, the daughter of his professor at Stuttgart, Paul Ewald; the family had emigrated to England in 1937 and Rose followed Bethe to the United States. Among their wedding guests were Richard Courant and his daughter, and Teller and his wife, Bethe's closest friends in America. Teller and Bethe had been students in Munich, met again in England and collaborated on several projects in the United States before they worked together on the Manhattan Project at Los Alamos.

Bethe became a US citizen in 1941 and was eager to contribute to the war effort. He produced a paper about the penetration of armour plating by projectiles, which was promptly classified as a document so secret that Bethe himself was not allowed to read it. He received his clearance to work on classified projects later that year, and in 1942 joined the Manhattan Project. It was Teller, who had worked on the bomb project right from the beginning, who put Bethe in the picture about the work that had been done.

Teller was continually throwing out ideas; Bethe, 'the Battleship', was renowned for his capacity to work steadily and at full steam on solving problems. On arriving at Los Alamos, Bethe, with his pragmatic approach, was chosen to take charge of the Theoretical Division; Teller never forgave either Oppenheimer for the appointment, or his old friend for superseding him, and their relationship never fully recovered.

In 1949, however, Teller urged Bethe to work with him on the H-bomb; Bethe at first refused, although in 1952 he spent eight months at Los Alamos working on the project after being persuaded that the Russians would be sure to build one. He tried unsuccessfully to dissuade Teller from giving evidence against Oppenheimer in 1954; their friendship suffered for years afterwards.

Bethe's career in the United States was long and successful. In 1967 he was awarded the Nobel Prize for his work on the sources of energy in the sun and the stars; he also won the President's Medal of Merit, the Max Planck Prize of the German Physical Society and the Enrico Fermi Award of the Atomic Energy Commission. In his old age Bethe has been greatly concerned with global energy problems. He recognizes that nuclear energy is not a complete solution to meeting the world's energy needs, and emphasizes the need for greater efforts towards conservation, the development of synthetic fuels and the safe disposal of nuclear waste.

ENRICO FERMI

Enrico Fermi was a late refugee from Europe, and one of the most influential of all the physicists who settled in America. The Italian scientist played a key role in the development of the atomic bomb.

Fermi's prodigious scientific talent had been recognized early in his career when he became the youngest member of the Royal Academy of Italy. He had studied with Max Born in Göttingen and with Paul Ehrenfest in Leiden from 1922 to 1924, then taught mathematics in Florence, before being appointed professor of theoretical physics in Rome in 1926 at the age of 25. His department became a leading centre for research, visited by many Europeans, among them Rudolf Peierls, who later achieved great fame.

While most of the great physicists who were Fermi's contemporaries specialized either in experimental or theoretical physics, Fermi was exceptional in being equally at home in the laboratory and with abstract paperwork. As a professional scientist, not as a cosmic thinker like Einstein or Bohr, he was one of the very greatest. He was also able to apply his mind to almost anything – on his deathbed he wished that he had given a little thought to politics – was prepared to invent devices of extreme sophistication and occasionally, in an un-American fashion, of childlike simplicity. It was this versatility that proved so crucial in his wartime experimental work with Leo Szilard.

After Chadwick's discovery of the neutron Fermi bombarded all the chemical elements with neutrons in turn. As early as 1934 he discovered that when he bombarded uranium atoms with neutrons using the medium of paraffin or water to slow the neutrons, up to 100 times as much radioactivity was produced. Fermi believed that he had made elements heavier than uranium, the heaviest element in the periodic table. In fact he had actually split the uranium atom, but neither he nor other scientists realized it, though the experiments aroused huge interest – at the time it was believed that only massive force could split the nucleus of a heavy atom.

The work won Fermi the 1938 Nobel Prize for 'his identification of new radioactive elements produced by neutron bombardment and for his discovery of nuclear reaction effected by slow neutrons'. By then Mussolini had tied Italy to Germany's anti-Semitic policies; although Fermi was not Jewish his wife, Laura, was, and he resolved to emigrate to the United States, where he had been offered a chair at Columbia University. He arranged this very elegantly – travelling first to Stockholm in December to collect his Nobel Prize, then, instead of returning to Rome, crossing the Atlantic to New York and his new life.

In January 1939, soon after his arrival, he returned to the New York docks to greet Niels Bohr, who was visiting the United States with momentous news of the work of the radiochemists Otto Hahn and Fritz Strassman in Berlin. They bombarded uranium with neutrons and achieved the 'bursting' of the nucleus, as Hahn first described the process. It was correctly interpreted by Lise Meitner and Otto Frisch in Sweden as fission. While there was huge interest in the discovery, it was almost universally believed at the time that the development of atomic energy or weapons was far in the future. In Chapter 10 we describe how Fermi, with his exceptional practical gifts, was pressed by Szilard, the brilliant ideas man, into the experiments with pure graphite that led him to create the first nuclear chain reaction in an atomic pile – and thence to the development of the bomb.

Fermi became a very popular leader of the atomic physicists at Los Alamos, where he moved in 1943. After the war he returned to peacetime theoretical physics at Chicago, but contracted cancer and died at the age of 53.

PETER DEBYE

Another immigrant to the United States who was in danger from the Nazis was the Dutch scientist Peter Debye (even though he was not Jewish). In 1933, when the exodus of German Jewish academics began, Debye was professor of experimental physics at Leipzig, where the young Werner Heisenberg was professor of theoretical physics at the time. In 1934 Debye became director of the Kaiser Wilhelm Institute for Physics in Berlin, a successor to Einstein and von Laue. The post required that he become a German citizen, but he managed to avoid this until 1940, when he realized that he was in danger after the invasion of the Netherlands. He travelled to Zurich, ostensibly on a lecture tour, then instead of returning to Germany, made his way to Milan and thence to the United States. He had no difficulty in finding a place at Cornell University, where he remained for the rest of his life. In 1946 Debye won the Nobel Prize for chemistry for his work on X-ray diffraction in gases.

He was a particularly clear expositor of ideas, and his honesty and clarity of thought are revealed in the following insight into the process of scientific discovery: 'Our science is essentially an art which could not live without the occasional flash of genius in the mind of some sensitive man, who, alive to the smallest of indications, knows the truth before he has the proof.'

Such was his dedication to his work that in his final illness he had a telephone installed in his oxygen tent.

OTTO MEYERHOF

Most refugees left Germany when they were relatively young, but Otto Meyerhof, born in 1884, was already a world-famous biochemist who had won the Nobel Prize jointly with A. V. Hill in 1922 for work on muscle metabolism. Although Meyerhof was Jewish he was not dismissed because he worked at the Kaiser Wilhelm Institute for Chemistry in Berlin, a non-governmental body which was not subject to the anti-Semitic legislation affecting the civil service, after which he was director of the new, well-equipped and successful Institute for Medical Research at Heidelberg. However, life under the Nazis became progressively more difficult and unpleasant until in 1938, not a moment too soon, he left Germany for France. The respite was only brief and in 1940, when the German army entered Paris, he escaped to the United States via Portugal by an arduous and dangerous journey, travelling partly on foot over the mountains. On his arrival, the Rockefeller Foundation arranged a post for him at the University of Pennsylvania, where he was made welcome and became a highly successful teacher and researcher.

FRANZ LIPMANN

Long before Otto Meyerhof escaped from Germany he had seen one of his most promising protégés go into voluntary exile, alienated by the increasing menace of the Nazi Party. Franz Lipmann, who could be called one of the last 'conventional' biochemists – i.e. before biochemistry was transformed by molecular biology – shared the 1953 Nobel Prize with another refugee, Hans Krebs. Born in East Prussia in 1899, Lipmann worked first with Meyerhof in Heidelberg, and later in exile, on intermediary metabolism (the innumerable intervening steps in the building up and breaking down of body constituents). This work led him to the discovery of the crucial co-enzyme A, which is involved in sugar and fat metabolism.

In 1932, alarmed by the growing popularity of the Nazis, he left

Germany for Copenhagen and was still there in 1939. By then Denmark was uncomfortably close to the spreading threat of the Third Reich and Lipmann moved again, this time across the Atlantic to a post at Cornell University. Two years later he transferred to the Massachusetts General Hospital, where he became professor of clinical chemistry in 1949. He moved again in 1957, to the Rockefeller Institute (later University) in New York, where he stayed until his death at the age of 87 in 1986.

Although Lipmann was never under direct personal threat in Germany, having left before Hitler came to power, the Nazis nevertheless deprived their country of his talent and presented it to the United States, where he was greatly and properly appreciated.

RUDOLPH SCHOENHEIMER

Rudolph Schoenheimer's story is both triumphant and tragic. He was a young biochemist of great promise who was head of physiological chemistry in Ludwig Aschoff's Institute of Pathology at Freiburg. There Schoenheimer met Hans Krebs. He described Krebs as a 'loner' – and predicted he would win a Nobel Prize, more than 20 years before Krebs actually did so. Schoenheimer had spent the academic year of 1930–1 at the University of Chicago, so his work was known in the United States, and when he was forced to leave Germany in 1933 he was invited to Columbia University by its head of biochemistry, Hans Clarke.

Schoenheimer's great contribution to biochemistry, and to biology generally, was to reveal that all body constituents are in a constant state of chemical renewal and that even the constituents of bone, previously believed to be static, are rapidly replaced. Chemicals appear and disappear even in adult organisms while the structure and form remain apparently unchanged. He studied this phenomenon by feeding or injecting chemical compounds such as calcium, which were 'labelled' with stable isotopes so that added molecules could be traced and distinguished from endogenous ones. The radioactive isotopes which make measurement quick and easy today were not available in the 1930s (and with them there was a remote danger from radioactivity). Schoenheimer's technique involved an enormous amount of work and the use of a mass spectrograph, an expensive and complicated machine which separated isotopes by means of their different weights.

The significance of Schoenheimer's research in the biochemistry department at Columbia University was widely admired and he was invited to give the Dunham Lectures at Harvard, a very high accolade. But they had to be read for him. He had been cursed with manic depression all his life and in 1941, at the age of 43, he killed himself. If he had lived he would have been a likely winner of a Nobel Prize.

These are some of the scientists whom Hitler drove from Germany to the United States. His actions led to the rapid decline of German science and the promotion of American. Until 1933, Germany was incontrovertibly the leading scientific nation in the world. Only 12 years later, after Hitler's persecution and his war, the United States was easily in the lead and has shown no sign of losing it.

Hitler did America some service!

8

Those Who Stayed

Your resignation would have no effect at the present time other than to ruin your career . . . If you do not resign . . . you will have a task of a quite different kind . . . You can gather young people around, teach them to become good scientists and thus help them to preserve the old values . . . if we can guide even small groups of talented and right-minded young through these horrible times, we shall have done a great deal to ensure Germany's resuscitation after the end.

Max Planck to Werner Heisenberg, who had asked for his advice about leaving Germany shortly after Hitler's accession. But, after the Second World War, Planck told Francis Simon: 'You were right to leave.'

William Feldberg, the neurophysiologist who, as we have seen, was expelled from his post in the physiology department at Berlin University at a few hours' notice in 1933, described himself as 'lucky'. The decision to stay or leave his work and his country would have been painful had he been given the option, but he was a Jew and he had no choice. Werner Heisenberg, the brilliant young physicist who was already a leader in German science in his early thirties, was not a Jew, and wrote later that he 'almost envied those of my friends whose life in Germany had been made so impossible that they simply had to leave. They had been the victims of injustice and would have to suffer great material hardships, but at least they had been spared the agonizing choice of whether or not they ought to stay on.'

As Jewish scholars were forced out of their jobs it quickly became clear that the Nazis had made many converts in the universities who were eager to replace them. National Socialism had deliberately extended its appeal to the middle classes, and there was no shortage of academics among them. The *völkisch* movement had become hugely popular with Germany's youth during the 1920s and students were already raucously demanding that the universities should fulfil 'national' aims. Physical and military prowess and unstinting support for the regime were the new order of the day, replacing study, thought and criticism.

Although the great majority of academics in the German universities were not Jewish or otherwise targeted by the Nazis, those who were still concerned with maintaining academic standards found themselves deeply compromised and torn between conflicting interests. There were so many Jewish academics that few of their colleagues could have been unaware of what was happening (unless they were determined not to know). Some, despite being repelled by the new regime's coarseness, violence and anti-intellectualism, hoped for the best, and initially at least believed that the movement could bring a kind of moral revival and salvation to Germany. Heisenberg wrote hopefully to Max Born in early 1933 that 'in the course of time the splendid things will separate from the hateful'. Carl Friedrich von Weizsäcker, a promising young physicist and protégé of Heisenberg's, was at first so strongly attracted to Hitler and the Nazis that he might have joined the Party if so many of his young Jewish colleagues had not been dismissed.

Most non-Jewish scientists did not consider leaving Germany, with the exceptions of Erwin Schrödinger (who was Austrian), Marthe Vogt, Martin Stobbe, Max Delbrück and Otto Krayer. Instead they saw their duty as staying on to uphold academic standards and to protect younger colleagues as far as they could, and in this they were often successful. A common reaction to the events of 1933 was to retreat into work, imagining that the Nazis could not last, or at least that their ferocity would abate, and that those who stayed would be able to hasten the process and help in the restoration of German science afterwards.

The theoretical physicists' position was especially disturbing, since they lost more scientists than any other discipline because there were so many Jewish physicists in the universities and research institutes. Also, while scientists in 'useful' fields such as chemistry, engineering or industrial physics had bargaining power with the Third Reich, theoretical physics was in a weak position because it apparently had no practical use and the Nazis had no inkling of its significance This position turned out to have advantages as well as disadvantages during the following decade.

With the coming of Hitler the opposition of Philipp Lenard and Johannes Stark to the new physics also became significant. Marginalized as cranks during the 1920s, these two malevolent outcasts were now in a position to inflict real damage on scientific scholarship. Both had been enthusiastic supporters of Hitler since the early 1920s, so they cannot be accused of climbing on the Nazi bandwagon. By 1933 Lenard was in his seventies and had retired, but the younger Stark set his sights on becoming head of German physics. Their main drive was to destroy the 'Jewish physics' of Planck and Einstein, Schrödinger and Heisenberg, and replace it with what they claimed was 'Aryan physics'.

Three men epitomized the predicament facing scientists of integrity who stayed on in Germany under the Third Reich. They were Max Planck, who embodied the Prussian traditions of loyalty to the state; Max von Laue, Planck's former student and his successor at the Kaiser Wilhelm Institute, who was seen as a hero of resistance both inside and outside Germany; and Werner Heisenberg, the outstanding young theoretical physicist who could well have moved to work anywhere in the world, but chose to stay in Germany.

MAX PLANCK

During the months of confusion and uncertainty in the academic sciences after Hitler became Chancellor, Max Planck, the godfather of German science, was the first figure to whom colleagues turned for support and leadership.[1] 'Now everyone counts on his help,' his wife Marga wrote to Paul Ehrenfest, Einstein's friend and associate at Leiden, whose deepening depression led him to commit suicide shortly before the war.

In 1933 Planck still held Germany's most important scientific offices as Secretary of the Prussian Academy of Sciences and President of the Kaiser Wilhelm Society, the national organization of research funding. At 75 he might have looked forward to a quiet retirement free of the heat of national politics. But he stayed on in these scientific organizations in order to prevent the disastrous prospect of the fanatical anti-Einstein faction, notably Johannes Stark, taking over German science.

Planck was in many ways the personification of the best in the Prussian tradition of duty to the community and the State and respect for education and achievement. This included a concept of personal honour which governed his life. No one doubted Planck's integrity and objective judgement; throughout his long career his decisions were made on a considered moral basis, never on grounds of personal advancement. An ardent German patriot, Planck based his loyalty to his country on duty and self-sacrifice rather than chauvinism and conquest.

His character was the product of a family background of lawyers, public servants and scholars, 'excellent, reliable, incorruptible, idealistic and generous men, devoted to the service of the Church and State'. Born in 1858, he was brought up in Kiel, but when he was nine the family moved to Munich in Bavaria, a part of Germany with a very different atmosphere – more relaxed and less authoritarian. There in the Gymnasium his interest in physics was fired by one outstanding teacher, as is so often the case in the life stories of great scientists. He was obsessed with 'laws of thinking' and questioned whether the outside world represented something independent of our observations, whether in fact there is an external reality outside ourselves. He was certain that this was the case and was determined to understand the laws which govern this 'absolute', as he called it. This determination became the driving force of his life.

The principle of the conservation of energy ('energy cannot be created or destroyed') was regarded by Planck as the first of the 'absolute' laws. It was his belief that the secrets of nature can be elucidated by pure thinking that led him to become a theoretical physicist. His early scientific papers were not well received, but gradually he gained respect and his textbook on thermodynamics, written when he was 39, became a standard and highly influential work. He was offered an extraordinary chair in theoretical physics at Kiel in 1885 and another in 1889 at Berlin University, a major advance in his career.

Planck's great contribution to physics was – as so often in science – a paradox. Through his persistent attempts to reconcile an apparent anomaly in classic thermodynamics, this most conservative-minded and cautious of scientists produced the most revolutionary idea in physics. He discovered the 'elementary quantum of action' – in other words, that energy is packaged in discrete amounts or quanta, not in a continuous process as had been universally assumed. Planck at once saw the importance of his achievement: 'Today I have made a discovery as important as that of Newton,' he told his son while they were out walking near Berlin, typically revealing himself only in private to his family; his modest and almost hesitant public demeanour, by contrast, made him appear doubtful of his own results.

This was no mean claim, but it was true. As Planck realized, it was impossible to reconcile the quantum of action with previous theories, with the result that classical physics would have to be rethought. It was some years before the implications were fully recognized; one of the first to see their significance was Einstein, whose theory of the photoelectric effect, published in 1905, led on from Planck's discovery to show that light itself was packed in 'corpuscles'. As early as 1906 Planck was championing Einstein's work, which he compared with Copernicus's discoveries, and between them they shaped the course that physics has taken since.

Planck was now internationally famous, and after he and Walther Nernst persuaded Einstein to move to Berlin in 1914 they made it the world's leading centre of theoretical physics. By then the first of many personal tragedies had afflicted Planck, who was a devoted family man and said only to be truly comfortable in family circles. His first wife died in 1909, and his eldest son Karl was killed in action in 1916. One of his twin daughters died in childbirth in 1917; her husband then married the second twin, who also died suddenly a year later, shortly after giving birth. One son, Erwin, was left; he died 27 years later, during the Second World War, in circumstances which finally broke even the stoical, deeply religious Planck.

A man who valued a clear conscience and the concept of unity in Germany above everything, Planck set out to restore German physics after the collapse of his country in 1918, which distressed him greatly. He was awarded the Nobel Prize in 1918. Planck's standing as diplomat, peacemaker and leader of German physics continued during the 1920s. By virtue of his reputation and his scientific offices, he was the man the scientists turned to when Hitler came to power.

In character and approach Hitler was repellent in every way to Planck. Nevertheless, the broad aims of the Nazis were attractive to him as a patriot: the reversal of Germany's humiliating international status, the introduction of a programme of full employment and especially the individual's submission to the common good. Moreover, Hitler had been appointed Chancellor by the Head of

State, Hindenburg, and Planck was not a man to favour un-constitutional action. However distasteful were the anti-Semitic policies and actions of the new government, Planck believed he might be able to ameliorate them and soften their consequences.

Perhaps partly as a result of his experience with the 'Appeal of the Ninety-three' in 1914, Planck could not later see the symbolic value of a public protest. During the war he had signed a chauvinistic manifesto, formally entitled the 'Appeal to the Cultured Peoples of the World', on the basis of the other signatories before he had read it; he came to regret this afterwards. Now, in July 1933, when the chemist Otto Hahn proposed a joint protest by 30 senior professors against the sackings of Jewish colleagues, Planck said that for every 30 who protested, 150 who wanted their jobs would come out against them. He took no account of the potential effect of a gesture on morale at home or on opinion abroad – in contrast with Einstein's highly public refusal. The difference fractured their friendship. Einstein could not forgive Planck's acquiescence. Planck could not condone Einstein's public protest. In Planck's view Einstein's attitude to Hitler's government was disloyalty to the German State, and the future of the Prussian Academy of Sciences as an institution must not be put at risk by individual members.

Planck's position was unenviable. He was aware that the Academy's record concerning Einstein's resignation did not look good to outsiders. His own apparent condoning of the Nazi government could be construed as neutralizing some of the efforts of foreign and émigré scientists against its policy. Conversely, with the great Planck freely in office and at work, the Nazis could claim that reports of their attacking science were no more than Jewish propaganda.

Meanwhile Planck's illusions about Hitler and the Nazis were steadily eroded. In the summer of 1933 Werner Heisenberg, like everyone else, came to see him in a mood to resign after the dismissal of a Jewish mathematician at Leipzig. Heisenberg was one of the brightest young stars among the scientists who stayed in Germany, already a Nobel Prize winner at 31 when Hitler came to power and world-famous for his formulation of quantum mechanics and the Uncertainty Principle. Planck seemed 'tortured . . . and tired'. Heisenberg's reconstruction of their conversation many years later was almost certainly an amalgam of several discussions with Planck and others over months in 1933; its interest lies in the prevailing arguments for those who stayed.

You have come to get my advice on political questions, but I am afraid I can no longer advise you. I see no hope of stopping the catastrophe that is about to engulf all our universities, indeed our whole country. Before you tell me about Leipzig – and, believe me, things couldn't be worse than they are here in Berlin – I would like to apprise you of my conversation with Hitler a few days ago. I had hoped to convince him that he was doing enormous damage to the German universities, and particularly to physical research, by expelling our Jewish colleagues; to show him how senseless and utterly immoral it was to victimise men who have always thought of themselves as Germans, and who had offered up their lives for Germany like everyone else. But I failed to make myself understood – or, worse, there is simply no language in which one can talk to such a man. He has lost all contact with reality. What others say to him is at best an annoying interruption, which he immediately drowns by incessant repetitions of the same old phrases about the decay of healthy intellectual life during the past fourteen years, about the need to stop the rot even at this late hour, and so on. All the time, one has the fatal impression that he believes all the nonsense he pours forth, and that he indulges his own delusions by ignoring all outside influences. He is so possessed by his so-called ideas that he is no longer open to argument. A man like that can only lead Germany into disaster.[2]

Heisenberg told him about the latest developments in Leipzig and about the plan of some of the younger staff members to resign. But Planck was convinced that all such protests had become utterly futile:

I am glad to see that you are still optimistic enough to believe you can stop the rot by such actions. Unfortunately, you greatly overestimate the influence of the university or of academicians. The public would hear next to nothing about your resignation. The papers would either fail to report it or else treat your protests as the actions of misguided and unpatriotic cranks. You simply cannot stop a landslide once it has started. How many people it will destroy, how many human lives it will swallow up, is a matter of natural law, even if we ourselves cannot predict its precise course. Hitler, too, can no longer determine the subsequent course of events; he is a man driven by his obsessions and not someone in the driver's seat. He cannot tell whether the forces he has unleashed will raise him up or smash him to pieces.

In these circumstances, your resignation would have no effect at the present time other than to ruin your own career – I know you are prepared to pay that price. But as far as Germany is concerned, your actions will only begin to matter again after the end of the present catastrophic phase. It is to the future that all of us must now look. If you resign, then, at best, you may be able to get a job abroad. What might happen at worst, I would rather not say. But abroad you will be one of countless emigrants in need of a job, and who knows that you would deprive another, in much greater need than yourself? No doubt, you would be able to work in peace, you would be out of danger, and after the catastrophe you could return to Germany – with a clear conscience and the happy knowledge that you never compromised with Germany's gravedigger. But before that happens many years will have passed; you will have changed and so will the people of Germany, and I don't know whether you will be able to adapt yourself to the new circumstances, or how much you will achieve in this changed world.

If you do not resign and stay on, you will have a task of quite a different kind. You cannot stop the catastrophe, and in order to survive you will be forced to make compromise after compromise. But you can try to band together with others and form islands of constancy. You can gather young people around you, teach them to become good scientists and thus help them to preserve the old values. Of course, no one can tell how many such islands will survive the catastrophe; but I am certain that if we can guide even small groups of talented and right-minded young people through these horrible times, we shall have done a great deal to ensure Germany's resuscitation after the end. For such groups can constitute so many seed crystals from which new forms of life can arise. I am thinking first and foremost of the revival of scientific research in Germany. But since no one knows what precise roles science and technology will play in the future, these remarks may apply to much wider fields of endeavour as well. I think that all of us who have a job to do and who are not absolutely forced to emigrate for racial or other reasons must try to stay on and lay the foundations for a better life once the present nightmare is over. To do so will certainly be extremely difficult and dangerous, and the compromises you will have to make will later be held against you, and quite rightly so. Naturally, I cannot blame anyone who decides differently, who finds life in Germany intolerable, who cannot remain while injustices are committed that he can do nothing to prevent. But in the ghastly situation in which Germany now finds herself, no one can act decently. Every decision we make involves us in injustices of one kind or another. In the final analysis, all of us are left to our own devices. There is no sense in giving advice or in accepting it. Hence I can only say this to you: No matter what you do, there is little hope that you can prevent minor disasters until this major disaster is over. But please think of the time that will follow the end.

On the journey back to Leipzig Heisenberg decided to stay, and the compromises began for him as for Planck. One of the commonest, simplest and most powerful was the simple matter of greetings. The physicist P. P. Ewald described Planck's dilemma at the opening of a new Kaiser Wilhelm Institute of Metals in Stuttgart in 1934: 'We were all staring at Planck, waiting to see what he would do at the opening, because at that time it was prescribed officially that you had to open such addresses with "Heil Hitler." Well, Planck stood on the rostrum and lifted his hand half high, and let it sink again. He did it a second time. Then finally the hand came up, and he said, "Heil Hitler". . . . Looking back, it was the only thing you could do if you didn't want to jeopardize the whole Kaiser Wilhelm Gesellschaft.'

There were many other unpleasant compromises. All official letters had to finish with 'Heil Hitler'. Speeches at the German Physical Society were made in front of enormous emblems of the swastika. Planck's colleague Walther Nernst was investigated (unsuccessfully) for non-Aryan ancestors. Academic posts were being filled by nonentities qualified mainly by Nazi Party membership. Stark's appointment as head of the Imperial Institute of Physics, Germany's biggest single laboratory, in May 1933, gave him a leading voice in the new order. When Stark defended the Nazi government's scientific policy in the British scientific journal *Nature* no German scientist dared to contradict him – giving observers abroad the impression that German science was in agreement.

However, by remaining President of the Kaiser Wilhelm Society until 1937 Planck was able to protect Jewish staff, among them Lise

Meitner, for several years. (This might have been a mixed blessing since, like other later refugees, she found that most available jobs and funds had gone to colleagues who had fled earlier.) He led the opposition to Stark and managed to keep the Kaiser Wilhelm Institute for Physics in Berlin going under the leadership of a non-Nazi, the Dutch physicist Peter Debye, for some time. In 1938 Planck resigned as Secretary of the Prussian Academy of Sciences.

Despite Planck's apparent acquiescence with the regime the Nazis were aware of his real feelings. Years later Goebbels wrote: 'It was a great mistake that we failed to win science over to support the new state' and blamed their failure on Rust, the Prussian Minister of Education. For all Planck's inherent 'piety and unbreakable attachment to the State' (his own expression) it was inconceivable that he would join Hitler and his henchmen in their assault on reason and humanity.

As the war continued, under intensified Allied bombing and the invasion of Germany itself, Planck's world collapsed physically as it disintegrated personally. His house in Berlin was bombed and his library and possessions destroyed while he was away on a lecture tour. Then his son Erwin, his last surviving offspring, who was a senior official in the German foreign office, was implicated in the 1944 plot to assassinate Hitler. The Nazis' ruthless hunt for all those who could possibly have been involved in the affair included Erwin, who certainly knew some of the instigators although he was probably not one of them. That was enough for him to be condemned to death. Planck set 'Heaven and Hell in motion' to have the sentence commuted, and believed he had succeeded; but on 18 February 1945, seven months after the assassination attempt, Erwin was executed, probably on the orders of an underling. Planck was shattered.

As the war reached its end his wartime home near Magdeburg was caught between the German and Allied lines and Planck, by now a sick man, and his wife had to hide in the woods nearby. A physicist in Göttingen, hearing of their plight, persuaded an American officer to send a car to collect them and take them to safety and hospital treatment in Göttingen. Through all his troubles Planck bore his 'Job-like fate' with fortitude, resigning himself to the will of God, his only consolation, which enabled him to endure until 'this insanity in which we are forced to live reaches its end.'

Planck's reputation remained untarnished after the war, and in 1946 he was the only German to be invited to London for the belated celebration at the Royal Society of the three-hundredth anniversary of Newton's birth. He died in 1947, six months short of his ninetieth birthday. His name was subsequently attached to the Kaiser Wilhelm Society so that today research institutes in science and the humanities all over Germany are known as Max Planck Institutes.

WERNER HEISENBERG

In 1933 Werner Heisenberg was at his peak, one of Germany's youngest and most brilliant physicists and with aspirations to be at the helm of German science. That year, at the age of 31, he received both the Max Planck Medal from the German Physical Society and the Nobel Prize. The great days of Planck and von Laue as research scientists were well past; Heisenberg's were still ahead, and his dilemma was all the greater because he could have easily found a position abroad.

Heisenberg was – and still is – world-famous for his formulation of the Uncertainty Principle. The culmination of a series of papers completed over two years from 1925 to 1927, it was immediately hailed as a new direction for atomic physics. Rudolf Peierls described his contribution: 'In 1925, at the age of 23, he wrote the paper that laid the foundations of quantum mechanics on which all subsequent generations have built.' It was not just an extension of previous work but a new direction for atomic physics. Heisenberg's early work, before the Uncertainty Principle, was crucial to quantum theory. Nearly three centuries of Newtonian physics had been contravened first by Max Planck with the idea of the quantum of energy, and then in 1913 by Niels Bohr, who realized that the quantum theory applied to matter as well as energy. But there were gaps and contradictions in their new theory. Newton's laws concerning the motion of the heavenly bodies and gravity were derived from precise, directly observable measurements; the atom was thought to be similar to the solar system, a central nucleus, like the sun, with orbiting electrons, like the planets, around it. It was assumed that similar laws applied to the infinitely minute subatomic particles with which theoretical physics was concerned.

By 1925 Heisenberg was 'convinced that one needed a theory which abandoned the classical description of the electron orbits inside the atom, and instead concerned itself with quantities that were accessible to observation . . .' That summer, laid low by an attack of hay fever, he escaped for a respite to the bare coast of Heligoland, and there he made the mathematical breakthrough that filled in crucial gaps in the existing quantum theory. 'Heisenberg discarded the concept of orbits, which could not in principle be observed – and he proposed that the physicist should deal only with observable things . . .' Max Born, Heisenberg's professor in Göttingen, was quickly won over by Heisenberg's new formulation, and with Pascual Jordan added another paper which completed the structure of matrix mechanics, as the new system came to be called.

In 1927 Heisenberg consolidated the theoretical structure of the new physics with the Uncertainty Principle, in which he said that the method of observation itself affected the results. An electron could not be seen; its presence and its movement could be deduced only by the effect it had on particles directed at it, which were deflected by the electron. The same was true for particles in a cloud chamber – the track of these particles when they hit something else gave information about them. Thus the act of observation altered the behaviour of the particle observed. Certain variables are related to each other – position and momentum, or energy and time – and the more precisely one such variable is measured, the less precise can be the simultaneous measurement of its related variable.

Although the term 'Uncertainty Principle' is universally used, Heisenberg himself in his original publication in 1927 called it the 'Inaccuracy Principle', which perhaps would have made the concept easier to understand. Most physicists were convinced by its revolutionary concept, although Einstein could never accept it and Schrödinger always hoped that 'some new development might avoid the need for this limitation of our concepts'.

Heisenberg's set of laws helped to seal the 'Copenhagen interpretation' of atomic theory, and made him second only to Einstein – deservedly so, for his work has been the basis of much of modern physical science and its practical application in the electronics industry, notably radio and laser technology.

Born in 1901, Heisenberg was still young during the chaotic

aftermath of the First World War, and the Youth Movement's patriotic ideals and aims for a better future left a lasting impression on him. He became a youth leader and even after becoming a famous scientist still went hiking with his group. He studied at Munich under Arthur Sommerfeld, then joined the famous seminar at Göttingen led by James Franck and Max Born. He studied in Copenhagen with Niels Bohr, who immediately recognized his brilliance. The two worked profitably together, 'work' often taking the form of discussions on country hikes. His string of papers, each more original than the last, confirmed his reputation, which grew so quickly that in 1927, at 26, he was offered two professorships, in Leipzig and Zurich. He chose Leipzig and rapidly started building up his own seminar there.

Heisenberg was an attractive, outgoing young man; Born said he looked like a bright-eyed farm boy. He excelled not only at science but also in music, languages and mountain-climbing, and played ferociously competitive table tennis with his colleagues. As a chemistry student in Vienna, Max Perutz describes going to a lecture by Heisenberg, who had recently received his Nobel Prize. Perutz was expecting to see 'a portly professor. In came a slim young man who looked like one of us students and was quite without pomp'.

After the dramatic exodus of his Jewish colleagues in 1933 Heisenberg did what he could to preserve the old atmosphere. But his sense of isolation was acute. 'The immediate pre-war years, or rather what part of them I spent in Germany, struck me as a period of unspeakable loneliness,' he wrote. The Third Reich's policies alienated its scientists from the rest of the world. There could be no hope of change from within, and as Germany became increasingly cut off from international dialogue by growing distrust, Heisenberg missed his contacts with the scientific fraternity abroad.

He had visited Britain, the United States and Denmark, in each of which countries the atmosphere of personal and political freedom beckoned; emigration to the New World was, he wrote decades later, 'a constant temptation'. But he decided to remain, and build up his own group of young scientists in order to ensure German participation in scientific advances and to make sure that 'uncontaminated science can make a comeback in Germany after the war'.

In 1935 Heisenberg was nominated as successor to his old teacher Sommerfeld in Munich, a tempting post in his early home town, to which he was very attached. But after virulent attacks by Stark, Lenard and the SS newspaper *Das Schwarze Korps* denouncing him and the theoretical physicists as 'white Jews', the authorities decided otherwise. The attacks grew so vicious that Heisenberg's mother, who knew Himmler's mother slightly, contacted her to ask for advice; on her recommendation Heisenberg wrote directly to Himmler to ask if Stark's actions had the support of the SS, in which case he would resign. After a long interval he heard in 1938 that Stark's attacks would stop, and he could stay. Even so, he did not move to Munich and he had to promise not to mention Einstein when teaching about relativity.

In 1939 he visited the United States because, as he later wrote, he wanted to see his friends there 'before the war started' and they might never meet again. He added another reason: 'If I was to help in Germany's reconstruction after the collapse, I would badly need their help.' This remark, made 25 years after the war, smacks of hindsight. According to Heisenberg, he was already sure that Germany would lose since the territory and resources controlled by Britain, the United States and the Soviet Union were overwhelming compared with Germany's capabilities. But in 1939 the United States was determinedly neutral, and that August the Soviet Union signed a pact with Hitler; so his comments about the inevitable defeat of Germany lack conviction.

While lecturing that summer in Ann Arbor and Chicago, Heisenberg met Enrico Fermi, who had only recently left Fascist Italy. Fermi tried hard to persuade him to stay in the United States, arguing that new immigrants like himself were in 'a larger, freer country where they could live without being weighed down by the heavy ballast of their historical past. In Italy I was a great man; here I am again a young physicist and that is incomparably more exciting.' Heisenberg understood his arguments and already knew that life under Hitler was hard; that the compromises he was forced to make with the regime would look bad to his scientific friends in the West; that if Germany lost he would have to take the consequences. The dilemma facing him was perhaps greater than for any other German scientist, since he was genuinely sought after in

10. *Right:* Max Born (*left*) and James Franck, *c.* 1937

11. Lise Meitner and Otto Hahn, 1920

12. Adoring crowd greeting Hitler, 1935

13. Niels Bohr, the
'Great Dane', *c.* 1945

14. Hans Krebs, 1967

15. Rudolf Peierls (*left*) and
Francis Simon, *c.* 1951

16. Erwin Schrödinger (*right*)
and Frederick Lindemann,
Lord Cherwell, 1933

17. Jews forced to scrub the streets

18. Max Perutz, 1990

20. *Right:* Internees on the Isle of Man, 1940

19. Professor Chadwick (*left*) and General Groves at Los Alamos, *c.* 1944

21. Model of atomic pile built by Fermi and Szilard, Chicago 1940

22. Edward Teller, 1983

23. Joseph Rotblat, 1995

24. Albert Einstein and Leo Szilard composing the letter to
President Roosevelt, August 1939

the West. Whatever one may think of his decision, his constancy was impressive.

On his return to Germany, Heisenberg was called up in September 1939, not to the Mountain Rifles, the regiment in which he had done his conscript service, but to the Army Ordnance department in Berlin. There the possible use of atomic energy was discussed and Hahn, the co-discoverer of atomic fission, declared, 'If my work should lead to a nuclear weapon, I shall kill myself.' It did, but he did not. At this time the Kaiser Wilhelm Institute for Physics became the centre for nuclear research – the 'Uranium Club', as it became known – and Heisenberg was a regular visitor. Peter Debye, its head, went on a lecture tour to Switzerland and the United States and never came back, and eventually (in April 1942) Heisenberg took over as director. His colleagues abroad concluded he had sold out to the Nazis, and the fact that he was the head of an established group of German atomic physicists in Berlin became a major spur to the efforts of his former colleagues to develop a bomb for the Allies, in the belief that his team might be doing the same for Hitler.

Since then there has been endless conjecture about how close the Third Reich came to producing its own atomic bomb, and why it failed. The story is complex, and Heisenberg was intimately involved in it. His own account of the war years is ambiguous, and he remains a problematic figure for historians, who have continued to speculate about his war record.

In particular, Heisenberg's visit to Copenhagen in the autumn of 1941 with his younger colleague, von Weizsäcker, ostensibly to give a lecture at the German embassy, but in fact to see his mentor and friend Niels Bohr, has aroused intense speculation ever since. In his play *Copenhagen* Michael Frayn makes Heisenberg say, 'There are only two things the world remembers about me. One is the uncertainty principle, and the other is my mysterious visit to Niels Bohr in Copenhagen in 1941. Everyone understands certainty. Or thinks he does. No one understands my trip to Copenhagen.' The play offers several intriguing variations on what could have happened during this fateful meeting.

After the lecture Heisenberg met Bohr at his house and took a walk with him. The two men remembered the occasion quite differently. Almost immediately the meeting went disastrously wrong. Both men knew that Bohr's house was under surveillance, and Bohr was suspicious of the German physicist's motives in making the visit. Meanwhile Heisenberg knew that any comment he made betraying Germany's war interests would be relayed to Berlin, where it would be regarded as treason.

While Heisenberg had to be extremely careful about what he said, Bohr was better at talking than at listening. He never wrote down an account of the occasion. According to Heisenberg's version, he asked if Bohr believed scientists would be justified in working on uranium research in wartime. Bohr, scientifically isolated in Denmark, had believed that practical application of nuclear fission was inconceivable in the immediate future. Aghast, he asked if Heisenberg believed the process could be used to make weapons; to which Heisenberg replied that he knew it was possible.

What were his motives in raising the subject? According to Heisenberg, Bohr was by then so shaken that he missed his main point, which was that enormous cost and technical effort would be needed to develop a bomb and that the physicists would have the terrible responsibility of advising their governments whether to go ahead or not. As Bohr understood it, Heisenberg was asking how far Allied research had got, and was proposing a common policy on both sides not to proceed with it. First Hitler had expelled Germany's Jewish physicists, and now that they were working in America on nuclear weapons research his chief atomic scientist was proposing to Bohr that they should stop!

The meeting ended abruptly, and back at his hotel Heisenberg, dismayed, told von Weizsäcker that the encounter had failed. In 1947 he visited Bohr again in Copenhagen to try to unravel the misunderstanding, but this meeting also ended in disaster. Whatever his motives had been – to seek 'absolution' from Bohr for going ahead with the project; to find out how far Allied scientists had got with developing a bomb; to arrange a secret bargain with them not to go any further – from then on he was regarded with suspicion by scientists abroad.

Given the situation in which the two physicists met – Heisenberg, from the invading power, visiting Bohr, the 'uncrowned king' of occupied Denmark – a friendly meeting was virtually inconceivable, and Heisenberg was remarkably insensitive in not anticipating this.

However, his tactlessness on other occasions is well recorded. Francis Simon recalled Heisenberg remarking to him after the war: 'The Nazis should have been left in power longer, then they would have become quite decent' – this after the discovery of the death camps, to a man who had lost relatives in them.

Meanwhile British and American Intelligence were intensely interested in the German team's progress on atomic research throughout the war, as we shall see in Chapter 10. There were clues that the Germans were trying to build an atomic bomb: the use of heavy water (needed to slow down neutrons), access to radioactive uranium ore in Czechoslovakia. But there were also contradictory clues: the relevant physicists mostly stayed at their separate universities rather than clustering in a single research centre. No one could be certain; no one wanted to take any risks; and no one could have the slightest doubt that if a German atomic bomb existed Hitler would use it.

Some have argued that Heisenberg and his colleagues held back from the project. It is true that he told Albert Speer, the Armaments Minister, in 1942, that Germany had no chance of developing an atomic bomb in wartime. Instead he and von Weizsäcker asked for relatively small funds for his team to work on an experimental nuclear reactor for atomic energy, which they then worked on for the duration of the war. This was indeed the case; the question is whether Heisenberg was hiding the fact that he believed a bomb programme was feasible, whether he actually hadn't made the fundamental calculations needed to 'start building a bomb', or whether – as he reported – he had concluded that the project could not be managed in time to be used during the war.

British Intelligence was fairly sure as early as January 1944 that the Germans were not carrying out any large-scale work on an atomic bomb. Nonetheless, General Leslie Groves, the American in charge of the Manhattan Project, took no chances. At his instigation the United States Air Force bombed the Kaiser Wilhelm Institute for Physics in Berlin, where the small-scale atomic research was being carried out, and Heisenberg and Hahn were listed as personal targets. Hahn's chemistry department was destroyed, though Hahn himself escaped injury, as did Heisenberg and his physics department.

As we now know, the German team came nowhere near to

developing an atomic bomb. Its failure was partly due to the immense size and complexity of the effort required to produce it, as Heisenberg said in 1939. The United States succeeded, but its situation was very different from that of Germany in that it had huge economic resources, vast space, immunity from air attack and numerous enthusiastic and highly trained scientists (including many refugees from Europe). Germany, on the other hand, after the first two years of the war was subjected to extremely heavy air bombardment. Under these circumstances, and with the Axis armies retreating and space contracting after late 1942, it is hard to see how Germany could have mounted the massive enterprise needed. Furthermore, Hitler thought only in the short term where weapons were concerned, and ordered that no enterprise was to be started that would not deliver the product to the army in less than nine months. So a project that would take years would never have been approved, and Heisenberg could tell Speer with a clear conscience that quicker production was impossible. Finally, the German scientists confidently believed that the Allies were nowhere near to producing nuclear weapons right up to the day the atomic bomb was dropped on Hiroshima – as we know from the *Farm Hall Transcripts* (see Chapter 10).

When Allied troops entered Germany in early 1945, a special intelligence force, the Alsos mission, was sent to identify the places and people (Heisenberg in particular) who would be working on a bomb if there was one. Its leading operator was Samuel Goudsmit, who, after searching the office of Heisenberg, his former colleague and friend, realized that the German team had got nowhere near to producing a bomb. Even so, American and British speculation about German research was still intense and at the end of the war the atomic physicists, including Heisenberg, von Laue, Hahn and von Weizsäcker, were captured in the French sector by the British, smuggled out to England and interned at Farm Hall, near Cambridge, formerly used by British Intelligence.

Whether the German physicists were held to prevent their capture by the Russians, or for the secrets they might reveal or both, every room was bugged and transcripts were secretly made of the recording cylinders. Not until 1992 were the files opened to the public and the English translation of the transcripts published.[3] The main revelations came when the bomb was dropped on Hiroshima on 6 August. The interned scientists were thunderstruck and Heisenberg at first refused to believe it was an atomic bomb. The transcripts show they had had no inkling that the Americans could have made the massive industrial and technological investment needed to produce atomic weapons so quickly. Their next reaction was to reproach themselves and one another for their own failure to make one. Von Weizsäcker alone suggested that they had held back for moral reasons but he was quickly contradicted.

Heisenberg, speaking privately with Hahn that night, confided that 'quite honestly I have never worked it out as I never believed one could get pure [uranium] 235 . . .' He now revised his estimate of the critical mass needed to create a fast chain reaction, which would dictate the size of a bomb, and a week later gave his colleagues the correct calculations in an informal seminar. Rudolf Peierls, a former student of Heisenberg's whose answer to the same question had launched the Allied bomb project in 1940, commented drily that 'Heisenberg, though a brilliant theoretician, was always very casual about numbers . . .' The German team had made other mistakes, notably in ruling out graphite as a moderator to slow down neutrons in a nuclear pile. In fact the graphite needed further purification, as Fermi and Szilard realized.

Heisenberg lived on for 30 years after the war, respected if no longer trusted – during a trip to the United States in 1949 half the guests invited to meet him at a reception organized by his former colleague Weisskopf stayed away rather than meet the man who had headed Hitler's atomic research team. His postwar career was outwardly successful. In Germany he opposed the development of atomic weapons while promoting the peaceful use of nuclear power, and helped to launch CERN, the European nuclear research centre. As director of the Max Planck Institute for Physics and Astrophysics he moved with it to Munich, his home city, in 1958 and stayed there until he retired in 1970.

When he had decided to stay in Germany in the 1930s he probably foresaw the risks – to his country from Hitler's uncontrollable aggression and to himself from inevitable contamination by his association with the Nazi state. Heisenberg was a patriot as well as a physicist: 'It would be [an] easy mistake to make, to think that one loved one's country less because it happened to be in the wrong,' as his dramatic counterpart comments in *Copenhagen*. He was caught by a relentless fate, and had his been a more profound or sensitive personality his predicament would have had the force of Greek tragedy.

Heisenberg's reputation was clouded by his failure to explain his wartime record satisfactorily. But then, whatever account he and his colleagues gave of the war years (apart from von Laue and Hahn, who thanked God that they had failed to make a bomb), they were trapped in a dilemma: they did not want the Allies to think they had worked on a bomb for Hitler, but were equally reluctant to face condemnation by their countrymen, either as traitors or as incompetents, for having failed to produce one.

MAX VON LAUE

Perhaps it was his high-principled Prussian background which made Max von Laue one of the very few scientists to stand up to the Nazis. His family were Junkers, the class of wealthy landowners from the eastern lands who were the backbone of old Prussia. They served in the administration or, more often, in the army – a calling in which von Laue proved himself hopelessly unsatisfactory, despite his military bearing, meticulous grooming and soldierly manner. Kurt Mendelssohn's biography of Walther Nernst recounts the story that:

> At one of the university festivities Nernst met a retired general whom somebody had brought along as a guest. Learning that Nernst was a physicist, the old man recalled that many years ago at the famous officers' training school at Lichterfelde they had had a cadet who had proved 'utterly useless at military life'. This was particularly sad since he had come from a good old Prussian family, and the fellow had then decided to study physics. The general felt that Nernst would probably never have heard of him, a certain Herr von Laue. Nernst told the general that not only did he know Laue but that Laue had received the Nobel Prize. At this the old man's eyes lit up and he said how glad he was for the family that the cadet whom they had to send away had after all proved 'not completely useless'.

Von Laue's indifference to danger and determination to do what was right during the years of the Third Reich became legendary – it was said, for instance, that he never left the house without carrying a package in each hand, so neither was free to give the Hitler salute. His solitary support for Einstein, his resignation from the Prussian Academy of Sciences, his public protest at the dismissal of Richard Courant from Göttingen, and his generous obituaries in praise of Fritz Haber in 1934, were all courageous acts of resistance in the first year of the Nazi regime, when opposition was already dangerous, if not yet fatal.

He continued to show resistance. He visited Jewish colleagues still in Germany, notably Dr Arnold Berliner, who was editor of the scientific weekly journal *Die Naturwissenschaften* (the German equivalent of *Nature*) until he was forced out of office in 1935. Conditions became progressively worse for Berliner and in 1942, when he was about to be evicted from his apartment, he committed suicide. Von Laue was one of very few who attended his funeral at the Jewish cemetery in Berlin.

As professor of theoretical physics in Berlin von Laue was in a position of authority and influence. He considered leaving Germany in 1933 but quickly decided that he should stay to do what he could to protect his science and his colleagues. Significantly for German physics, he was also opposed to Johannes Stark's election to the Prussian Academy of Sciences, a position in which Stark could have done great damage. Von Laue argued that Stark had shown that he aimed to control German physics, to the extent of overseeing all articles published in the scientific journals – in effect, censoring them. If Stark was successful, theoretical physics research, in which Germany had led the world, was in danger of disappearing from the Third Reich. Von Laue's determined stand saw off Stark's election; and Stark's inability to avoid falling out even with his own allies at the Education Ministry thwarted his ambitions to head German science.

Like Planck and Heisenberg, von Laue urged to stay those of his Jewish colleagues who were allowed to keep their jobs, in the hope that the anti-Semitic laws would be moderated and the damage to German science contained. As one of the presidents of the German Physical Society during the Third Reich, he, along with others, managed to protect the Society from Nazi infiltration; its officials continued to be self-selected and it still had Jewish members until as late as 1940. When colleagues were forced to leave he made every effort to help, passing on their details to visitors from the British Academic Assistance Council and visiting the organization's offices in London on their behalf. In so doing he earned the admiration and respect of Tess Simpson and her colleagues, for whom he symbolized honourable opposition to Hitler's regime.

Despite his known views about the Nazis von Laue was left untouched by the regime, because he kept just within acceptable bounds of opposition; to have overstepped them would have been suicide. (He wrote wryly to Einstein that he was still teaching his students the theory of relativity – adding that it had originally been written in Hebrew.) Unlike Heisenberg, who had the ambitions of a younger man, von Laue kept to himself, and made few of the public concessions forced on the others. He was greatly admired by his colleagues, and was the only German scientist Einstein was prepared to recognize after the war. Reflecting in a letter to Max Born in 1944 on the behaviour of German scientists during the previous decade, Einstein remarked that the conduct of the rare few who stood apart from the regime was 'not due to their reasoning powers but to their personal stature, as in the case of Laue. It was interesting to see the way in which he cut himself off, step by step, from the traditions of the herd, under the influence of a strong sense of justice.'

Von Laue's relationship with Einstein went back to 1905 when, aged 26, he was one of the first physicists to recognize the importance of the work of the unknown patent clerk in Switzerland on the electrodynamics of moving bodies and relativity. He had accepted Einstein's special theory of relativity by 1907, long before most of his colleagues.

His own great discovery concerning the diffraction of X-rays by crystals arose when he was asked to write a chapter on wave optics in an encyclopaedia of mathematics. In February 1912 he speculated that X-rays might be electromagnetic waves of a wavelength similar to the distance between neighbouring atoms in crystals. If that were so, the crystals would act as diffraction gratings for X-rays. Von Laue asked Friedrich and Kripping, two assistants of Wilhelm Röntgen, who held the chair of experimental physics in Munich, to try the experiment. They obtained a striking pattern of diffracted X-rays from a crystal of zinc blende. Hearing the results of the experiment, von Laue rushed to the laboratory, and as he walked home he worked out the mathematical solution of the effect. Röntgen himself, the discoverer of X-rays, visited the laboratory to inspect the results; he had had the same idea 15 years earlier, but his X-ray equipment had not been powerful enough to show the effect.

The news of von Laue's discovery spread quickly by the standards of those days, reaching the British Association in three months. Over the next decades it led to a revolution in our comprehension of chemistry, mineralogy and metallurgy. It brought the solution of the structures of many minerals, so that 20 years later scientists knew the atomic arrangement in most minerals that constitute the earth's crust.

Like Planck, von Laue was something of a father figure to Heisenberg, as he was to other colleagues who stayed in Germany. P. P. Ewald, who later left for Britain, suggested that as a patriot von Laue greatly regretted the loss to Germany of so many of her best scientists during the Hitler years, but his human loyalty prevailed over his patriotism. 'To all of us minor figures,' he added, 'the very existence of a man of Laue's stature and bearing was an enormous comfort. Compare it to the comfort the presence of just one man gave during the war, Churchill. You felt that as long as he stood up, not all was lost.'

Despite the high standing in which others held him, for von Laue it was impossible not to feel compromised by his wartime record. Long afterwards he confided in a letter to Lise Meitner: 'We all knew that injustice prevailed, but we did not want to see it, we deceived ourselves and should not then be surprised that we must pay for it.' Listing his reasons for staying in Germany, von Laue wrote that: 'above all, I wanted to be there once the collapse of the Third Reich – which I always foresaw and hoped for – allowed the possibility of a cultural reconstruction upon the ruins this Reich created.'

He did just that, although immediately after the war ended he was captured by the British and taken to Farm Hall, near Cambridge, with the other physicists suspected of working on an atomic bomb. On his release he returned to Germany, where he was appointed director of the Max Planck Institute for Physics (formerly Kaiser Wilhelm Institute) at Göttingen. Five years later he went back to Berlin as director of the Institute of Physical Chemistry, named after

Fritz Haber. Further honours were heaped on him: he became the only honorary president of the International Union of Crystallography at Harvard in 1948 and was elected as a foreign member of the Royal Society of London.

Death came when he was 80, in a strange if not altogether surprising way. Von Laue was famous for his reckless driving: for many years he travelled to his office by motorcycle at high speed. Later he bought a car, which he drove equally fast but safely – until 8 April 1960, when he collided with a motorcycle. The motorcyclist died immediately; von Laue a fortnight later.

OTTO WARBURG

A discussion of those who stayed in Germany during the Hitler period could include nearly the whole population – except the Jews. Few non-Jews left; hardly any Jews who were able to emigrate stayed. One who did was Otto Warburg. He stands out in contrast to all the others. This famous physiologist was a Jew and made no secret of the fact. He took no action against the Nazis and they took none against him. Why they did not remains a puzzle.

Warburg, like so many of his fellow scientists, was an assimilated Jew; he thought of himself, and was regarded by others, as German. He was one among many in the professional and middle classes who did not practise the Jewish religion and had no sympathy with Zionism; they often chose to be baptized, and some had actually forgotten their Jewish background. The crude racial categories of the new laws seemed utterly irrelevant to people who identified completely with German society and the culture of Bach and Goethe. Their rejection by the German State under Hitler was a gross affront to lifetimes of loyalty and achievement; that this was only the prelude to greater tragedy seemed inconceivable.

Like Fritz Haber, the Jewish chemist who had contributed so much to Germany's military-industrial expansion during the First World War, Warburg was a fervent patriot who cultivated the traditional Prussian military bearing and manner. He did not regard his time in the army as wasted; on the contrary, he commented 50 years later that he had worn 'one of the finest uniforms of the old Prussian army', and had served as orderly officer to 'several of our great commanders. In the course of this I got to know the realities of life which had escaped me in the laboratory. I learned to handle people; I learned to obey and to command. I was taught that one must be more than one appears to be.' Wartime allegiances run deep; Warburg's pride in his military experience reinforced his loyalty to the German state, and left him with a lifelong preference for military ways: straight talking, 'elimination of humbug' and dislike of inefficiency.

His father came from a celebrated Jewish family which could be traced back four centuries. Recent generations had excelled in banking and art history, and Otto Warburg's father, Emil, was one of Germany's leading physicists, holding the physics chair at Berlin University. By the time Hitler became Chancellor, Otto was a world-famous biochemist who had won his Nobel Prize, dominated German physiology and was universally respected.

As a war veteran Warburg was initially exempt from the dismissals under the civil service law; unlike his German Jewish contemporaries, who were also exempted but could not stomach staying at their work while their colleagues were sacked, Warburg held on. He was left unscathed throughout the years of the Third Reich – even though as a biochemist he could not contribute directly to the German war effort.

From childhood Warburg was highly ambitious, though not for the conventional rewards of rank and power; perhaps to avoid competing with his father, his goal was the achievement of great scientific discovery. On the strength of his record as an outstanding student in science and medicine at Heidelberg he was invited to become head of the research department at the Kaiser Wilhelm Institute in Berlin. There he had no teaching or administrative duties and was completely free to choose his subject of research. Having chosen its scientists carefully, the Institute left them to follow whatever avenue of interest they preferred in exchange for opportunity, security and independence. The policy reaped rich rewards, attracting some of the supreme talents who achieved spectacular results.

Apart from his four years in the army, Warburg stayed at the KWI for the rest of his working life. He pioneered methods of measuring cellular respiration, including the 'Warburg apparatus', which is still in use, and the study of tissue slices to measure the metabolism of living tissues. He also identified the function of structures within cells which are vital to their metabolism, and the profound importance of these continues to be revealed. A second major interest was photosynthesis, the process of forming chemical entities through the absorption of light, the fundamental life cycle of plants on which all life depends.

Warburg was brilliant at devising experiments. His interest in the rate of metabolism in cells led him to attack the problems of cells which were abnormally active – cancer cells. He was determined to understand the process which led them to excessive growth and thus to malignancy.

In 1931 he won the Nobel Prize for his studies on cell respiration – hearing the news, he commented that it was 'about time' – and by 1933 his reputation was unassailable. Professional considerations were disregarded by the Nazis in respect of other Jewish scientists, but somehow they seem to have counted for Warburg. Possibly Goering – who had declared, 'I decide who is a Jew' – protected the scientist by reclassifying him as only a quarter Jewish, though to be classed as 'a quarter Jewish' was enough to destroy others. Perhaps Warburg's work on cancer gave him some protection, since Hitler was terrified of cancer, although here again the importance of the work others were doing was not enough to save them. Whatever its reasons, the machinery of Nazi bureaucracy banned him from teaching – a matter of indifference to him since he did not teach, and did not want to – but nothing was taken from him in the way of workspace, apparatus or funds. His working life continued unchanged.

Warburg seems to have had no objection to accepting the 'mercy' of the Third Reich, although he knew that he was bitterly criticized for it outside Germany. He made sardonic remarks about Hitler's regime, and indeed he scored one small but notable point against it. He was to attend the International Physiology Congress at Zurich in 1938 (at which British physiologists successfully lobbied for the release of Otto Loewi, who had been imprisoned when Austria was occupied), but was then forbidden to do so. After being told to cancel his trip without specifying why, he blandly cabled the Congress: 'Instructed to cancel participation without giving reasons.' The message was clearly received by the world scientific community.

That was apparently Warburg's only gesture in defiance of the Third Reich. Perhaps he was even protected by it, in view of the pressure that might have been exerted on him if he had gone to the conference at Zurich, where Jewish and other scientists could have lobbied him to leave Germany.

Why the Germans allowed him to stay is one mystery; why he chose to remain is another. Perhaps that question could be asked of all non-Jewish German scientists, the vast majority of whom did stay. In Hitler's early years as Chancellor his astonishing transformation of Germany must have impressed Warburg, the super-patriot. By 1936 Hitler had effectively restored German prosperity and security, recreated the German army, symbol of national pride, and his massive programme of public works was the envy of the world. Warburg could be expected to appreciate efficiency in the Third Reich – and a man who chose soldiers rather than scientists as his friends could well favour a leader who presented himself as a 'simple soldier'.

It is far harder to understand how Warburg could square this with the Nazis' treatment of his Jewish colleagues, of the Jews generally – even the treatment of his own relatives. Aby Warburg, a cousin, had founded the Warburg Institute of the History of Art, which moved to London when the Nazis came; other relatives who came to London were Sigmund Warburg, the banker, and Frederick Warburg, who set up the publishing company Secker & Warburg.

Warburg's own life was totally dedicated to his scientific research. The memoir of Warburg by Hans Krebs,[4] who worked with him for more than four years, describes a man of unbending routine whose universe centred around his laboratory, his home and the country house where he spent his holidays. The temperament that made him ideally suited to a lifetime of laboratory research also made him singularly impervious to the march of history.

His very adherence to convention became in the end a form of eccentricity. Deviation from his habits was apparently unthinkable. He would arrive at the laboratory at eight sharp after an hour's horseriding when daylight allowed, and work until six or later, expecting his team at the laboratory to do the same. His workforce tended to be technicians rather than scientific collaborators and he preferred to spend available funds on equipment rather than extra manpower.

Warburg was, he said, 'too busy to get married'; as a student he apparently once fell in love, but thereafter showed no romantic interest in women. Yet despite his solitary existence every aspect of his life rooted and tied him to Germany. He was looked after at home by his devoted companion Jacob Heiss, and was deeply attached to his horses and dogs; he managed to maintain a horse throughout the war. His research into cancer made him suspicious of chemical additives in food, and household produce all came from his kitchen garden.

During the war a senior official of Hitler's Chancellery, Reichs-leiter Boubler, protected Warburg when he was attacked for making critical remarks about the regime. The scientist could have emigrated to England or the United States earlier: his work in Berlin had been supported by the Rockefeller Foundation, which offered to set him up elsewhere; but Warburg refused. After the war he made enquiries about moving to the United States when his laboratory was taken over by American occupying forces, but his approach was rebuffed.

Warburg did not underestimate the value of his work, and in a memoir of another scientist he wrote revealingly that some scientists are irreplaceable. When the war was over he justified having stayed in Germany on the grounds that his work on cancer with his laboratory team was indispensable; yet soon afterwards he brutally sacked his collaborators on the suspicion that they had denounced him to the Nazi authorities. His ruthless treatment of his staff was confirmed by his aggressive attitude to many scientific colleagues. Although he was often right he believed himself always to be so; his explanations were always correct, and he regarded himself as the 'victor' in every contest. His papers, which he typed himself, were rarely collaborative, and his refusal to brook argument eventually left him intellectually isolated.

The discipline and self-sufficiency that imposed a lifetime's hard work were one side of a character whose opposite face was a rigid inability to adapt to change or criticism. Warburg's self-contained existence insulated him from the monstrous activities of the Third Reich; he was a man so set in his ways that even the Nazis did not dislodge them. Like Lise Meitner, who always rejected attempts to associate her distinguished record with her Jewish origins, saying she had never identified herself with being Jewish, Warburg lived according to his own definition of himself. He was fortunate in that the Nazis let him do so.

CARL FRIEDRICH VON WEIZSÄCKER

One of the atomic physicists who stayed in Germany, Carl Friedrich von Weizsäcker is still alive, and we visited him at his home near Munich in 1993. He met Heisenberg when he was only 15 and immediately fell in love with him and with physics. Later he studied under Heisenberg in Leipzig and was still only 20 when the Nazis came to power. After two of Heisenberg's assistants left because they were Jewish, Heisenberg appointed von Weizsäcker.

Von Weizsäcker had been impressed by Hitler, who seemed the 'strong man' that the times demanded. Feeling he should do something, he joined the *Arbeitsdienst*, the labour service, a semi-military organization which gave young men training for a few months, a way of getting round the limitations on the size of the German army permitted under the Versailles Treaty. Students could join for three months in their vacation.

However, he was saved from the temptation to join the Nazi Party by two things. Having already had some experience of university life, he had met many Jewish physicists and in particular he knew, by name at least, the great leaders of German physics of the period: Einstein, Born, Franck and others.

The second factor was his father. Ernst von Weizsäcker was principal State Secretary in the German Foreign Office, the top civil servant. He warned his son about Hitler: 'Please be careful, please do not be impressed by him.' Von Weizsäcker senior knew that Hitler had a great power over people; those determined to tell him of some great error he had made or was proposing caved in completely in his presence. This warning was just enough to hold young von Weizsäcker from joining the Nazi Party, which probably would have made no difference to his career over the next dozen years but might have impeded him after the war. His father was tried in one of the later Nuremberg trials and sent to prison for five years.

Von Weizsäcker has no recollection of ever joining the Party; when he applied for a US visa in 1949, the American consul said: 'You have been a member of the Party, we have the documents.'

Von Weizsäcker never knew what the documents were or even if they existed, but they did not prevent his being allowed into the United States. So there must be some doubt about what actually happened.

So much in the shadow of Heisenberg was von Weizsäcker that we have found it difficult to assess his own role in atomic research. He was extremely able and was involved in research into the possibilities of nuclear fission from the beginning. He went with Heisenberg on the disastrous trip to Copenhagen in 1941. Von Weizsäcker continued in the inner councils of Germany's atomic research until the end of the war and was interned in Farm Hall, near Cambridge, afterwards.

A postscript: Carl Friedrich's younger brother Richard was President of Germany from 1984 to 1994.

OTTO HAHN

We include a short story of Otto Hahn not because there was ever a serious possibility that he would leave Germany, as far as we know, but because he had an independent spirit, made no show of cooperation with the regime and he played such an important role in German physics. With Fritz Strassman he discovered nuclear fission when he was head of the radiochemistry department at the Kaiser Wilhelm Institute in Berlin in 1938. As a young man he had made a name for himself working with Sir William Ramsay at University College, London, then with Ernest Rutherford, and from 1904 to 1906 in Montreal. He was joined by the brilliant young Austrian Lise Meitner, and they worked together for 32 years.

After the Anschluss Meitner, as a Jew, was no longer protected by her Austrian nationality and had to leave Germany in a hurry. This was before Hahn and Strassman had made their crucial observation of the splitting of uranium by bombardment with neutrons. The essential observations had been made several times before, for example by Enrico Fermi and Irène Curie, but, like Hahn and Strassman, no one had done a sufficiently sensitive chemical analysis of the elements produced by the irradiation of uranium with neutrons. Hahn and Strassman's analysis led to the astonishing discovery that the principal products were isotopes of barium, an element of no more than half the atomic weight of uranium. This clearly implied, though Hahn and Strassman's paper does not say so, that the uranium nucleus had split in half. Meitner and Frisch named the process fission and calculated the enormous energy that it would release.

Hahn shared the horror of many physicists in all countries at the possibilities of the unrestricted use of atomic energy and strongly advocated its control. This was after the dropping of the atomic bomb on Hiroshima on 6 August 1945, which he had not in the least expected. He was as astonished as the other German scientists interned at Farm Hall when they heard what had happened.

Hahn won the Nobel Prize in 1944 and the Fermi award with Strassman and Meitner in 1966.

When he returned to Germany after the war from internment in England he was elected the first president of the Max Planck Society, the successor of the Kaiser Wilhelm Institute. He died in 1968 aged 89.

9

Internment

What I feel about this internment is that it is an
awful thing for the innocent ones, but it is very
hard for them to distinguish between innocent and
guilty, and the only thing is to intern everyone. I
am sure people like you will put up with this for
the sake of England.

*A letter written to John Wilmers in 1940, then aged 20.
'That is precisely what I thought about internment,'
he later commented.*

In April 1940 the war had been going for seven months, but nothing seemed to be happening. When Germany attacked Poland on 1 September 1939 it overran the whole country in three weeks. The Polish army had been thought to be formidable, especially its cavalry, but cavalry no longer had any role in war and the army crumpled before the onslaught of tanks and planes. This was the beginning of a new style in war – the blitzkrieg. But then the war went quiet. Hitler actually wanted to attack in the West immediately but for once his generals restrained him. The effort in the east and the need to shift everything to the west gave him too little time. Britain and France were taking no significant initiatives. This was the 'phoney' war, as the Americans called it.

Then on 9 April 1940, without the Allies having any idea of what was afoot, the Germans attacked Denmark and Norway. Denmark surrendered within hours and Norway within days. The whole of Norway's 1000-mile coastline was occupied. It seems that the German triumph was helped by traitors in Norway. A Norwegian army major, Quisling, proclaimed himself a Nazi and head of the government; his name has passed into history as synonymous with treachery.

The Allies were overwhelmed by German military power – and by fear of treachery within their own countries. If the Germans had been helped by spies and traitors to overcome Norway so quickly, might not the same be true in France, the Low Countries – or Britain? After all, there were enough Germans living in Britain, mostly refugees from Nazi Germany who had fled there over the previous seven years after Hitler came to power.

The problem did not come out of the blue. There had been a similar one at the beginning of the First World War, when, in a mood of anti-German hysteria and amid much confusion, 30,000 Germans or people with German-sounding names had been interned. The British government did not want a repeat performance when the Second World War began. It set up tribunals all over the country to investigate the refugees and divide them into Category A: hostile and to be interned if there was any threat of invasion; Category B : to be watched and interned if things went badly; and Category C: friendly aliens, sympathetic to Britain, who were to be left at liberty. By March 1940 73,500 cases had been examined and 64,200 (87 per cent) put into Category C. These people followed their normal lives, most, being ardently anti-Nazi, trying to get into war work. Many of the scientists in particular were already working on projects related to the war, including atomic energy.

The public mood was calm – too calm perhaps. Neville Chamberlain, the Prime Minister, announced complacently in March: 'Hitler has missed the bus.' This was two weeks before the invasion of Norway. There was no anti-German hysteria. None of the refugees was pestered or intimidated, nor did any lose their job.

When Norway was invaded the Allies realized they had been caught napping. But far worse was to come. On 10 May the Germans attacked in the west: France, Belgium and the Netherlands were assaulted with overwhelming force. The French army, which had been assumed to be mighty, mightier even than the German army, collapsed. The small British Expeditionary Force in France advanced into Belgium but Belgian defences were overrun and within five days the country had surrendered. The Netherlands also gave up within days and by the end of the month the British army had been evacuated through Dunkirk and the French army had fallen back and was awaiting the knockout, which came on 20 June when the French leader, Pétain, surrendered.

This sudden, overwhelming and totally unexpected defeat in the West created near-panic in some British government departments about the refugees. Most of the Cabinet stayed calm, but others and some military leaders did not. They favoured interning the refugees, so did Winston Churchill, by now Prime Minister, who used the phrase 'collar the lot'. The cause of calmness was not aided by the British ambassador to the Netherlands, Sir Nevile Bland, who claimed that the Dutch collapse had helped by traitors ('fifth columnists'), in particular that they had helped German parachutists. Parachutists had not been used in great numbers before and they provoked great fear, increased by rumours that they came disguised as civilians or in the uniforms of their enemies. Bland broadcast on 30 May:

> It is not the German or Austrian who is found out who is the danger. It is the one, whether man or woman, who is too clever to be found out. That was apparent in Holland – where . . . many of the obvious fifth columnists were interned at the outbreak of war – but where there still remained a dreadful number at large to carry out the instructions they had from Germany.
>
> . . . be careful at this moment how you put complete trust in any person with German or Austrian connections. If you know people of this kind who are still at large, keep your eye on them; they may be perfectly all right – but they may not, and today we can't afford to take any risks . . .

In the face of this kind of agitation and of the more discreet but powerful concerns of the military, especially military intelligence, internment of refugees living near the east coast of England began within a few days. Max Perutz, then a postgraduate research worker at Cambridge, was one of those arrested. He wrote:[1]

> It was a cloudless Sunday morning in May of 1940. The policeman who came to arrest me said that I would be gone for only a few days, but I packed for a long journey. I said goodbye to my parents.
>
> From Cambridge, they took me and more than a hundred other people to Bury St Edmunds, a small garrison town twenty-five miles to the east, and there they locked us up in a school. We were herded into a huge empty shed cast into gloom by blacked-out skylights thirty feet above us. A fellow-prisoner kept staring at a blank piece of white paper,

and I wondered why until he showed me that a tiny pinhole in the blackout paint projected a sharp image of the sun's disc, on which one could observe the outlines of sunspots. He also taught me how to work out the distances of planets and stars from their parallaxes and the distances of nebulae from the red shifts of their spectra. He was a warm-hearted and gentle German Roman Catholic who had found refuge from the Nazis at the Observatory of Cambridge University. Years later he became Astronomer Royal for Scotland. In the spring of 1940, he was one of hundreds of German and Austrian refugee scholars, mostly Jewish and all anti-Nazi, who had been rounded up in the official panic created by the German attack on the Low Countries and the imminent threat of an invasion of Britain.

After a week or so at Bury, we were taken to Liverpool and then to an as yet unoccupied housing estate at nearby Huyton, where we camped for some weeks in bleak, empty semi-detached two-storey houses, several of us crowded into each bare room, with nothing to do expect lament successive Allied defeats and worry whether England could hold out. Our camp commander was a white-moustached veteran of the last war; then a German had been a German, but now the subtle new distinctions between friend and foe bewildered him. Watching a group of internees with skullcaps and curly side-whiskers arrive at his camp, he mused: 'I had no idea there were so many Jews among the Nazis'. He pronounced it 'Nasis'.

Lest we escape to help our mortal enemies, the Army next took us to Douglas, a seaside resort on the Isle of Man, where we were quartered in Victorian boarding houses. I shared my room with two bright German medical researchers, who opened my eyes to the hidden world of living cells – a welcome diversion, lifting my thoughts from my empty stomach. On some days, the soldiers took us out for country walks, and we ambled along hedge-flanked lanes two abreast, like girls from a boarding school. One day near the end of June, one of our guards said casually: 'The bastards have signed'. His terse message signified France's surrender, which left Britain to fight the Germans alone.

In general the arrests, carried out by the police, not military intelligence, were quiet and courteous. Most of those arrested were told, like Perutz, that it was only for a few days, they need not bring much luggage, they would probably soon be released. This was the general story, but it was not true: most of those interned spent months or years behind bars. The worst burden for many of them was that they were told nothing, so they did not know where they were going nor what was happening to their families.

They were searched, money and valuables taken and, although a receipt might be given, the money in many cases was not seen again. Refugees from all over the country were, like Max Perutz, taken to Huyton, whence many were sent to the Isle of Man. Some were maltreated or insulted on the way by the army and even, in a few cases, by the police, and many had possessions stolen. But the worst suffering for the internees was the ignorance, not even knowing what was happening in the war. When they had been interned they knew things were going very badly, but since then? After all, these were the people the Nazis would have murdered first if they had invaded. They did not even know of the efforts of their friends and colleagues to get them released, which had begun within days of the first internment.

The total number of those interned was 27,000 – incidentally less than in the First World War. Aside from Huyton and the Isle of Man, there were smaller internment centres in Scotland and elsewhere, but the Isle of Man, with 20,000 internees, was by far the largest. The Governor of the island was a figure reminiscent of earlier years who believed that the 'only good Hun was a dead Hun'. In the face of this attitude the dozen or so Germans living on the island opted for internment.

The Isle of Man had housed internees in the Great War. It was a very suitable place, being a holiday resort with a large number of hotels and guest houses. They were largely unoccupied as few people were taking holidays in the summer of 1940. The internees provided a substantial source of income.

The commander of the camps on the Isle of Man issued a notice to the internees which was clear and fair:

It is my wish that every man who enters internment on this Island shall be assured that nothing avoidable will be done that might add to his discomfort or unhappiness.

It must be obvious to you all that a uniform code of discipline is essential if a community of men is to live together successfully. That code will be mine and will be obeyed. There is, however, a good reason for every order and there will be no aggression. The officers and troops who are given charge of you are men of understanding. In any case, it is not a British characteristic to oppress the man who is unable to retaliate, and you will find no one anxious to foster a spirit of enmity which, within the confines of an Internment Camp, can achieve nothing.

The measure of your co-operation and good behaviour will decide the measure of your privileges and the consideration shown for your welfare. In all events, you are assured of justice.

The internees soon started arranging things for themselves. Within days they had created a university with organized teaching in English, Spanish, Russian, telegraphy, advertising and the theory of numbers. They organized a concert and an art exhibition, and they produced a newspaper. The newspaper complained of the lack of communication with the outside world – they had no newspapers and could not listen to the radio. They were limited to two letters a week, which were often delayed, even those between husbands and wives in separate camps on the island. The rules in the women's camps were often stricter than in the men's.

Gradually conditions improved. Husbands and wives were allowed to meet once a month. In late July the Home Secretary said in the House of Commons that internees would be allowed to apply for release. In the next few days came several indications of a relaxation and of a change of mind by the government. Sir John Anderson spoke of 'the very greatest reluctance and regret' with which the policy of internment had been imposed and said: 'I am not here to deny for a moment that most regrettable and deplorable things have happened. They had been due partly to the inevitable haste with which the policy of internment, once decided upon, had to be carried out. They have been due in some cases to the mistakes of individuals and to stupidity and muddle. These matters all relate to the past. So far as we can remedy mistakes, we shall remedy them.'

The first prisoners had been released from the Isle of Man on 5 August; by the end of the month 1000 had been released and two months later 4000 had left.

The most intimidating and frightening experience came to those who were deported. The government looked frantically for somewhere abroad to send them. There was not enough room in Britain and, thinking that some of them were really potential spies, they wanted them out of the country. Pressure was put upon the Canadians and Australians, who, more or less reluctantly, agreed to accept them, thinking that they were taking dangerous people out of Britain. In fact the internees who were deported were Category C, 'friendly' aliens. As far as is known, there were no spies or traitors among the internees.

The government also asked New Zealand to take internees, but that country's Prime Minister refused on the grounds that 'the presence of a large number of prisoners in New Zealand would be likely to tempt Hitler to try to induce Japan [not yet in the war] to rescue them'. No one can have believed this extraordinary excuse but the New Zealanders were indirectly supported in their opposition by the United States.

Four ships went to Canada, the *Arandora Star*, the *Ettrick*, the *Duchess of York* and the Polish liner *Sobieski*, and the *Dunera* went to Australia. The ships were overcrowded, carrying about twice as many internees as they had carried passengers. Some prisoners were kept entirely below decks, some fenced in by barbed wire and some were maltreated by the guards. But not all. Perutz was on the *Ettrick*, and wrote about his experiences in the *New Yorker* magazine (see Appendix III):

Suspended like bats from the mess decks' ceilings, row upon row of men swayed to and fro in their hammocks. In heavy seas, their eruptions turned the floors into quagmires emitting a sickening stench. Cockroaches asserted their prior tenancy of the ship. To this revolting scene, Prince Frederick of Prussia, then living in England, restored hygiene and order by recruiting a gang of fellow-students with mops and buckets – a public-spirited action that earned him everyone's respect, so that he, grandson of the Kaiser and cousin of King George VI, became king of the Jews. Looking every inch a prince, he used his royal standing to persuade the officers in charge that we were not the Fifth Columnists their War Office instructions made us out to be. The commanding colonel called us scum of the earth all the same, and once, in a temper, ordered his soldiers to set their bayonets upon us. They judged differently and ignored him.

The worst event of the whole internment story came at seven o'clock on the morning of 2 July when the *Arandora Star*, with 1600 internees and 200 crew on board, was torpedoed 200 miles off the west Scottish coast. About 650 men were lost. The survivors were taken back to Liverpool, where a number were promptly put on the *Dunera*, which set off for Australia eight days later. The terror of going to sea again so soon after being torpedoed was made even worse when the *Dunera* was herself attacked by another submarine, but this time, because she made a sudden change of course when she was in the U-boat's sights, both torpedoes missed.

When the internees reached Canada their experiences were varied. The Canadian authorities had been told that these were dangerous Nazis and it took them some time to realize that the bedraggled, rather gentle and passive people were as far from being Nazi as it was possible to be. Expecting spies, they had got scientists. There were many petty persecutions in the Canadian internment camps, but there were compensations. The situation of one of the camps beside the St Lawrence River was magnificent. Gradually the extremely talented men (there were no women) among the internees formed themselves into a mini university. Perutz, the 'dean', organized the teaching. Among his 'staff' was Hermann Bondi, later Fellow of the Royal Society, Chief Scientist to the (British) Ministry of Defence and Master of Churchill College, Cambridge. He was a brilliant mathematician who had come to Cambridge from Vienna before the Anschluss, having decided as a schoolboy that he wanted to study mathematics at Trinity College. After he was released he was immediately transferred to secret scientific work on radar; he commented on the contrast between being held behind barbed wire because he was so dangerous and then behind barbed wire because the work he was doing was so secret! Another of the 'staff' was Thomas Gold, later Professor of Astronomy at Cornell University, and another Klaus Fuchs. Ten years later Fuchs was discovered to be a spy but before that he had done brilliant physics and made important contributions to the development of the atomic bomb.

The *Dunera* was the only ship to take internees to Australia. She carried 450 survivors from the *Arandora Star* and 2100 others. The *Arandora Star* men were disembarked at Melbourne and sent 100 miles to the north to Tatura. The rest sailed on to Sydney, whence they were sent across the Nullarbor Plain to a desolate spot called Hay. There they created their own camp conditions, 'a small working republic', as one internee described it. The internees arranged such things as allocation of huts according to nationality, politics, sexual preference; they set up a shop which sold sweets, fruit and cigarettes and made a profit, which was used to help the old and the sick. They even designed their own banknotes, showing a sheep on one side and on the other a kangaroo and an emu surrounded by barbed wire.

Inmates made furniture from eucalyptus wood and sandals from old rubber tyres. One man ran a vegetarian restaurant and others painted portraits for modest fees. The cultural and intellectual life was richer even than at the Onchan or Hutchinson camps on the Isle of Man. There were lectures on chemistry, astronomy, atomic research, Shakespeare, Italian, Russian, Chinese. The concert pianist Peter Stadlen gave recitals and transposed orchestral works so that they could be performed by male-voice choirs. A maths professor made a dozen whistles from eucalyptus wood and another internee carved a working violin. They combined forces with Stadlen to perform Handel's oratorio *Israel in Egypt*. The actors staged *The Good Soldier Schweik* and the anti-war drama *Journey's End*, which left the Australian camp commander, seated as a guest of honour in the front row, in tears.

There were similar efforts by the ex-*Arandora Star* men at Tatura. The Collegium Taturensium was founded and offered a range of lectures almost as diverse as Hay's; one of the most popular series was on political philosophy, given by a veteran of the International Brigade who fought in the Spanish Civil War.

After a few months, when the refugees in Canada and Australia were beginning to think that their imprisonment might last the whole war, the tide turned and releases began. The internees could not know this, but protests and questions about internment started within weeks of 10 May. As so many of them came from Cambridge and London they were known to senior figures there, professors, vice-chancellors, Members of Parliament. In those days Oxford and Cambridge Universities had their own MPs; one of the two for Cambridge University was A. V. Hill. He had been elected, as an 'independent conservative' only in April 1940 and had not, therefore, much political experience. But, as Vice President of the Academic Assistance Council, he had been involved in the rescue of refugee scholars from the beginning. He felt strongly about the issue, knew many of the internees and was determined to act. He was all the more effective for being extremely courteous.

Hill and the Society for the Protection of Science and Learning (as the AAC now was) went to work at once. The SPSL's Secretary, Walter Adams, wrote to the Home Office on 6 June, within four weeks of the first internments, saying that they understood the reasons behind the action but urging the earliest possible release of some of the refugees for reasons to do with Britain's war effort. They offered to guarantee 20 selected scientists whose internment had led to the cessation of work of national importance and who had been near naturalization (which had stopped at the beginning of the war). Cambridge had been particularly badly hit because in the first wave of internment refugees living near the east coast had been targeted as being a special risk in the event of invasion.

Hill had been in the USA but went into action on his return. Tess Simpson had written to him on 20 June. Four days later he told her that he had been on a delegation to the Home Office and had offered to prepare a list of aliens whom they could vouch for and the Home Office agreed. The SPSL asked the Home Office to consult them before deporting any more people to Canada (although this was not done). A committee was set up with the Royal Society to deal with internments and releases and the Home Office conceded that this could apply to anyone whose work was important for science or learning, not to scientists only.

Although the Home Office was outwardly cooperative, Hill and the SPSL were not told of many of the things that were going on, in particular of further internments and deportations. This was not due to any perfidy on the part of the Home Office, which was engaged in a struggle with the military to control the whole internment programme. The Home Secretary, Sir John Anderson, had been holding off the more extreme efforts of the 'collar-the-lot' forces, MI5 and, at first, Winston Churchill. Thanks to repeated questions in Parliament from Hill and other MPs, Eleanor Rathbone, Josiah Wedgwood, George Strauss and Victor Cazalet, press comments and comments from Canada about the apparent lack of danger posed by the internees sent there, the mood in the government began to alter. This was helped by the change, slight but steady, in the military situation. In May invasion was an immediate threat; by July the danger seemed to be lessening. The acute fear of traitors and spies was decreasing and ministers were beginning to realize that they had overreacted. Churchill had become less insistent and Neville Chamberlain, who was now Lord President of the Council and oversaw policy towards refugees, changed Churchill's mind, and together with Lord Halifax, Foreign Secretary, and Sir John Anderson, they tipped the balance.

One of the most remarkable contributions to the change of policy came from a 20-year-old man, Merlin Scott, a soldier who shepherded internees on to the *Dunera*. These were men who had survived the *Arandora Star* nine days before, and many were Italians who had lived in Britain for years. They had been hurriedly interned after 10 June when Mussolini declared war and when the confusion and agitation about spies was at its height. Scott wrote to his father on 11 July:[2]

I thought the Italian survivors were treated abominably – and now they've all been sent to sea again to Canada [*sic*], the one thing nearly all were dreading, having lost fathers, brothers etc the first time. Many valuable men I think have been packed off. We had a certain Martinez who had been head of the Pirelli Cable and Tyre factories and who knows more about armaments than most – there were many others who had just been rounded up without any sort of inquiry.

When they got down to the ship their baggage was naturally searched, but what I thought so bad was that masses of their stuff – clothes etc was simply taken away from them and thrown into piles out in the rain and they were only allowed a handful of things. Needless to say various people, including policemen, started helping themselves to what had been left behind.

They were then hounded up the gangway and pushed along with bayonets, with people jeering at them. It was, in fact, a thoroughly bad show. I think largely due to some of those useless hard-bitten bogus Majors who were standing around in large numbers!

Masses of telegrams came for them from relatives nearly all just saying 'Thank God you are safe', and they were not allowed to see them.

Although written in English they had to go to a Censor's office, and as the ship has now sailed, I know they will never get them. Some of them said they had had no mail for six weeks.

The letter had an immediate effect as Scott's father was Assistant Under-Secretary at the Foreign Office. No one at the Foreign Office or Home Office even knew that the survivors of the *Arandora Star* had been sent to sea again. This came a few days after the debate in the House of Commons on internment when government statements had been flatly contradicted by Eleanor Rathbone and others and when Anthony Eden, then Secretary of State for War, had had to say lamely that he would look at the matter again. The Foreign Secretary, Lord Halifax, on reading Merlin Scott's letter, had said: 'It speaks for itself – and discloses a state of affairs that we should all find it quite impossible to defend.'

The policy began to change but its effects were slow: it was one thing to lay hands on aliens, quite another to find them in prison camps here or in Canada or Australia and return them to Britain. But the internees soon noticed a difference. Alexander Paterson, a senior Home Office official, was sent to Canada to sort things out. He was a kindly man and soon after his arrival on 25 November changes began. Category C internees were to return promptly to England or in a few cases offered the chance to go to the United States.

In Australia it was the same. Julian Layton had been sent out to facilitate the internees' return and to help those who wanted to go to the United States. At first both Paterson and Layton thought those wishing to go there would be able to do so but then Breckinridge Long, Assistant Secretary of State, blaming opposition from the American Legion, refused to take any. It was clearly his own decision, albeit cloaked in a political hypocrisy which included other members of the US administration and members of Congress influenced by a mixture of economic, xenophobic and anti-Semitic motives. As if this were not enough, the United States not only refused the refugees' entry but also hampered their return to the United Kingdom by refusing to allow any ships carrying enemy aliens, whether friendly or not, to pass through the Panama Canal following the Japanese attack on Pearl Harbor.

In the camps in Canada and Australia hopes were raised once

Paterson and Layton arrived to start things moving. Max Perutz was called to the Commandant's office in his camp at Sherbrooke in Canada and feared bad news. But this time the news was good. The Home Office had ordered his release, and he could go to the new School for Social Research in New York or he could return to England. He opted to return to England, leading the Commandant to say that he would make a fine soldier. Max Perutz, hardly a military type, ruefully remarked that it was the only time such a comment had been made about him.

The return journey from Canada was better than the outward trip. For them there was no need to go through the Panama Canal and Perutz and some of his fellow internees travelled on a small, comfortable Belgian liner, the *Thysville*. The Canadian authorities insisted on a military escort, so one unarmed British officer, assisted by four of the internees (one of whom, a Dutchman, had escaped to Britain in 1940 by rowing across the Channel by himself in an open boat), escorted the 280 men. When they got back to Britain some of the internees had to spend more days on the Isle of Man, but most were soon united with their families and friends. When he got home in January Perutz was met at Cambridge railway station by his faithful laboratory technician with the news that his father had been released and his mother was also safe.

Many of those who returned joined the Pioneer Corps, originally intended as an auxiliary labour unit of low status but now becoming almost an army university, so many professors and lecturers having joined it. Others went into more dangerous units such as the airborne forces. By then they had changed their names and identities. It was dangerous enough to be in a front-line regiment without being a refugee German Jew who would get very short shrift if captured.

Perutz had been interned from May 1940 until January 1941. Many were held for longer; a few were released early, one getting back to Cambridge in time for the start of the Michaelmas term. In the summer of 1941 there were still 7000 internees left on the Isle of Man out of a total of 27,000. The last camp was closed in September 1943.

Not all the academic refugees were interned, however. Marthe Vogt was one. She was exceptional in that she was not Jewish, and had come voluntarily because she hated the Nazis, not because she had to. In 1935 she was research assistant and head of the Chemical Division at the Kaiser Wilhelm Institute in Berlin. She had no political interests but she could not believe that such a man as the author of *Mein Kampf* could get and keep power. When Hitler did so she knew she must get out.

Vogt left Germany when she was given a Rockefeller Fellowship to go to England. Many of her Jewish friends had already left. They had mostly been replaced by inferior scientists who were anxious to take their jobs. With the fellowship Vogt had the chance to work at the National Institute for Medical Research in London under Sir Henry Dale, one of the leading pharmacologists in the world and a future Nobel Prize winner. Six months later she transferred to Cambridge to work under E. B. Verney, Professor of Pharmacology – another world leader. At the end of that year, when her Rockefeller Fellowship came to an end, Vogt had no intention of returning to her previous appointment in Germany, although under the conditions of the Rockefeller Fellowship she should have done so. Verney got her a research fellowship in Cambridge for a year and then she was given a fellowship at Girton College for three years – 'an eternity'. Now she felt free and at home, she was no longer pestered with political questions, and she was successful and happy, with many new British friends and old German ones who had settled in England.

Then came the war and the Tribunals for categorizing all 'enemy aliens', which she still was, not having had time to become naturalized. The judge at the Tribunal did not understand the situation. Because Vogt had had a permanent appointment in Germany she had automatically been made a member of the German Workers' Front; she resigned her membership of the Front, but the Nazi official refused to accept it on principle and left her name on the organization's list. When British Intelligence discovered this she was classified Category A, which meant immediate internment.

She was taken by a policeman from Shire Hall in Cambridge to the police station to be interned. At the first traffic lights the policeman said: 'You know you can appeal.' The police gave her three days to find a lawyer and outside support.

That was enough; her friends sprang into action. E. B. Verney, Henry Dale, Wilhelm Feldberg and Edith Bülbring moved at once.

These were people of great distinction. Verney went to see Henry Dale at Hampstead. He telephoned the Home Secretary, Sir John Anderson, who agreed to see them at once, but was not encouraging. 'We are very busy, you know. I am not sure there is anything I can do, but I will look into it,' he said. By the time Verney had got back to Cambridge Vogt had already been told by the police that she would not be interned. Characteristically, she criticized her friends for wasting the time of the British government at such a crucial time!

During the war Vogt was Reader in Pharmacology at Edinburgh University. In March 1947 she was naturalized and, at last, she was British instead of merely feeling British. She went on to a very distinguished career in pharmacology, in London and Cambridge and was elected a Fellow of the Royal Society in 1952.

What should we make of the internment of 1940?

As far as we know, none of the German refugees who were interned was, or intended to be, a spy or a traitor. They were, on the contrary, Hitler's fiercest enemies. That does not mean that the Nazis might not have tried to infiltrate spies among them. If they did, they were not discovered.

The British authorities overreacted to the danger. Although the problem of refugees from enemy countries had loomed since the start of the war and even before it, when the crisis came their handling was confused and callous. Most individual policemen and soldiers behaved well. There was some roughness and thieving both here and overseas, but there were no outrages and no one was seriously mal-treated. There was stupidity, callousness, even occasionally cruelty, in the process of internment. But there was also kindness, not only from colleagues and friends but also from officers. A case of police kindness was that of a young man who was studying in the summer of 1940 and was marked for internment. A policeman called at his house when he was out and told his mother to keep him out of the house all day. After about two weeks of this the young man got a job with a government minister and was no longer in danger.

The deportations were badly organized and executed. The civil authorities, particularly the Home Office, often did not know what was happening: Who had been arrested? How were they selected? Where were they sent? Much unnecessary suffering was caused by families and friends being kept in ignorance (because the Home Office was) of where the internees were. The lack of news of loved ones was one of the hardest things to bear. It was mostly due to confusion and the long delays caused by censorship. The sending of the *Arandora Star* survivors on the *Dunera* to Australia within days of the sinking was outrageous.

Some of the fiercest criticism of the internment policy and its execution came at the time, both in public and private. On the policy of locking up the country's friends because they happened to be foreign, one newspaper headline said: 'Why not lock up General de Gaulle?' and there was persistent questioning in Parliament of government policy and practice. A. V. Hill, fed with information by Tess Simpson and supported by other MPs, was a relentless, while understanding, critic.

The critics eventually carried the day because those in authority, particularly those in government, were decent, humane men. They did not want to impose harsh and unnecessary suffering. Those who at first favoured a fierce policy came round to seeing its error, futility and harmfulness. Perhaps they were slow to unscramble the eggs they had broken in May 1940 – but they had other matters on their minds. Britain was facing its greatest crisis. Hitler was only 20 miles away. He was seemingly all-powerful and was poised to invade.

Many people, including the refugees themselves, were greatly impressed that at such a time Parliament and the press should concern themselves with the fate of a few thousand foreigners (about 0.05 per cent of the population). It is perhaps almost too obvious a point to make that the concern of the government and people in the case of internment in Britain contrasts with the lack of public or private concern in Germany with the fate of the Jews and others imprisoned there. When the internees, having heard nothing since their imprisonment about what was going on in the outside world, learned that their case were being raised in Parliament, they were immensely encouraged. One of the internees, Heinz Schild, later a professor of pharmacology and an FRS, happened to see a newspaper with a report of Hill's parliamentary questions. It raised his hopes: the war situation could not be so bad if Parliament was concerning itself with the predicament of people like him. The fact is that the situation was desperate, yet Parliament did concern itself with people like Schild.

François Lafitte wrote a Penguin Special, *The Internment of Aliens*,[3] which was published as early as the first week of November 1940. The book sold widely and had a large influence. Forty-eight years later Lafitte republished it with a new introduction in which he accepts that military panic was 'understandable' but the notion that refugees were a menace was not:

> That can be explained only if we understand the mental make-up of the Establishment of the day – that combination of ignorance and prejudice against foreigners so prevalent among the civil and military Upstairs-Downstairs set who had run Britain during the past decade with their tendency to assume that foreigners who disliked Hitler ... and Mussolini ... were very likely to be Communists wanting to overthrow the established order.

Class bias hardly explains the actions of Stalin in moving ethnic Germans from the Baltic States to Poland in 1939 and from southern Russia to Siberia when the Nazis invaded the Soviet Union in 1941; nor does it explain the action of the Americans who moved ethnic Japanese on the west coast of the USA inland after Pearl Harbor. Far more Japanese-Americans were involved than German refugees in Britain. Most of the 112,000 were removed and interned, although they were actually US citizens (no refugees in Britain who had acquired British nationality were interned). The American general involved regarded their danger as proved by the fact that there were no subversive actions.

If class bias underlay the British internment of refugees should it not be credited with the early, loud, persistent and successful pressure for its abolition? It is hard to imagine that there was a single explanation for the complexities of such a varied, callous, un-necessary, incompetent, stupid but understandable operation as internment.

Looking back, even at the time the overall judgement of the internees seems to have been strikingly fair. One internee, John Wilmers, then aged 20 and later a leading QC, received a letter from a friend in the very early days of internment:[4] 'What I feel about this internment is that it is an awful thing for the innocent ones, but it is very hard for them to distinguish between innocent and guilty, and the only thing is to intern everyone. I am sure people like yourself will put up with this for the sake of England.' Wilmers later wrote: 'That is precisely what I thought about internment.'

It says something for the girl who wrote that letter that she could say this directly to her friend and know it would be understood, and it says even more for him that he did.

That confidence and understanding seems to have been the overwhelming reaction of the British people and of the victims of the internment of 1940.

10

The Bomb

Birmingham, March 1940. Two physicists:
Otto Frisch: 'If you had enough uranium 235, how
much would you need to make an atomic bomb?'
Rudolf Peierls, after a brief calculation: 'About 1lb.'

Of all the brilliant physicists working in Germany in the early 1930s, Leo Szilard stands out as eccentric.[1] It was Szilard who 'did the most amongst scientists of his generation to foresee, then create and control the atomic bomb'. But he never concentrated on one problem – he had so many ideas that they spilled over. Often he picked them up and gave them to other people.

After the need to help place Jewish scientists in English universities became less urgent, Szilard was tempted to go into biology. What stopped him was a remark Lord Rutherford had made at the British Association in September 1933 which was reported in *The Times*: 'anyone who looked for a source of power in the transformation of atoms was talking mere moonshine'.

Szilard pondered this statement as he wandered about London. The concept of a nuclear chain reaction came into his head as he waited to cross Southampton Row in Holborn, and watched the traffic lights change from red, through amber to green. He later wrote: 'It suddenly occurred to me that if we could find an element which is split by neutrons and which would emit two neutrons when it absorbs one neutron, such an element, if sufficiently large mass, could sustain a nuclear chain reaction.' The idea never left him. From then on the need to find an element whose nucleus would split and emit two neutrons when hit by one obsessed him. After this, 'physics became too exciting for me to leave it'.

Szilard stayed for some months in the Strand Palace Hotel in London, in a room without a private bath, so each morning at nine he occupied a bathroom down the corridor. He wrote: 'There is no place so good to think as the bath tub. I would just soak there and think, and around 12 o'clock the maid would knock and say "Are you all right, sir?"' Then he would get out of the bath, make a few notes and speculate about experiments which might test the chain-reaction theory.

In 1935 he patented the idea of the chain reaction and assigned it to the British Admiralty. He brooded constantly about how the energy from the reaction might be controlled and used peacefully, perhaps even to bring abundant energy to poor developing countries; he also worried that it might be used by the Nazis in the manufacture of atomic bombs. He tried to interest the General Electric Company in the commercial application of the chain reaction – but his presentation left them unimpressed. He asked Professor G. P. Thomson at Imperial College to find him a laboratory for his chain-reaction experiment; this came to nothing because Szilard feared the risk of results being read by scientists in Germany.

At last a chance meeting with F. L. Hopwood, director of the physics laboratory at St Bartholomew's Hospital, London, enabled Szilard to work there during the summer of 1934. He and Thomas A. Chalmers, a young physicist, successfully bombarded the element beryllium with neutrons from a small amount of radium; they also discovered a brilliantly simple method of separating an element into its isotopes. This work brought the offer of a fellowship at Oxford, and a big contract for a patent on the method of isotope separation.

Szilard continued to work on nuclear fission for a while, but he could not settle. He spent much of his time searching for a rich man to finance his chain-reaction research. He half decided to work in Manchester with his old friend from Berlin, Michael Polanyi. After applying for a place at the Clarendon Laboratory at Oxford, and failing, he crossed the Atlantic in February 1935 to try his luck in New York. Finally Frederick Lindemann offered him a research fellowship at the Clarendon Laboratory, which he accepted.

There Szilard continued with research designed to discover how neutrons interact with atomic nuclei. It turned out very well: Niels Bohr called the work 'beautiful' and it established Szilard as a serious nuclear physicist, consulted by John Cockcroft, one of the first physicists to split the atom, and by his Hungarian colleague Eugene Wigner and the Italian physicist Enrico Fermi. But after a few months he tried to change his full-time Oxford fellowship for one which would allow him to spend six months of the year in the United States. Even the courteous James Franck reproved him in a letter for vacillating, warning that he was becoming difficult to help and should make up his mind to choose a problem and get on with it. Szilard's decision was to emigrate to America.

In January 1938 he arrived in New York, and spent the following months invading the laboratories of different universities, possessed by the idea of the nuclear chain reaction, embarking on experiments, while all the time preaching the need for secrecy about the results of atomic research.

By December he was extremely depressed. Nobody would take seriously the commercial potential of the chain reaction – partly because of his preoccupation with keeping the work secret. He had filed his patent in 1935 to produce a nuclear chain reaction from either indium or beryllium. On 21 December 1938 he wrote gloomily to the British Admiralty to cancel it. On the very same day, in the Kaiser Wilhelm Institute in Berlin, Otto Hahn and Fritz Strassman bombarded uranium with neutrons; it split and released extra neutrons. Szilard had been right about the chain reaction all along – he had just tested the wrong elements for his demonstration.

What Hahn and Strassman were expecting to do when they bombarded uranium with neutrons was to create new, 'transuranic' elements. What actually happened was that they produced an element which at first they could not identify. Then they suspected it was barium, an element about half the atomic weight of uranium. This was incredible. Hahn wrote to Lise Meitner, his former colleague: 'Perhaps you can suggest some fantastic explanation . . . it really can't break up into barium.'

It was natural that Hahn and Strassman should turn to Meitner, who had fled to Sweden with the help of her Dutch colleague Dirk Coster, for she and Hahn had long worked together before her flight. Now she was in Sweden, where she was spending Christmas 1938 with her nephew and fellow refugee Otto Frisch, who was visiting her from England.

Discussing Hahn's hot news from Berlin during a cold walk in the woods, the pair realized that Hahn and Strassman had produced what Frisch named 'atomic fission', and that this process released vast amounts of energy. Frisch immediately told Niels Bohr at the Copenhagen laboratory, and on 16 January 1939 Bohr arrived in New York with the news of the tremendous discovery of fission. He announced it on 27 January at the Fifth Congress on Theoretical Physics in Washington. Before he had even finished speaking, members of his audience were leaving the meeting and hurrying back to their own laboratories in order to repeat the experiment. But although the physics community was buzzing with the news, it was still a very long way from designing a bomb. Those who thought about it at all believed the idea was entirely impractical.

Szilard, who learned the news a few days later from Wigner in Princeton, was the exception. He was stunned. Both he and Wigner realized that they were on the threshold of war, and he was now sure that the chain-reaction process which he had warned the Admiralty about could create violent explosions. So he cabled London again, asking the director of navy contracts to cancel his instruction of 21 December and reinstate his patent application.

Szilard then undertook some fission experiments of his own. He borrowed $2000 from Benjamin Liebowitz, a friend and successful inventor, and got permission from George Pegram, the Professor of Physics at Columbia University in New York, to set up the necessary equipment. Szilard was not a skilled technician and he knew it, so he enlisted Walter Zinn, a Canadian physicist, as his collaborator.

On the evening of 3 March 1939 Szilard and Zinn set up an experiment in which they bombarded uranium with slow neutrons from beryllium irradiated with gamma rays of radium while they watched for the results on a monitoring screen. If the uranium split and neutrons were emitted they would appear as small grey streaks on the screen, showing that the atomic chain reaction was possible. When they switched on the monitor, nothing happened – to Szilard's great relief, since no chain reaction meant there could be no bomb. Then Zinn began checking: they had forgotten to plug the screen into the mains. Once the equipment was connected, the grey flashes appeared. So the atomic chain reaction was not 'moonshine': it was a real possibility.

Szilard had no doubt that war between Germany and Britain was not far off and he was obsessed with the possibility that fission might be exploited in Germany to make an atomic weapon. Hahn and Strassman had published their results, but they did not work out the amount of energy released by the fission. Meitner and Frisch were the first to calculate that energy, and Frisch was the first to verify it experimentally. The joint paper by Meitner and Frisch and another by Frisch alone were published in *Nature* in February 1939. A third paper, which Frédéric Joliot, Hans Halban and Lew Kowarski sent to *Nature* in April 1939, showed that absorption of a single neutron by a uranium nucleus led to fission accompanied by the release of at least two neutrons. That meant that a chain reaction was possible. The title contained the words 'Nuclear Fission', despite Szilard's pleas for secrecy. As Szilard put it, 'the cat wasn't quite out of the bag, but its tail was showing'.

That spring Bohr continued to work on the problem, and at a meeting of the American Physical Society in April 1939 he publicly announced that the rare uranium isotope 235, bombarded by slow neutrons, could set off a chain reaction and an enormous explosion. The *Washington Post* relayed the news in the headline 'Physicists here debate whether experiments will blow up two miles of landscape', and the *New York Times* reported that 'a tiny amount of uranium would be enough to wipe out the entire city of New York'.

Separating enough rare uranium 235 to make a bomb was still believed to be impossible. Nevertheless governments began buying all the uranium they could lay hands on; Germany annexed Czechoslovakia, which had rich deposits of uranium; by September 1939 German scientists were studying how nuclear fission might be used to make weapons and how heavy water might be used as a moderator of the explosion.

By July 1939 Szilard and Wigner were alarmed enough about the dangers of the whole situation to ask advice from Einstein, who was staying on Long Island in a cottage belonging to some friends. Driving out to Long Island the two geniuses of physics became hopelessly lost and had to be directed by a small boy to where Einstein lived.

It was 34 years since Einstein had published his first theory of relativity and here in America he had not kept up with atomic research. When his visitors explained to him how fission of an uranium nucleus releases energy in an explosive chain reaction which could be exploited to make nuclear bombs, Einstein is reported to have said, 'I had never thought of that' (*'Daran habe ich gar nicht gedacht'*) – he had not believed that atomic energy would be released in his lifetime.

This meeting led to the famous letter to President Roosevelt, drafted by Szilard, Wigner and Teller and signed by Einstein:

August 2nd, 1939
Sir:
Some recent work by E. Fermi and L. Szilard, which has been communicated to me in manuscript, leads me to expect that the element uranium may be turned into a new and important source of energy in the immediate future. Certain aspects of the situation which has arisen seem to call for watchfulness and, if necessary, quick action on the part of the Administration. I believe therefore that it is my duty to bring to your attention the following facts and recommendations:

In the course of the last four months it has been made probable – through the work of Joliot in France as well as Fermi and Szilard in America – that it may become possible to set up a nuclear chain reaction in a large mass of uranium, by which vast amounts of power and large quantities of new radium-like elements would be generated. Now it appears almost certain that this could be achieved in the immediate future.

This new phenomenon would also lead to the construction of bombs and it is conceivable – though much less certain – that extremely powerful bombs of a new type may thus be constructed. A single bomb of this type, carried by boat and exploded in a port, might very well destroy the whole port together with some of the surrounding territory. However, such bombs might very well prove to be too heavy for transportation by air.

The United States has only very poor ores of uranium in moderate quantities. There is some good ore in Canada and the former Czechoslovakia, while the most important source of uranium is Belgian Congo.

In view of this situation you may think it desirable to have some permanent contract maintained between the Administration and the group of physicists working on chain reactions in America. One possible way of achieving this might be for you to entrust with this task a person who has your confidence and who could perhaps serve in an inofficial [*sic*] capacity. His task might comprise the following:

a) to approach Government Departments, keep them informed of the further development, and put forward recommendations for Government action, giving particular attention to the problem of securing a supply of uranium ore for the United States.

b) to speed up the experimental work, which is at present being carried on within the limits of the budgets of University laboratories, by providing funds, if such funds be required, through his contacts with private persons who are willing to make contributions for this cause, and perhaps also by obtaining the co-operation of industrial laboratories which have the necessary equipment.

I understand that Germany has actually stopped the sale of uranium from the Czechoslovakian mines which she has taken over. That she should have taken such early action might perhaps be understood on the ground that the son of the German Under-Secretary of State, von Weizsäcker, is attached to the Kaiser-Wilhelm-Institut in Berlin where some of the American work on uranium is now being repeated.

Yours very truly,

Albert Einstein

They chose Dr Alexander Sachs, an investment banker and already an adviser to the President, to deliver the letter, but the war Szilard had dreaded for so long started on 1 September, before a meeting could be arranged. It was not until 11 October that Sachs met the President.

As a first result of the meeting with Sachs, Roosevelt created a government Advisory Committee on Uranium to study the problems raised in Einstein's letter. The three refugees from Hungary, Szilard, Wigner and Teller, were invited to join. By the end of October $6000 of government money was provided to buy the uranium and graphite needed for the large-scale experiment. Six years later the bill for testing the first atomic bomb in Los Alamos came to over $2 billion and 200,000 people were employed on the Manhattan Project.

The amount of matter needed to create a chain reaction was

crucial. If the mass was too small the neutrons would escape and nothing would happen. Physicists were deterred from pursuing atomic bomb research by their doubts about the size of the critical mass necessary to create a chain reaction. The effort involved, particularly the separation of the uranium isotope 235 from the mass of U238, was too great, they thought. It would require vast effort and in the end the weapon, even if it could be produced, was likely to be useless because of its size.

This was the situation in March 1940 when Otto Frisch[2] met his friend Rudolf Peierls[3], another refugee physicist living in Britain and at that time Professor of Physics at Birmingham.

The earlier careers of Peierls and Frisch we have mentioned in Chapter 5. Both physicists were dedicated to the destruction of Nazism and desperate to help the war effort, but neither was fully engaged in the struggle. Then, as we have seen, one day in Birmingham Frisch asked Peierls, 'If you had enough uranium 235 how much would you need to make a bomb?' In a very short time Peierls had made his calculation: 'About 1lb.' (This was a small underestimate: the first bomb actually weighed 15kg.) The two men stared at each other. Peierls was 'frightened', as well he might be.

On three typed foolscap pages Peierls and Frisch wrote a memorandum to Oliphant, the Australian professor of physics at Birmingham, explaining the situation and specifying the methods, implications and costs of making a bomb, which we have given in full in Appendix II; this information turned out to be astonishingly accurate. The paper also warned of the dangers from radioactive fallout and suggested that the effects of an explosion would be so drastic that Britain might find the weapon morally unacceptable. Oliphant took the Frisch-Peierls Memorandum to Sir Henry Tizard, the government's chief scientific adviser, who suggested that a small committee should 'sit soon to advise what ought to be done, who should do it, and where it should be done'. The committee, headed by G. P. Thomson, met for the first time on 2 April 1940, and its investigations launched the atomic bomb project.

Peierls also spoke to Francis Simon in Oxford. Simon took him to see Lindemann, who, after May 1940, was in a highly influential position as the Prime Minister's chief scientific adviser. Lindemann was famously taciturn; Peierls told him the story, but said afterwards,

'I do not know him sufficiently well to translate his grunts correctly.' Despite his apparently noncommittal reaction, Lindemann was convinced, and set about persuading Churchill, whose memorable minute to his Chief of Staff – dated 30 August 1940, in the middle of the Battle of Britain – was: 'although personally I am quite content with the existing explosives, I feel we must not stand in the path of improvement'. He ordered the project to go ahead – but it was a year before the government finally made the decision to start building an atomic bomb. This would be doubly momentous because it provided the incentive for the United States to move ahead with its own atomic bomb project.

The core of fissionable material inside the bomb which exploded over Hiroshima on 6 August 1945 consisted of uranium 235, which normally occurs in only seven of every 1000 nuclei. The separation and concentration of uranium 235 was a dangerous and difficult problem, which was partly solved by Simon.

Until 1940 Simon and his colleagues had had no professional way of helping Britain's war effort; now they could make their contribution to atomic research. Their work involved handling the hexafluoride compound of uranium, which was corrosive and unstable. They relied on gaseous diffusion through a membrane perforated with very fine pores. In the great scientific tradition of extemporizing, Simon brought his wife's wire kitchen strainer into the laboratory one day, beat it out into a flat surface and tested its ability to separate carbon dioxide and water vapour. His findings from this homely equipment led him to commission ICI to produce membranes of 2–3 feet square, each containing 160,000 holes to the square inch.

His family having gone to Canada, alone in Oxford, Simon longed to give his 'whole force to the struggle for this country'. His paper on the separation of uranium isotopes reached the Cabinet advisory committee late in 1940; this provided the basis for the process which, after the bomb project was transferred to the United States, produced enough U235 to fuel a bomb. Simon's report, like that of Peierls and Frisch, reached Churchill through Lindemann.

Considerable development work was done in Britain before Simon's report reached Churchill. Metropolitan Vickers was brought in to build a prototype separation plant in the village of Mold in north Wales before it was realized that Britain was too small and resources too stretched by the other effects of war, including aerial bombardment, for the necessary large-scale development to proceed there.

Thus two of the most crucial steps in the early development of the atomic bomb came from papers by German Jewish refugees in Britain: Peierls and Frisch in March, and Simon in December 1940; while Szilard, another escaper to Britain, was responsible for helping to make the US government aware of the significance of the latest atomic research.

Refugee scientists also contributed to aspects of atomic research in other countries. In France research under Frédéric and Irène Joliot-Curie had been aimed at using heavy water (deuterium oxide), rather than graphite, to slow the fast neutrons – without some slowing agent the neutrons would escape without impact, and there would be no explosion. Heavy water was produced at a manufacturing plant in Vermok, Norway and transferred to Paris before the plant was sabotaged by the Norwegian underground and finally bombed by the US Air Force in 1944. When France was invaded in May 1940 the containers of 'Product Z', as the heavy water was known in code, were smuggled out of France by two of the Joliot-Curies' staff, Hans Halban (who had studied in Copenhagen with Frisch and Bohr) and Lew Kowarski. On the way to Bordeaux they stored the containers overnight in the death cell at Riom State Prison, and during the voyage by destroyer from Bordeaux to Britain the canisters were strapped, in case of enemy attack, to a special raft improvised by the scientific attaché at the British Embassy in Paris, the Earl of Suffolk. After arriving safely in England Halban and Kowarski moved to Cambridge, where they continued their research. It was then discovered that in their French reactor they had produced a new fissionable element, plutonium, which was actually used in the second atomic bomb.

In assessing the rights and wrongs of developing atomic energy and the atomic bomb, we need to think back to the position of the Allies in mid-1940. Half of France was occupied by German troops and British forces had suffered defeat at Dunkirk, with heavy losses, especially of arms. The United States was neutral and the Soviet Union was committed to stay out of the conflict by the German-

Soviet pact of 1939. Britain had no realistic prospect of defeating Germany's vastly superior numbers and weaponry, even with American industrial help. The Nazi threat was deadly and overwhelming. Any means that could be devised against it had to be exploited. That reasoning is as valid today as it was in 1940.

There was another powerful consideration. News about the successful discovery of atomic fission had galvanized the world community of physicists in the summer of 1939, and German scientists would understand the military potential of the discovery as clearly as any others. There was nothing anyone in Britain or the United States could do to ablate that knowledge or prevent others from developing it. The failure of Heisenberg's fellow physicists to persuade him to stay in America during his visit in the summer of 1939 left them extremely concerned.

The refugee physicists, who had suffered persecution at first hand under the Third Reich, were among Hitler's most determined opponents. Their academic life had been brutally interrupted by political fanaticism in the early 1930s, and the experience gave them both insight into the horrors of the Nazi regime and the motivation to do everything in their power to destroy it. As aliens in Britain, they were prevented from working on the secret radar research that was the top priority for most British scientists; but the Maud Committee work was subcontracted to the universities where they were working. Ironically, they were deflected into a field which would prove even more decisive to the outcome of the war, yet at this stage was less shrouded in secret: the atomic bomb.

Almost the whole of the early drive and research into the atomic bomb was powered by refugee scientists from Germany, Austria and Hungary, as well as scientists from Britain, most of them Jewish. Those most closely involved at the time had few doubts about their work. As Otto Frisch put it: 'We were at war and the idea was reasonably obvious; very probably some German scientists had had the same idea and were working on it.' He added: 'Responsible men who properly and understandably feared a dangerous enemy saw their own ideas reflected back to them malevolently distorted. Ideas that appeared defensive in friendly hands seen the other way round appeared aggressive. But they were the same ideas.'

As the project progressed the Allies were desperate to know how far the Germans had got with their atomic research. Rudolf Peierls had an ingeniously simple idea for assessing this. As in Britain and the United States, an atomic bomb project would require the participation of all the leading physicists in Germany, who would have to be concentrated in one research centre as they could not conduct their work in separate laboratories. So Peierls suggested that the German scientific journals, obtainable through neutral countries, should be searched to see whether the leading atomic physicists were still publishing their findings and if so, where they were based. The answer was clear. The members of the 'Uranium Club' were publishing separate studies from different universities. That made it highly unlikely that an authorized concerted atomic initiative was under way – highly unlikely, but not certain, and nothing less than certainty was acceptable to the Allies.

The Japanese were also involved in research into atomic energy. Their programme started in 1941, before they entered the war. It ended when their research institute was destroyed in an American air raid on Tokyo. It is hard to see how a Japanese atomic programme could have succeeded given the economic and military circumstances and the drenching raids by American bombers.

Of the refugee scholars' community in Britain only Max Born, whose wife was a Quaker and a pacifist, refused to work on the project from the beginning; Lise Meitner, who remained in Sweden, also refused to take part in nuclear weapons research. Apart from ethical considerations, there were practical arguments against going ahead with building a bomb, always assuming it were possible. The economic and military effort required was gigantic and would therefore detract from other military effort. Perhaps more important, the United States was not at war and until then had no military imperative to proceed. Even in Chicago, where Fermi and Szilard were at work in the University's Metallurgical Laboratory, they had not caught up with development work in Britain.

The Frisch-Peierls Memorandum and the Maud Reports, which followed it in June and July 1941, were the earliest seeds of Britain's position as a nuclear power. In 1941 Professor Harold Urey, from Columbia University, made a visit to Britain. He was very impressed by how far the British atomic scientists had got. His report on their research to his colleagues and the US government produced a crucial change in attitude, providing the drive that led to the concentration of the entire project in the United States. By the time it was realized that Britain was too small (and too preoccupied by the immediate threat from Germany) to cope with the project, Pearl Harbor had been bombed and the Americans had joined the war. It is fascinating, if fruitless, to speculate what would have happened to the bomb project (and to the war itself) if Japan had not attacked the United States on 7 December 1941, and if Hitler, in an act of folly, had not declared war on the Americans three days later.

The subsequent combined effort was by no means easy or simple. By the summer of 1942 the British realized that their early work was a dwindling asset in the growing American project. Even on commercial grounds, some US companies were suspicious that their British rivals, especially ICI, were planning to exploit the wartime collaboration to their advantage after the war. In Britain the Maud Committee had foreseen that having the bomb would be crucial after the war and the government was concerned that it was losing control of atomic research to the Americans. Full cooperation was not established until Churchill and Roosevelt met at Quebec in 1943, after which the joint effort was based entirely in the United States and the British end of the operation ceased. The first four-man team of atomic experts – Simon, Peierls, Chadwick and Oliphant, two Germans, a Briton and an Australian – arrived in New York the day after the agreement was signed.

The Manhattan Project to develop an atomic bomb had started in the Metallurgical Laboratory at Chicago, to which Szilard had moved. Enrico Fermi, after leaving Italy, had also moved there from Columbia and he and his assistant tested the extra-purified graphite which Szilard had insisted on using as a moderator of the exploding of atomic energy. (Szilard's self-appointed job was to bombard manufacturers for supplies of graphite.) It was a good moderator: it slowed down the bombarding neutrons just as they had hoped. Fermi and Szilard quarrelled about the need for secrecy: Fermi wanted to publish; Szilard feared the information would help the Germans to produce a bomb. Luckily Szilard won.

It took another two years, until December 1942, before the world's first atomic 'pile' – bricks of graphite with uranium spheres set into the pile, and cadmium strips inserted to absorb escaping neutrons – designed by Fermi and Szilard, began to produce a chain reaction in a disused squash court under a football stadium in Chicago. Wigner produced a bottle of Chianti, which they drank from paper cups, but there was no rejoicing. When the others had gone, Szilard and Fermi shook hands. 'This day will go down as a black day in the history of mankind,' Szilard said.

Having worked feverishly to develop the bomb technology, Szilard now put equal energy into his efforts to control the use of the bomb as a weapon, to prevent its being dropped on Japan and to remove atomic energy from military control to the Atomic Energy Control Commission. He wrote to his partner Trude that he was 'terribly awfully tired'; but he went on badgering anyone, especially high-ups, who might listen, with memos, telephone calls, articles, petitions and lectures.

All this time, inept military security checks were kept on Fermi and Szilard. In September 1942 General Leslie Groves took command of the Metallurgical Laboratory and of the entire Manhattan Project, based at Los Alamos. He took an instant dislike to Szilard. Groves considered Szilard to be a 'villain' and Szilard in return thought Groves the 'biggest fool' in the Manhattan Project. Groves's dislike grew to paranoia and before the war was over he drafted a letter to Henry Stimson, Secretary of State for War, asking to have Szilard classified as a spy who should be interned or exiled. Stimson sensibly refused, no doubt aware of the irony that the man most passionate about atomic secrecy should be suspected of spying.

Even when Szilard became an American citizen on 29 March 1943, two FBI agents tailed him to the ceremony in Manhattan, and they tailed him to Washington when he went to see Lord Cherwell, Szilard's former supervisor in Oxford. The agents' reports were ludicrous: 'he had a fondness for delicacies', 'speaks occasionally in a foreign tongue' and 'associates mostly with people of Jewish extraction'. Szilard knew he was being followed: once he offered one of the agents a ride in his taxi and another time a share of his umbrella in a rainstorm.

Five months after his naturalization Szilard was told that he would be dismissed from the Metallurgical Laboratory unless the patents he had taken out on his various inventions were assigned to the army. He was to return all secret notebooks and reports and was not to talk to the other scientists. In addition Groves demanded that he should sign the Espionage Act. Szilard refused; but in order to keep his work in the Metallurgical Laboratory he was obliged to sign over and sell his patents to the army, while protesting to Groves about duress. The patent attorney who drew up the papers declared that Groves's treatment of Szilard was abominable, like the 'stiff-arm tactics of the Nazis'.

Later Szilard worked on the breeder reactor which produced the new element plutonium when uranium 238 was bombarded by neutrons. Plutonium was used in the bomb dropped on Nagasaki on 9 August 1945. Szilard began to concentrate on the politics of controlling atomic energy. Like Bohr, Franck and others working on the project, he looked to the future, and foresaw a postwar nuclear arms race, unless international control of uranium could be established.

JOSEPH ROTBLAT

The atomic bomb had been developed largely in response to the German threat. When Germany surrendered on 8 May 1945 many of the scientists who had worked on it assumed there was now no need to contemplate its use. Joseph Rotblat was one of them. He was a Polish physicist who had come to England in April 1939 to work with Sir James Chadwick in Liverpool. That August he had returned to Poland to fetch his wife but she was taken acutely ill and he had to return to Britain without her two days before war broke out. As he could not return home he stayed in Britain.

Chadwick was the leading atomic physicist who had discovered the neutron. In due course he became head of the British team at Los Alamos, and in February 1944 Rotblat was chosen to go with him to the United States. In March 1944 Rotblat heard General Groves, head of the Manhattan Project, declare that even after the end of the war in Europe the bomb would still be developed for use as a political, if not as a military, weapon against the Russians. Rotblat, whose wife was still in Poland, was profoundly shocked, and that autumn he resigned from the atomic programme.

His resignation was unprecedented, and it caused a great stir. His motives were immediately suspect. He was accused of being involved in a fantastic plot which included returning to England, joining the RAF and then somehow getting himself flown to the Soviet Union, where he would pass on the 'secret' of the atomic energy programme. (In fact it had already been betrayed by Klaus Fuchs and others.)

Eventually this absurd accusation was dropped and the more credible explanation of 'family reasons' was substituted. Now that Poland was in the process of being liberated, Rotblat intended to go back to find his wife. He never discovered what happened to her, and assumed she must have died in one of the camps. He never remarried.

After Los Alamos he moved into the study of medical aspects of physics; although his career was probably affected by his resignation from the atomic bomb project he made major contributions in his field, and became a world authority on radiation. His final and sweet reward was to win the Nobel Prize in 1995, not for physics, as many of his colleagues had done, but for peace. The prize was well deserved.

At present Joseph Rotblat is President of the Pugwash Conferences on World Affairs, an organization founded in 1957 in response to a manifesto produced by Albert Einstein and Bertrand Russell two years earlier in order to bridge the gap between physicists of the rival nuclear powers, the USA and the Soviet Union. He was knighted in 1998.

There was much discussion after the war about the respective contributions of the United States and Britain to the atomic bomb. There is no doubt that the American effort was by far the greater in the bomb's construction. General Groves said the British contribution was 'helpful but not important' and the Manhattan Project's Official History said it was 'in no sense vital and actually not even important'. These may be fair estimates of the contribution of the two countries to the building of the bomb but certainly not to its concept and design. On the contrary, all the early work on atomic energy, the potential use of atomic fission in a bomb, which could be small enough to be carried in a plane, the use of very pure graphite and the method of separating highly concentrated uranium 235 – all these came from the work of the Europeans.

Incidentally, three divisions at Los Alamos were headed by Europeans, Frisch, Peierls and Bethe, while Teller, a Hungarian, was the main drive behind the H-bomb. It seems bizarre to play down the European contribution. The most crucial advances in the whole process of making an atomic bomb were, we believe, the discovery of Peierls and Frisch that building an atomic weapon was feasible and Simon's work on the separation of uranium isotopes.

Epilogue

No sum of money can adequately and appropriately
express our gratefulness to the British people . . .
What this country of our adoption gave us was not
just a new home and livelihood . . . we also found a
new and better way of life coming from an
atmosphere of political oppression and persecution
. . . we found here a spirit of friendliness, humanity,
tolerance and fairness. It is this way of life with
which some of us, I for one, fell in love. We were
given a new home – not merely a shelter but a true
home. Home is where one strikes roots, where one
has the opportunity of doing the things which . . .
one feels one ought to do in order to fulfil one's life
and thereby gain true happiness.

*Hans Krebs on presenting a cheque from the Jewish
refugees to the British Academy in 1965*

Considering the number, eminence and achievement of German Jewish scientists it is extraordinary that the suicidal policy of anti-Semitism did not do even more damage to Germany than it did. There was an immediate falling-off of standards in German universities in teaching and research but they were not paralysed. It is impossible to estimate what might have happened without anti-Semitism but we do know, according to Admiral Dönitz, head of the German navy, that Germany fell behind the Allies in the U-boat conflict as the war progressed. The Allies were developing new U-boat detection methods using airborne radar against which the German navy had no defence.

For many ex-Germans even to visit their homeland after the war was too much. When he went back to Vienna for a meeting, Max Perutz described to the authors his feelings of doubt and unease. He saw colleagues, acquaintances or even people in the street and wondered what they had done during the war. Had they been Nazis? Had they committed crimes? Had they joined the Jew-baiters? It is a horrible thing to lose confidence in people you expect to trust – hosts, colleagues, anybody.

As a junior army medical officer in Germany in 1948, David Pyke visited Berlin on leave and was shown round a large hospital by a very courteous chief surgeon. It was some years later that Pyke discovered that the surgeon had committed atrocities and was a war criminal. It was difficult to comprehend that an apparently friendly colleague could be such a character.

One story nicely illustrates the depths of some refugees' feelings, even if rather illogically. A woman ex-refugee (mother of the current President of the Royal College of Physicians) living in England found an ingenious way round the difficulty of what to do about returning to Germany. She did not want to go but she and her family were going to Czechoslovakia. They couldn't fly. They could drive across Germany or go all the way round. She finally agreed to drive across the country provided the car windows were kept shut!

One obvious question is: How many of the refugee scientists returned to Germany (or Austria) after the war? The answer is 'hardly any'. A few returned to visit in the early postwar years but none resumed their careers there. Some, such as Franck and Born, did what they could to resurrect the teaching of science in the universities, but they were not always welcomed by the students. In the early days there was often resentment at their defeat. Hitler after all received strong support from the student body.

Many of the scientists not only stayed away from Germany after the war but remained hostile and suspicious, Einstein especially. Nearly all had lost relatives in the Holocaust. The refugees had long since established themselves in the West and their loyalties were fully engaged there. They did not want to go back.

Gradually things improved. Max Delbrück, for example, who was not Jewish and had gone to the USA from scientific choice, helped to set up phage research in German universities, but that was 15 or more years after the end of the war. Wilhelm Feldberg's Foundation, which he created with restitution money he received from the German State, did much to bring individual scientists together in the annual exchange of British and German professors. Feldberg had many close friends and admirers among German physiologists, but they were mostly much younger and had escaped the terrible tarnish of living under Hitler.

Thus Germany not only lost the services of the scientists it forced out of the country in one way or another: it lost them for ever. A whole generation was swept away and replaced only slowly.

The damage that Hitler did to German science, and the slowness of its recovery, is shown by the number of Nobel Prizes Germany won after he came to power.

As we saw in Chapter 1, in the years between 1901 and 1932 Germany won one third of all the science prizes, 33 out of 100. In the next 27 years to 1960 – i.e. including 15 years after the war, she won only eight. (In this period Britain won 21). These were:

1935	H. Speman	Physiology/Medicine
1938	R. Kuhn	Chemistry
1939	G. Domagk	Physiology/Medicine
1944	O. Hahn	Chemistry
1950	O. Diels	Chemistry
1950	K. Alder	Chemistry
1953	H. Staudinger	Chemistry
1954	W. Bothe	Physics

Gradually, very gradually, Germany became once again an equal partner in European and world science.

Research on the atom bomb was a special subject. It is irresistible to speculate on whether Germany could have built a bomb if the Jews had not been expelled – irresistible but futile. Certainly the refugee scientists, from Einstein onwards, contributed enormously to the early developments. Nearly all the preliminary work on the bomb came from European scientists. Indeed, as we know, the realization that a weapon could be made at all came from two German Jews working in England in 1940. From then on an atomic bomb was on the agenda. Its actual construction depended predominantly on the United States. Even then, with all the American commitment, wealth, space and freedom from bombing, they did not build a bomb before the end of the war against Germany.

In our reading and interviewing while writing this book we have often been tempted to criticize – not just the Nazis but the German people for having supported Hitler so overwhelmingly, even German academics for not coming to the help of their Jewish colleagues. It is easy to do so. What would we have done if we had been in the power of such a ruthless, evil regime? After all, the British government did precious little to help before 1939. It did not even understand what manner of force it was up against but thought Hitler was a reasonable being who could be conciliated long after it should have been clear that was impossible. Furthermore, the policy of appeasement was widely supported in Britain until the invasion of Czechoslovakia in March 1939.

The corresponding policy in the United States was detachment – isolation from Europe's problems was highly popular and President Roosevelt, even if he wanted to, could do little to help.

What should individual non-Jewish German scientists have done? It is easy to criticize Heisenberg, for example, for having stayed in Germany in 1939 when war was looming and he had invitations to stay in America. The arguments against his leaving were forcefully put by Max Planck (in the quotation at the head of Chapter 8). Heisenberg can certainly be criticized for things he said – for example, that the Nazis should have been left in power for 50 years then they would become 'quite decent' – to Francis Simon, who had lost relatives in the Holocaust. His reasons for staying in Germany were powerfully, if not predominantly, idealistic; he wanted to preserve what he could of German science. Max Planck, the dean of German science, could never have brought himself to leave Germany, so overwhelming was his feeling for preserving German science, but this attitude brought him into head-on collision with Einstein. Planck finally admitted after the war that Simon, who had left in 1933, had been right to leave.

Certainly outspoken support of Jewish colleagues was rare among non-Jewish academics. Otto Krayer's case shows well the position they were in. When he, an assistant professor in Berlin, refused to accept a senior position vacated by the expulsion of a Jewish colleague in Düsseldorf and wrote publicly to give his reasons, he was dismissed from the university and expelled instantly. It had not been an easy decision for him to make. He was not then famous and his future was uncertain – he had no job to go to and had to move his family to an entirely new environment. Fortunately, through Feldberg and other friends, he found jobs in England and Beirut before reaching the United States, where he eventually became head of pharmacology at Harvard, a more eminent appointment than any in Germany. Even then some Americans criticized Harvard for appointing a non-American.

The decision to leave Germany therefore can never have been easy. Heisenberg may have been speaking a truth when he said he almost envied his Jewish colleagues – they had no choice. Feldberg felt the same. 'I was very lucky,' said this perennial optimist.

We have concentrated on the effect of the Nazis on the refugees' careers. But it was, of course, more than merely work, vital though it was, which was affected. Their family life was disrupted, marriages destroyed and children left without parents.

Hans Krebs, when he left Germany in a hurry in 1933, left behind his father, who had recently remarried and had a young daughter. His father besought Krebs to take care of his young wife and child in the future, but Krebs did not see them again until after the war, when he sought them out in the wreckage and took care of them.

In some cases when refugees said goodbye to their relatives who were staying (or could not find anywhere to go) they never saw them again. There were few refugees who, however promptly they emigrated and tried to bring relatives with them, did not lose family members in the Holocaust. It is easy for us to realize that all German Jews were in danger from the moment Hitler came to power, but things were by no means so clear in the early months and years – the fury would pass, calmer voices would prevail – nothing like Hitler's anti-Semitism had ever happened before. Many may have wanted to leave Germany but left it too late.

Some children were sent to England alone under the famous *Kindertransports*. This organized journeys shortly before the outbreak of war to rescue children of parents trapped in Germany or Austria. Some never saw their parents again; most seem to have made a splendid adaptation to English life.

One boy of 13 was put on a *Kindertransport* from Vienna to Britain in 1939. He didn't see his parents for 12 years, including the whole period of the war and six years afterwards. By that time he had qualified as a doctor at Edinburgh and was thoroughly at home in his new family there. One reason for mentioning this young man is that he grew up to be one of the most original professors of metabolic medicine in Britain. He even showed that something the great Krebs had said could not happen did happen (lactate was converted into glycogen in muscle). This man is still alive and well. He is Robert Mahler, great nephew of the composer. He is not only a brilliant academic but an equally good and kindly clinician. This is not an invariable combination. His early traumatic transplantation from home and country does not seem to have done him any harm.

Another Jewish boy who left Germany at about the same age and time and also achieved great success in England was Leslie Brent. Life had become so impossible for Jewish children in Berlin by 1936 that his parents put him in a Jewish orphanage. After *Kristallnacht*, two years later, many *Kindertransport* groups left Berlin and Leslie Brent was selected for the first one, whose destination neither he nor his parents knew. It was Dovercourt in Kent and when he got there he was selected by the headmistress of a German-Jewish co-educational school which had moved there five years earlier. He was kindly treated and kept in touch with the headmistress for many years but he never saw his parents or sister again. He joined the army as soon as he could and became an officer at 19 while still an enemy alien. After the war he studied zoology at Birmingham University, where in 1951 Peter Medawar took him on as a postgraduate student. Within two years he had his name on the paper in *Nature* reporting immunological tolerance. This was the basis of transplantation biology and won Medawar the Nobel Prize. So Leslie Brent made a very quick contribution in this country's science at the highest level. Later he became Professor of Immunology at St Mary's Hospital Medical School, London.

We have come across tragic and amusing stories of marriages broken or manipulated in the process of emigrating.

Cornelius Medvei was Hungarian. He moved to Vienna, as so many Hungarians did, to advance his career (in endocrinology). He was doing very well when Hitler came in 1938 and he had to leave. His wife was not Jewish and decided not to go with him. Medvei spent the rest of his career in London, much of it at St Bartholomew's Hospital. He married an English girl soon after coming to England and they were blissfully happy until she died 40 years later. Soon after the war ended Medvei heard from his first wife that she would now like to join him. It was too late.

Elizabeth Beck was a laboratory technician in Berlin. She was due to marry a doctor who was not Jewish and did not know that she was. Her mother made her tell him. She did, all was well and they got married, but did not have any children. When official anti-Semitism got worse they agreed to a divorce of convenience. They would go on living together. As war threatened they drifted apart and he moved to Munich. While there he told a friend he had never intended to have children by 'that Jew'. Elizabeth Beck moved to England just before the war, and did very well in neuropathology, working at the Institute of Neurology in London on brain anatomy as studied in patients who had undergone frontal lobectomy. Soon after the war ended she got a letter from a Munich lawyer saying that her ex-husband was coming before a de-Nazification court and would she testify that he had never been a Nazi supporter. She refused.

Another marriage broken in a similar way was that of a pair of dentists in Mainz, he Jewish, she Catholic. They were earning very well, much of their income going on Rhenish wine, in which she was a great expert. When he left for England just after *Kristallnacht* she said that she would join him when he earned enough to keep her in the wine to which she was accustomed. In the meantime, for reasons of political prudence, she would officially divorce him. After the war she wanted to resume their marriage in England but by this time he was happily married to an English girl. They sent her food parcels, which did not include bottles of wine.

With Egon Kodicek and his wife the situation was reversed: they had a divorce of convenience. He was a Jewish nutritionist and had to get out of Prague. She was not Jewish and could leave only if she divorced him. She started proceedings only to stop them when she heard that he had escaped – they stayed married for the rest of their lives.

Some in the West were very willing to be deceived. During the 1936 Olympic Games in Berlin the ferocious anti-Semitism was put under cover. The many competitors and spectators were shown the soft, smooth face of Germany and were duly impressed. Immense trouble and expense had been taken and a huge new stadium built. Jews, previously excluded from the German team, were allowed to compete and some who had fled to England were brought back and included among the competitors. Outsiders who had been suspicious about coming to the Games could see perfectly well that they were being deceived but did not object.

Anti-Semitic slogans on the streets and in the newspapers were forbidden for the two months of the Games. There were some revealing episodes such as Hitler's refusal 'to shake hands with this Negro' (Jesse Owens, the champion sprinter and long jumper of the Games) but few people noticed them. The 1936 Olympics were a propaganda triumph for Hitler. The millions of visitors were persuaded that the horror stories they had heard at home of maltreatment of Jews and others were untrue, or at least greatly exaggerated.

When the Games were over the reality quickly re-emerged. The apparent gullibility came from an 'active willingness to be deceived' which was, partially, understandable: it was still less than 20 years since the horrors of the First World War. Another war would presumably be a repetition of that, only worse. It took some courage in those days to proclaim that to be ready for another war was the only way to stop Hitler.

There were many reasons why we in the West were slow to oppose Hitler fully. Sixty years later we cannot tell how we would have acted in the great difficulties of those times. We know how we *ought* to have acted and, before it was too late, we did. In these pages we have hesitated to criticize those who were slow to see the right course of action. The people who found the situation most difficult were the refugees themselves. They had had the horror of escaping from their country and then finding themselves in another which seemed to have no idea of the danger of Hitler. If they could not rouse their host country to realize what was happening in time the refugees would be the first to be destroyed.

In A. V. Hill's (unpublished) papers at the Royal Society is a comment in a note he sent to a colleague from his days at the Academic Assistance Council: 'If a similar crisis were to happen again, the same people would come running.' That nicely sums up the reaction of the British scientific community to the great challenge of the Nazis' persecution. The great majority of the scientific emigrants were young and unknown people. 'Those who later made worthwhile contributions were able to do so because their host countries generously gave them the chance that Germany denied them.'

In the end this extraordinary story of the scientific refugees comes out well. That was largely because of the rescue of the refugees by the quick-acting amateurs of the AAC, William Beveridge and A. V. Hill, helped by the ever-active Tess Simpson and many others.

This was Britain at its best.

Appendix I
Nobel Prize Winners
Who Left Their Universities

Seven already had the Prize; 20 won it later.

Name	Nationality	Emigrated to	Date of Prize
R. Willstätter	German	Switzerland	1915
F. Haber	German	UK	1918
A Einstein	German	USA	1921
O. Meyerhof	German	France/USA	1922
G. Hertz	German	Germany★	1925
J. Franck	German	USA	1925
E. Schrödinger	Austrian	UK	1933
O. Loewi	Austrian	UK/USA★★	1936
P. Debye	Dutch	USA	1936
V. Hess	Austrian	USA	1936
E. Fermi	Italian	USA	1938
O. Stern	German	USA	1943
G. de Hevesy	Hungarian	Sweden	1943
W. Pauli	Austrian	Switzerland/USA	1945
E. Chain	Russian/German	UK	1945
F. Bloch	Swiss	USA	1952
H. Krebs	German	UK	1953
F. Lipmann	Russian/German	Denmark/USA	1953
M. Born	German	UK	1954

E. Segrè	Italian	USA	1959
M. Perutz	Austrian	UK	1962
H. Bethe	German	UK/USA	1964
K. Bloch	German	Switzerland/USA	1964
M. Delbrück	German	USA	1969
B. Katz	German	UK	1970
G. Herzberg	German	Canada	1971
D. Gabor	Hungarian	UK	1971

★ He went to work for Siemens, Berlin.
★★ Before Hitler came to Austria.

Appendix II
The Frisch-Peierls Memorandum

This is the memorandum which Rudolf Peierls and Otto Frisch wrote in March 1940 anticipating the possibility of an atomic bomb. They foresaw its features and implications with astonishing accuracy. The memorandum was sent to the chief scientist in the British government and was the trigger which set the whole atomic bomb project in action.

The attached detailed report concerns the possibility of constructing a 'super-bomb' which utilises the energy stored in atomic nuclei as a source of energy. The energy liberated in the explosion of such a super-bomb is about the same as that produced by the explosion of 1,000 tons of dynamite. This energy is liberated in a small volume, in which it will, for an instant, produce a temperature comparable to that in the interior of the sun. The blast from such an explosion would destroy life in a wide area. The size of this area is difficult to estimate, but it will probably cover the centre of a big city.

In addition, some part of the energy set free by the bomb goes to produce radioactive substances, and these will emit very powerful and dangerous radiations. The effects of these radiations is greatest immediately after the explosion, but it decays only gradually and even for days after the explosion any person entering the affected area will be killed.

Some of this radioactivity will be carried along with the wind and will spread the contamination; several miles downwind this may kill people.

In order to produce such a bomb it is necessary to treat a substantial amount of uranium by a process which will separate from the uranium its light isotope (U235) of which it contains about 0.7 percent. Methods for the separation of such isotopes have recently been developed. They are slow and they have not until now been applied to uranium, whose chemical properties give rise to technical difficulties. But these difficulties are by no means insuperable. We have not sufficient experience with large-scale chemical plant to give a reliable estimate of the cost, but it is certainly not prohibitive.

It is a property of these super-bombs that there exists a 'critical size' of about one pound. A quantity of the separated uranium isotope that exceeds the critical amount is explosive; yet a quantity less than the critical amount is absolutely safe. The bomb would therefore be manufactured in two (or more) parts, each being less than the critical size, and in transport all danger of a premature explosion would be avoided if these parts were kept at a distance of a few inches from each other. The bomb would be provided with a mechanism that brings the two parts together when the bomb is intended to go off. Once the parts are joined to form a block which exceeds the critical amount, the effect of the penetrating radiation always present in the atmosphere will initiate the explosion within a second or so.

The mechanism which brings the parts of the bomb together must be arranged to work fairly rapidly because of the possibility of the bomb exploding when the critical conditions have just only been reached. In this case the explosion will be far less powerful. It is never possible to exclude this altogether, but one can easily ensure that only, say, one bomb out of 100 will fail in this way, and since in any case the explosion is strong enough to destroy the bomb itself, this point is not serious.

We do not feel competent to discuss the strategic value of such a bomb, but the following conclusions seem certain:

1. As a weapon, the super-bomb would be practically irresistible. There is no material or structure that could be expected to resist the force of the explosion. If one thinks of using the bomb for breaking through a line of fortifications, it should be kept in mind that the

radioactive radiations will prevent anyone from approaching the affected territory for several days; they will equally prevent defenders from reoccupying the affected positions. The advantage would lie with the side which can determine most accurately just when it is safe to re-enter the area; this is likely to be the aggressor, who knows the location of the bomb in advance.

2. Owing to the spread of radioactive substances with the wind, the bomb could probably not be used without killing large numbers of civilians, and this may make it unsuitable as a weapon for use by this country. (Use as a depth charge near a naval base suggests itself, but even there it is likely that it would cause great loss of civilian life by flooding and by the radioactive radiations.)

3. We have no information that the same idea has also occurred to other scientists but since all the theoretical data bearing on this problem are published, it is quite conceivable that Germany is, in fact, developing this weapon. Whether this is the case is difficult to find out, since the plant for the separation of isotopes need not be of such a size as to attract attention. Information that could be helpful in this respect would be data about the exploitation of the uranium mines under German control (mainly in Czechoslovakia) and about any recent German purchases of uranium abroad. It is likely that the plant would be controlled by Dr K. Clusius (Professor of Physical Chemistry in Munich University), the inventor of the best method for separating isotopes, and therefore information as to his where-abouts and status might also give an important clue. At the same time it is quite possible that nobody in Germany has yet realized that the separation of the uranium isotopes would make the construction of a super-bomb possible. Hence it is of extreme importance to keep this report secret since any rumour about the connection between uranium separation and a super-bomb may set a German scientist thinking along the right lines.

4. If one works on the assumption that Germany is, or will be, in the possession of this weapon, it must be realized that no shelters are available that would be effective and that could be used on a large scale. The most effective reply would be a counter-threat with a similar bomb. Therefore it seems to us important to start production as soon and as rapidly as possible, even if it is not intended to use the bomb as a means of attack. Since the separation of the necessary

amount of uranium is, in the most favourable circumstances, a matter of several months, it would obviously be too late to start production when such a bomb is known to be in the hands of Germany, and the matter seems, therefore, very urgent.

5. As a measure of precaution, it is important to have detection squads available in order to deal with the radioactive effects of such a bomb. Their task would be to approach the danger zone with measuring instruments, to determine the extent and probable duration of the danger and to prevent people from entering the danger zone. This is vital since the radiations kill instantly only in very strong doses whereas weaker doses produce delayed effects and hence near the edges of the danger zone people would have no warning until it is too late. For their own protection, the detection squads would enter the danger zone in motor-cars or airplanes which would be armoured with lead plates, which absorb most of the dangerous radiation. The cabin would have to be hermetically sealed and oxygen carried in cylinders because of the danger from contaminated air. The detection staff would have to know exactly the greatest dose of radiation to which a human being can safely be exposed for a short time. This safety limit is not at present known with sufficient accuracy and further biological research for this purpose is urgently required.

As regards the reliability of the conclusions outlined above, it may be said that they are not based on direct experiments, since nobody has ever built a super-bomb yet, but they are mostly based on facts which, by recent research in nuclear physics, have been very safely established. The only uncertainty concerns the critical size for the bomb. We are fairly confident that the critical size is roughly a pound or so, but for this estimate we have to rely on certain theoretical ideas which have not been positively confirmed. If the critical size were appreciably larger than we believe it to be, the technical difficulties in the way of constructing the bomb would be enhanced. The point can be definitely settled as soon as a small amount of uranium has been separated, and we think that in view of the importance of the matter immediate steps should be taken to reach at least this stage; meanwhile it is also possible to carry out certain experiments which, while they cannot settle the question with absolute finality, could, if their result were positive, give strong support to our conclusions.

Appendix III
'That Was the War: Enemy Alien'

The account of his internment by Max Perutz
(published in the *New Yorker*, 12 August 1985)

It was a cloudless Sunday morning in May of 1940. The policeman who came to arrest me said that I would be gone for only a few days, but I packed for a long journey. I said goodbye to my parents.

From Cambridge, they took me and more than a hundred other people to Bury St Edmunds, a small garrison town twenty-five miles to the east, and there they locked us up in a school. We were herded into a huge empty shed cast into gloom by blacked-out skylights thirty feet above us. A fellow-prisoner kept staring at a blank piece of white paper, and I wondered why until he showed me that a tiny pinhole in the blackout paint projected a sharp image of the sun's disc, on which one could observe the outlines of sunspots. He also taught me how to work out the distances of planets and stars from their parallaxes and the distances of nebulae from the red shifts of their spectra. He was a warm-hearted and gentle German Roman Catholic who had found refuge from the Nazis at the Observatory of Cambridge University. Years later, he became Astronomer Royal for Scotland. In the spring of 1940, he was one of hundreds of German and Austrian refugee scholars, mostly Jewish and all anti-Nazi, who had been rounded up in the official panic created by the German attack on the Low Countries and the imminent threat of an invasion of Britain.

After a week or so at Bury, we were taken to Liverpool and then to an as yet unoccupied housing estate at nearby Huyton, where we

247

camped for some weeks in bleak, empty semi-detached two-storey houses, several of us crowded into each bare room, with nothing to do except lament successive Allied defeats and worry whether England could hold out. Our camp commander was a white-moustached veteran of the last war; then a German had been a German, but now the subtle new distinctions between friend and foe bewildered him. Watching a group of internees with skullcaps and curly side-whiskers arrive at his camp, he mused, 'I had no idea there were so many Jews among the Nazis.' He pronounced it 'Nasis.'

Lest we escape to help our mortal enemies, the Army next took us to Douglas, a seaside resort on the Isle of Man, where we were quartered in Victorian boarding houses. I shared my room with two bright German medical researchers, who opened my eyes to the hidden world of living cells – a welcome diversion, lifting my thoughts from my empty stomach. On some days, the soldiers took us out for country walks, and we ambled along hedge-flanked lanes two abreast, like girls from a boarding school. One day near the end of June, one of our guards said casually, 'The bastards have signed.' His terse message signified France's surrender, which left Britain to fight the Germans alone.

A few days later, tight-lipped Army doctors came to vaccinate all the men under thirty – an ominous event, whose sinister purpose we soon learned. On July 3, we were taken back to Liverpool, and from there we embarked on the large troopship *Ettrick* for an unknown destination. About twelve hundred of us were herded together, tier upon tier, in one of its airless holds. Locked up in another hold were German prisoners of war, whom we envied for their Army rations. On our second day out, we learned that a German U-boat had sunk another troopship, the *Arandora Star*, which had been crammed with interned Austrian and German refugees and with Italians who were being deported overseas. More than six hundred of the fifteen hundred people aboard were drowned. After that, we were issued life belts.

Suspended like bats from the mess decks' ceilings, row upon row of men swayed to and fro in their hammocks. In heavy seas, their eruptions turned the floors into quagmires emitting a sickening stench. Cockroaches asserted their prior tenancy of the ship. To this revolting scene, Prince Frederick of Prussia, then living in England, restored hygiene and order by recruiting a gang of fellow-students with mops and buckets – a public-spirited action that earned him everyone's respect, so that he, grandson of the Kaiser and cousin of King George VI, became king of the Jews. Looking every inch a prince, he used his royal standing to persuade the officers in charge that we were not the Fifth Columnists their War Office instructions made us out to be. The commanding colonel called us scum of the earth all the same, and once, in a temper, ordered his soldiers to set their bayonets upon us. They judged differently and ignored him. One day, I passed out with a fever. When I came to, in a clean sick bay that had been established by young German doctors, we were steaming up the broad estuary of the St Lawrence River, and on July 13 we finally anchored off gleaming-white Quebec city. The Canadian Army took us to a camp of wooden huts on the citadel high above the town, close to the battlefield where the English General James Wolfe had beaten the French in 1759. The soldiers made us strip naked so they could search us for lice, and they also confiscated all our money and other useful possessions, but I forestalled them by dropping the contents of my wallet out the window of the hut while we were waiting to be searched, and went around to pick them up the next day, when the soldiers had gone. Sometimes jewels are safest on a scrap heap.

In Canada, our status changed from that of internees to that of civilian prisoners of war, entitling us to clothing – navy jackets with a red patch on the back – and army rations, which were welcome after our first two days when we were without food. Even so, the fleshpots of Canada were no consolation for our new status, which made us fear that we would remain interned for the duration of the war and, worse still, that in the event of England's defeat we would be sent back to Germany to be liquidated by Hitler. To have been arrested, interned, and deported as an enemy alien by the English, whom I had regarded as my friends, made me more bitter than to have lost freedom itself. Having first been rejected as a Jew by my native Austria, which I loved, I now found myself rejected as a German by my adopted country. Since we were kept incommunicado at first, I could not know that most of my English friends and scientific colleagues were campaigning to get the anti-Nazi refugees, and especially the many scholars among them, released. I had come to Cambridge from Vienna as a graduate student in 1936 and had begun my life's research work on the structure of proteins. In March of 1940, a few weeks before my arrest, I had proudly won my Ph.D. with a thesis on the crystal structure of hemoglobin – the protein of the red blood cells. My parents had joined me in Cambridge shortly before the outbreak of war; I wondered when I would see them again. But, most of all, I and the more enterprising among my comrades felt frustrated at having to idle away our time instead of helping in the war against Hitler. I never imagined that before long I would be returning to Canada [*sic*] as a free man, engaged in one of the most imaginative and absurd projects of the Second World War.

Our camp offered a majestic panorama of the St Lawrence and of the lush green country stretching away to the south of it. As one stifling-hot languid day followed another, freedom beckoned from the mountains on the horizon, beyond the United States border, I remembered the Bishop's advice to King Richard II: 'My lord, wise men ne'er sit and wail their woes, but presently prevent the ways to wail.' How could I escape through the barbed-wire fence? Suppose I surmounted that hurdle without being spotted by the guards, who stood on watchtowers with their machine guns trained on us? Who would hide me after my absence had been discovered at the daily roll call? How could I persuade the Americans to let me join my brother and sister there, and not lock me up on Ellis Island? These questions turned over and over in my mind as I lay on my back in the grass at night, listening to the faint hooting of distant trains and watching the delicately colored flashes of the northern lights dance across the sky. Soon I began to dream of jumping on goods wagons in the dark or of fighting my way across the frontier through dense mountain forests – or just of girls.

As a Cambridge Ph.D. of four months' standing, I found myself the doyen of the camp's scholars, and organized a camp university. Several of my Quebec teaching staff have since risen to fame, though in different ways. The Viennese mathematics student Hermann Bondi, now Sir Hermann, taught a brilliant course in vector analysis. His towering forehead topped by battlements of curly black hair, he arrived at his lectures without any notes and yet solved all his complex examples on the blackboard. Bondi owes his knighthood to his office as chief scientist at Britain's Ministry of Defense, and his fame to the steady-state theory of the universe. This theory postulates that, as the universe expands, matter is continuously being created, so that its density in the universe remains constant with time. A universe like that need not have started with a big bang, because it would never have known a beginning and it would have no end. Bondi developed that ingenious theory with another Viennese interned with us – Thomas Gold, who, like him, was still an undergraduate at Cambridge, and who is now professor of astronomy at Cornell University. The theory's third author was Fred Hoyle, the Cambridge cosmologist and science-fiction writer.

Theoretical physics was taught to us lucidly by Klaus Fuchs, the tall, austere, aloof son of a German Protestant pastor who had been persecuted by Hitler for being a Social Democrat. Klaus Fuchs himself had joined the German Communist Party shortly before Hitler came to power, and fled to England soon afterward to study physics at Bristol University. After his release from internment in Canada, he was recruited to work for the atomic-bomb project, first in Birmingham and then at Los Alamos, and when the war was over he was appointed head of the theoretical-physics section of the newly established British Atomic Energy Research Establishment, at Harwell. Everywhere, Fuchs was highly regarded for his excellent scientific work, and at Harwell he was also noted for his deep concern with security. Then, in the summer of 1949, just before the explosion of the first Russian atomic bomb, the Federal Bureau of Investigation found reason to suspect that a British scientist had passed atomic information to the Russians, and the Bureau's description in some ways fitted Fuchs. After several interrogations, Fuchs broke down and confessed – in January of 1950 – that from the very start of his work he had passed on to the Russians most of what he knew of the Anglo-American project, including the design of the first plutonium bomb. A few days after Fuchs' conviction for espionage, the Prime Minister, Clement Attlee, assured Parliament that the security services had repeatedly made 'the proper inquiries' about Fuchs and had found nothing to make them suspect him of being a fanatical Communist. Neither had I gathered this during my contacts with him in Canada, but when I recently said so to an old colleague he told me that Fuchs and he had belonged to the same

Communist cell while they were students at Bristol. 'The proper inquiries' cannot have been all that searching.

Having no inkling of the tortuous mind that later made Fuchs betray the countries and the friends that had given him shelter, I simply benefited from his excellent teaching. In my own lectures, I showed my students how to unravel the arrangement of atoms in crystals, and I spent the rest of my time trying to learn some of the advanced mathematics that I had missed at school and at the university.

The curfew was at nine-thirty. The windows of our hut were crossed with barbed wire. Its doors were locked, and buckets were put out. Stacked into double bunks, about a hundred of us tried to sleep in one room where the air could be cut with a knife. In the bunk above me was my closest friend from student days in Vienna. We had roughed it together in the mosquito-ridden swamps of northern Lapland and had almost suffered shipwreck on a small sealer in the stormy Arctic Ocean. These adventures had inured us to the physical hardships of internment, but the exhilarating sense of freedom that they had instilled in us made our captivity even harder to bear. Lacking other forms of exercise, we made a sport of reading our jailers' regulation-ridden minds. One day, the prisoners were told that each could send a postcard to his next of kin in England, but two weeks later all the postcards were returned – without explanation, at first. The camp seethed with frustration and angry rumors, but my friend and I guessed that after leaving the postcards lying around for a couple of weeks the Army censor returned them all because not every card carried its sender's full name. It took a month more before my card reached Cambridge, with the laconic message that Prisoner of War Max Perutz was safe and well.

In time, we learned through rumor that our scenic and efficient camp was to be dismantled and we were to be divided between two other camps. Would friend be separated from friend? By age or by the alphabet? It occurred to me that the pious Quebecois might divide us into believers and heretics – that is to say, into Roman Catholics and the rest – and my hunch was soon confirmed. Since my Viennese friend was a Protestant and I was a Roman Catholic, we were destined for different camps. Adversity tightens friendships. Our familiar Viennese idiom, my friend's keen sense of the ridiculous, and shared memories of carefree student days with girls, skiing and mountain climbing, had helped us to escape from the crowd of strangers around us into our own private world. I decided to stay with the Protestants and the Jews, who also included many scientists, and soon found a Protestant who preferred to join the Catholics. Like Ferrando and Guglielmo, the handsome young swains in *Così Fan Tutte*, we swapped identities. The false Max Perutz was sent with the faithful to the heaven of a well-appointed Army camp, while I, the real one, was dispatched with the heretics and Jews to the purgatory of a locomotive shed near Sherbrooke, Quebec. To start with it had five cold-water taps and six latrines for seven hundred and twenty men.

Some weeks later, our comedy of errors was unmasked. The stern camp commander, though he was impressed by the purity of my motives, sentenced me to three days in the local police prison. Here was privacy at last – yet not quite. They locked me up in a cage resembling a monkey's in an old-fashioned zoo. It had no chair, no bed – only some wooden planks to rest on. Unlike the prisoner in Oscar Wilde's *Ballad of Reading Gaol*, I did not look

> With such a wistful eye
> Upon that little tent of blue
> Which prisoners call the sky,
> And at every drifting cloud that went
> With sails of silver by

because I never even saw the sky. But I had smuggled in several books inside my baggy plus fours, so I was not as bored as the poor soldier who had to march up and down on the other side of the iron grille to guard me. My reading was undisturbed and my sleep interrupted only by the occasional drunk; the little mites burrowed into my skin without waking me. Only when they had made themselves at home there during the weeks that followed did the scabies rash keep me awake at night.

Back in the Sherbrooke camp, where my spirits sagged at the prospect of wasted years, the camp commander summoned me again – this time to tell me that my release had been ordered by the British Home Office and that I had also been offered a professorship by the

New School for Social Research, in New York City. He then asked me if I wanted to return to England or remain in the camp until my release to the United States could be arranged. I replied that I wanted to return to England, and this drew the admiring comment that I would make a fine soldier. I have never heard that said by anyone else, before or since, but what led me to my decision was that my parents and my research were in England, and from the safe distance of Sherbrooke the U-boats and the blitz did not frighten me. My American professorship had been arranged by the Rockefeller Foundation as part of a rescue campaign for the scholars whom the foundation had supported before the war broke out, and in principle it would have qualified me for an American immigration visa, but I was sure that as a prisoner of war without a passport I would never get it. The camp commander raised my hopes that I would be sent home soon.

From our perch on the citadel of Quebec, we had been able to watch the ships go by on the St Lawrence, but in the locomotive shed we could only watch the men line up for the latrines. In Quebec, we had had a room in a hut set aside for quiet study, but here among the milling, chatting crowd of men my assaults on differential equations petered out in confusion. Camp committees, locked in futile arguments over trivial issues, were chaired by budding lawyers fond of hearing themselves talk. In excruciating boredom, I waited impotently from day to day for permission to leave, but weeks passed and my captivity dragged on. There was little news from home except for hints that my father, who was then sixty-three and had been an Anglophile from youth, had been interned on the Isle of Man. He shared that fate, I learned afterward, with a frail, meticulous old Viennese with sensitively cut features who was distraught at having his life's work interrupted for a second time. This was Otto Deutsch, the author of the then incomplete catalogue of Franz Schubert's collected works. He finished it in later years at Cambridge.

Early in December, I was among some prisoners destined for release from my camp and from several others who were at last put on a train going east. From its windows, the snow-clad forest looked the same each day, so that we seemed to move merely to stay in the same place, like Alice running with the Red Queen. I had been sad at leaving my Viennese friend behind but was overjoyed to find his father – whom he had feared drowned on the *Arandora Star* – among the prisoners on the train. Some weeks earlier, the father, on discovering that his son was interned in another Canadian camp, had asked to be transferred there, and he was disconsolate that instead the Army had now put him on a train carrying him even farther away. The train finally dumped all of us in yet another camp – this one in a forest near Fredericton, New Brunswick. No one told us why or for how long. In the Arctic weather, I contracted a bronchial cold that made the dark winter hours seem endless. My father had taught me to regard Jews as champions of tolerant liberalism, but here I was shocked to run into Jews with an outlook as warped and brutal as that of Nazi Storm Troopers. They were members of the Stern Gang, which later became notorious in Israel for many senseless murders, including the murder of the Swedish Count Folke Bernadotte, whom the United Nations had appointed as mediator in the Arab-Israeli conflict.

At Christmas, we were finally taken to Halifax, where we were met by one of Britain's prison commissioners – the shrewd and humane Alexander Paterson, sent out by the Home Office to interview any of the internees who wanted to return to Britain. His mission was stimulated by public criticism – 'Why not lock up General de Gaulle?' was one of the sarcastic headlines in a London paper that helped to make the War Cabinet change its policy. Paterson explained that it had been impossible to ship any of us home earlier, because the Canadians had insisted that prisoners of war must not be moved without a military escort, yet had refused either to release us in Canada or to escort us to England, on the ground that our internment was Britain's affair. The British War Office had now fulfilled the letter of the regulation by detailing a single Army captain to take us home.

Chaperoned by one urbane captain, two hundred and eighty of us embarked on the small Belgian liner *Thysville*, which had been requisitioned by the British Army complete with its crew, including a superb Chinese cook. From this moment, we were treated as passengers, not prisoners, but I became fretful once again when days passed and the *Thysville* had not cast off her moorings; no one had told us that we had to wait for the assembling of a big convoy. As we finally steamed out to sea, I counted more than thirty ships, of all kinds and sizes, spread over a huge area. At first, Canadian destroyers escorted us, but we soon passed out of their range, and our remaining escort consisted of only one merchant cruiser – a passenger liner with a few guns on deck – and a single submarine, neither of them a match for the powerful German battleships *Scharnhorst* and *Gneisenau*, which, so our radio told us, prowled the Atlantic not far from our route. We steamed at only nine knots – the speed of the slowest cargo boat – and took a far-northerly course, trusting to the Arctic night to hide us. Both my Viennese friend and his father were on board.

Early in the voyage, I stood at the rail imagining a torpedo in every breaker. Like the Ancient Mariner,

Alas, (thought I, and my heart beat loud)

How fast she nears and nears

But time soon blunted my fears, and I began to enjoy the play of wind and waves. I slept in a warm cabin between clean sheets, took a hot bath, brimful each morning, ate my meals from white table linen in my friends' company, walked in the bracing air on deck or retired to read in a quiet saloon. Toward the end of the third week, we were cheered by the sight of large black flying boats of the Coastal Command circling over us, like sheepdogs running around their flock, to keep the U-boats at bay. One gray winter morning, the entire convoy anchored safely in Liverpool Harbor. On landing, I was formally released from internment and handed a railway ticket to Cambridge, and I was told to register with the police there as an enemy alien. When I presented myself at a friend's house near London that night, she found me looking so fit that she thought I must have returned from a holiday cruise, but then she admired the elaborate needlework by which I had kept my tweed jacket in one piece for all those months, so as not to have to wear the prisoners' blue jacket with the large red circle on the back. Next morning, at the Cambridge station, our faithful lab mechanic greeted me not as an enemy alien but as a long-lost friend; he brought me the good news that my father had been released from the Isle of Man a few weeks earlier and that both he and my mother were safe in Cambridge. That was in January of 1941.

Selected Bibliography

Arms, Nancy, *A Prophet in Two Countries* (Pergamon, 1966).

Bentwich, N., *Rescue and Achievements of Refugee Scholars* (Nijhoff, The Hague, 1953).

Beveridge, W., *A Defence of Free Learning* (Oxford University Press, 1959).

Beyerchen, A. D., *Scientists Under Hitler: Politics and the Physics Community in the Third Reich* (Yale University Press, 1977).

Born, M., *My Life: Recollections of a Nobel Laureate* (Taylor & Francis, 1978).

——*Born–Einstein Letters* (Macmillan, 1971).

Chargaff, E., *Heraclitean Fire* (Rockefeller, 1978).

Clark, R.W., *JBS: The Life of J.B.S. Haldane* (Hodder & Stoughton, 1968).

——*Einstein: The Life and Times* (Hodder & Stoughton, 1979).

——*The Greatest Power on Earth* (Sidgwick & Jackson, 1980).

——*Chain: The Life of Ernst Chain* (Weidenfeld & Nicolson, 1985).

Duggan, S. and Drury, B., *Rescue of Refugee Scholars* (Macmillan, 1948).

Engelmann, B., *Germany Without Jews* (Bantam, 1984).

Fermi, Laura, *Illustrious Immigrants: The Intellectual Migration from Europe* (Chicago University Press, 1968).

Fest, J. C., *The Face of the Third Reich* (Penguin, 1972).

Fleming, D. and Bailyn, B., *The Intellectual Migration* (Harvard University Press, 1967).

Friedländer, S., *Nazi Germany and the Jews, 1933–9* (Weidenfeld & Nicolson, 1997).

Frisch, O., *What Little I Remember* (Cambridge University Press, 1979).

Gillman, P. and L., *'Collar the Lot': How Britain Expelled its Wartime Refugees* (Quartet Books, 1980).

Gowing, Margaret, *Britain and Atomic Energy* (Macmillan, 1964).

Grunberger, R., *A Social History of the Third Reich* (Penguin, 1971).

Hartshorne, E. Y., *The German Universities and National Socialism* (Allen & Unwin, 1937).

Heilbron, J. L., *The Dilemmas of an Upright Man: Max Planck as Spokesman for German Science* (University of California, 1986).

Jungk, R., *Brighter Than a Thousand Suns* (Harcourt Brace, 1958).

Klemperer, V., *I Shall Bear Witness* (Weidenfeld & Nicolson, 1998).

Krebs, H. (with Anne Martin), *Reminiscences and Reflections* (Oxford University Press, 1981).

Lafitte, F., *The Internment of Aliens* (Penguin, 2nd edn. 1988).

Lanouette, W. with Silard, B., *Genius in the Shadows: A Biography of Leo Szilard* (Scribners, 1992).

Mendelssohn, K., *The World of Walther Nernst: The Rise and Fall of German Science* (Macmillan, 1973).

Moore, W., *Schrödinger: Life and Thought* (Cambridge University Press, 1984).

Müller-Hill, B., *Murderous Science* (Oxford University Press, 1988).

Nachmansohn, D., *German-Jewish Pioneers in Science, 1900–1933* (Springer, 1978).

Peierls, R., *Bird of Passage* (Princeton University Press, 1985).

Perutz, M., 'That Was the War: Enemy Alien', *New Yorker*, 12 August 1985.

Powers, T., *Heisenberg's War: The Secret History of the German Bomb* (Penguin, 1993).

Rhodes, R., *The Making of the Atomic Bomb* (Penguin, 1980).

Schrödinger, E., *What is Life? Mind and Matter* (Cambridge University Press, 1967; 1st edn. 1944).

Sherman, A. J., *Island Refuge* (Frank Cass, 1973).

Simpson, T. (ed. Cooper), *Refugee Scholars* (published privately, 1992).

Uhlman, Fred, *Reunion* (Harvill Press, 1971).

Weisskopf, V., *The Joy of Insight* (Basic Books, 1991).

Wheeler-Bennett, J. W., *The Nemesis of Power* (Macmillan, 1956).

Wistrich, R. S., *Anti-Semitism: The Longest Hatred* (Schocken Books, 1991).

Notes

1: German Science Before Hitler
1. K. Mendelssohn, *The World of Walther Nernst: The Rise and Fall of German Science* (Macmillan, 1973).
2. Rudolf Peierls, *Bird of Passage* (Princeton University Press, 1985).

2: The Coming of the Nazis
1. Fred Uhlman, *Reunion* (Harvill Press, 1971).
2. Victor Klemperer, *I Shall Bear Witness* (Weidenfeld & Nicolson, 1998).
3. Ferdinand Sauerbruch, *A Surgeon's Life* (André Deutsch, 1953).
4. H. A. Krebs and Anne Martin, *Reminiscences and Reflections* (Oxford University Press, 1981).
5. M. Born, *Born–Einstein Letters* (Macmillan, 1971).

4: Rescuers
1. Cabinet Papers.
2. W. Beveridge, *A Defence of Free Learning* (Oxford University Press, 1959).
3. V. Weisskopf, *The Joy of Insight* (Basic Books, 1991).
4. O. Frisch, *What Little I Remember*, p.76 (Cambridge University Press, 1979).
5. Beveridge.

5: Refugees to Britain – Physicists

1. K. Mendelssohn, *The World of Walther Nernst: The Rise and Fall of German Science* (Macmillan, 1973).
2. W. Moore, *Schrödinger: Life and Thought* (Cambridge University Press, 1984).
3. Moore.
4. E. Schrödinger, *What is Life? Mind and Matter* (Cambridge University Press, 1967; 1st edn. 1944).

6: Refugees to Britain – Biologists and Chemists

1. H. A. Krebs and Anne Martin, *Reminiscences and Reflections* (Oxford University Press, 1981).
2. H. A. Krebs and Anne Martin.
3. Ronald W. Clark, *Chain: The Life of Ernst Chain* (Weidenfeld & Nicolson, 1985).

8: Those Who Stayed

1. J. L. Heilbron, *The Dilemmas of an Upright Man: Max Planck as Spokesman for German Science* (University of California, 1986).
2. W. Heisenberg, *Physics and Beyond* (Allen & Unwin, 1971).
3. 'Operation Epsilon' in *Farm Hall Transcripts*, introduced by Sir C. Frank (British Institute of Physics, 1993).
4. H. A. Krebs and Roswitha Schmid, *Otto Warburg* (Oxford University Press, 1981).

9: Internment

1. M. Perutz, 'That Was the War: Enemy Alien', *New Yorker*, 12 August 1985.
2. Letter by Martin Scott, quoted in P. and L. Gillman, *'Collar the Lot': How Britain Expelled its Wartime Refugees* (Quartet Books, 1980).
3. F. Lafitte, *The Internment of Aliens* (Penguin, 2nd edn. 1988).
4. *John Wilmers by Himself and June Wilmers* (published privately by June Wilmers, 1993).

10: The Bomb

1. W. Lanouette, with B. Silard, *Genius in the Shadows: A Biography of Leo Szilard* (Scribners, 1992).

2. O. Frisch, *What Little I Remember* (Cambridge University Press, 1979).
3. R. Peierls, *Bird of Passage* (Princeton University Press, 1985).

Index